PT Cruiser

Chrysler's classic design for a modern age

Robert Ackerson

First published in February 2007. Veloce Publishing Ltd., 33 Trinity Street, Dorchester DT1 1TT, England. Fax 01305 268864/e-mail veloce@veloce.co.uk/web www.veloce.co.uk
ISBN 978-1-84584-039-6/UPC 6-36847-04039-0
British Library Cataloguing in Publication Data –
A catalogue record for this book is available from the British Library.
Typesetting, design and page make-up all by Veloce on Apple Mac.
Printed by Replika Press in India.

PT Cruiser

Chrysler's classic design for a modern age

Robert Ackerson

VELOCE

Contents

Introduction

In 2003, when the California Cruiser concept was making the rounds of the auto show circuit, an Australian automotive journalist noted that it seemed almost impossible that Chrysler, after creating numerous special editions, could still come up with new variations on the PT Cruiser design. Then, almost as an afterthought, he observed that other manufacturers should be so lucky.

After what seemed an endless string of dull-looking, uninspired and uninspiring small cars, the PT Cruiser broke the mold of what could be expected inside and out of a small car by casting aside virtually all existing conventions of auto design.

Whether it was pure luck, brilliant marketing analysis, a once-in-a generation gathering of creative energy, or simply a matter of good timing, the PT Cruiser's combination of style and utilitarian versatility has said "Buy Me Now!" to over one million customers, regardless of income, gender or age.

For many people, their first look at a PT Cruiser was the classic 'love-at-first-sight/just-gotta-have-one' experience. Others weren't so sure, however, initially experiencing a case of 'dislike-at-first-sight'. But many of those who were less than thrilled with the Cruiser's lines returned for a second look, and then a third, and soon, shapes and forms that looked pretty darn good on cars 50 years ago looked even better on an automobile in the new millennium.

My most memorable encounter with a PT Cruiser took place in Avondale, Arizona, a suburb of Phoenix, on an August night in 2001. My wife, Grace and I, along with daughter, Lynn, son-in-law Randy, and their Sheltie dog Cheyenne, were strolling the streets near their home. Arizona doesn't observe Daylight Saving Time, so it was much darker at 9PM than native New Yorkers like my wife and I were accustomed to during the peak of summer. However, the combination of a warm Arizona evening and the last remnants of twilight intertwining with the pleasure of enjoying the companionship of family made for an unforgettable evening. The evening got even better when we turned a bend and had our attention captured by a Silver PT Cruiser parked in a driveway. Even with the car only dimly Illuminated by the lights from an open garage, it was impossible to mistake it for any other car.

In that mix of man-made and natural lighting, with neighbors gathered around and the Cruiser's owners obviously in seventh heaven, it was crystal clear that Chrysler had created a modern marvel. The PT Cruiser was practical, compact, and inexpensive. But with styling unlike anything else on the road, it possessed an abundance of the elements making for a 'cool car'.

But unless DaimlerChrysler plans to follow the path of Citroën which produced its Traction Avant model in virtually unchanged form for over two decades, there will be, in the not-too-distant future, a second-generation PT Cruiser. On the day it debuts the debate over how well DaimlerChrysler answered the question "how do you 'update' a retro-design?" will begin.

Happily, there's no debate over the contributions to this book's content by these good people at DaimlerChrysler Media: Dan Bodene, Ed Saenz, Dave Elshoff, Sam Locricchio and Kristin Starnes. Special thanks also goes to Jackie Allard at DaimlerChrysler Media UK for her help in securing detailed information on the PT Cruiser models sold in the UK.

But as far as providing the day-by-day support, encouragement and advice essential to the completion of this book, my sincere appreciation goes to my wife, Grace, who patiently endured her husband's preoccupation with the PT Cruiser.

In similar fashion, my daughter Susan and her husband Chris deserve kudos for their good-natured tolerance of what must have seemed a never-ending parade of reports on the book's progress. For more Sunday mornings than he probably cares to recall, Chris was my breakfast companion at Jackie's Diner in beautiful downtown Milford, NY, where, along with a steady dose of baseball talk, the major topic of conversation was – you guessed it – the PT Cruiser. Thanks for being such a good listener, Chris.

Robert C Ackerson, Schenevus, NY.

Chapter 1 – Creating the coolest thing on wheels

When Chrysler introduced the Plymouth Pronto at the North American International Auto Show in Detroit, Michigan, on January 5, 1997, the company suggested that "future car buyers looking for an affordable five-door, four-passenger sedan with an instantly recognizable personality might want to take a look at the 1997 Plymouth Pronto concept car." Those attributes were to make the PT Cruiser, which was a direct descendent of the Pronto, an overnight sensation and success when it was introduced just three years later.

A major influence upon the sequence of developments leading to the PT Cruiser was Tom Gale's appointment as Chrysler's Vice-President of Design in April 1985. The importance of his promotion to this influential position became evident in the late eighties and early nineties when Chrysler, preparing to move beyond reliance upon the K-car era, introduced new production models along with numerous Gale-influenced concept cars. Auto show visitors were soon able to preview what could be expected from an reinvigorated Chrysler Corporation.

One example, the Dodge Viper, after receiving a tumultuously favorable reception on the 1989 auto show circuit as a concept car, went on sale as a $50,000 production model early in the summer of 1991. All were red in color, and their appearance and 488cid V10 engines amply justified portrayal as "a no-excuses car for no-excuses people." Reinforcing this image was the sight of a Viper pacing the 75th Indianapolis 500 race.

After tempting the public with a series of concept cars with cab-forward architecture, a new LH series of sedans with only slightly toned down designs were introduced in 1993 as the Chrysler Concorde, Dodge Stratus and Eagle Vision. Conspicuously absent from this line of attractive and highly publicized automobiles was a Plymouth version.

When the Prowler was introduced in 1997, it appeared that Plymouth's role in the new scheme of things at Chrysler might be as a producer of vehicles with a decidedly retro-theme. This view gained credence when the Pronto, with a grille design similar to the Prowler's, was identified as a Plymouth.

Comments by John E Herlitz, Chrysler Corporation's Vice-President of Product Design, and K Neil Walling, Chrysler's Design Director at the Pronto's introduction supported this notion. "Pronto – as a concept car", said Herlitz, "is another clever response to Plymouth's calling for unique, affordable transportation."

Referring to the implications of the Prowler's influence upon the Pronto's front end, Walling noted that "much in the same fashion that we seasoned the Dodge brand with Viper cues, we will seek opportunities to season the Plymouth brand with Prowler cues."

Herlitz had no difficulty explaining why the Pronto's appearance, dominated by its tall "architecture", and Prowler-motivated front end dramatically contrasted with the anonymous styling of most contemporary four-sedans. "Before setting out to create Pronto," he said, "we gathered guidelines and specs for designing traditional four-passenger sedans. Once we studied all of this information, we threw it out and built a new vehicle from the ground up for our next generation."

Although overshadowed by its appearance, the Pronto's

The Plymouth Pronto, with a Cool Vanilla finish, had a roll-back fabric roof. Its interior color combination was Vanilla with Sage accents. It was fitted with front bucket seats with split-back fold-down rear seats designed to fold flat, creating a large rear cargo area. When this photo was released on January 5, 1997, Chrysler suggested that any production derivative would be a Plymouth by noting that the Pronto "is another clever response to Plymouth's calling for unique, affordable transportation." (Courtesy DaimlerChrysler Media Services)

This depiction of the Chrysler Pronto Cruizer was released prior to its debut at the Geneva Motor Show on March 3, 1998. (Courtesy DaimlerChrysler Media Services)

major specifications, as noted in the following table, were indicative of the basic proportions of any new production model based on the Pronto.

But the Pronto was far more than a concept car with a spectacular and controversial appearance. Within its compact dimensions was a spacious interior made possible by a high roofline, the forward windscreen position, and taking full advantage of minimal front and rear overhang.

Attracting a great deal of favorable reaction were the Pronto's seats that, by fully

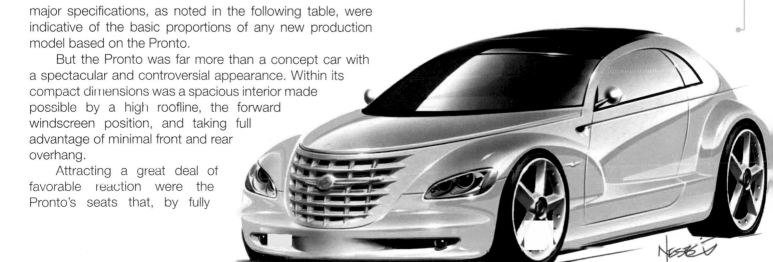

Wheelbase:	101.0in
Overall length:	148.9in
Overall width:	64.7in
Overall height:	58.0in
Front track:	57.4in
Rear track:	57.4in
Front suspension:	Strut
Rear suspension:	Multi-link
Brakes:	ABS, front disc, rear drum
Wheels:	6 x 18in cast aluminum
Tires:	P185/50R18
Engine:	Single overhead cam, 4-cylinder
Horsepower:	132
Transmission:	3-speed automatic

Plymouth Pronto specifications.

utilizing the available height, positioned their occupants noticeably higher than in most current sedans. The result, said Chrysler, provided them with more of a "command-of-the-road feeling."

Summing up the efforts that resulted in the Pronto, as well as offering an unerringly accurate explanation for the subsequent success of the PT Cruiser, Walling said: "We studied driving habits of future first-time car buyers and learned that they're interested in a vehicle unlike any other on the road today. They want a vehicle that was built just for them, a vehicle with a fun, distinctive personality."

In spite of the enthusiasm shown by Herlitz and Walling for a production version of the Pronto to appear as a Plymouth, it was not to be. Plymouth was headed for extinction, with the end of the line coming in 2001. When the Plymouth Pronto's derivative, the Pronto Cruiser appeared at the Geneva Motor Show on March 3, 1998, it bore the winged Chrysler badge.

The Pronto Cruizer's exaggerated grille and fenders encouraged comparison with the Prowler.
(Courtesy DaimlerChrysler Media Services)

The Cruizer's aggressive stance, combined with its flowing lines created the appearance of movement when it was stationary. When the Cruizer was underway, the impression that it was an American street rod at full song was undeniable. (Courtesy DaimlerChrysler Media Services)

The Cruizer's running boards, which flowed into the fenders, were reminiscent of 1940s vehicle architecture. The use of 18in front and 19in rear tires contributed to the car's wedge-like stance. (Courtesy DaimlerChrysler Media Services)

The Aztec Yellow Cruizer had a roll-back fabric top. Its interior space was larger than that of a production model Neon. Both cars had the same 104in wheelbase, yet the Cruizer's exterior length was considerably shorter. (Courtesy DaimlerChrysler Media Services)

Overall length:	167.2in (4247mm)
Overall width:	68.4in (1737mm)
Overall height:	58.5in (1486mm)
Wheelbase:	104in (2642mm)
Front and rear track:	59.1in (1501mm)
Front wheels:	18 x 7in, cast aluminum
Front tires:	205/55R18
Rear wheels:	18 x 7.5in, cast aluminum
Rear tires:	215/55R19
Suspension:	McPherson Strut
Engine*:	
Displacement:	1.6-liter
Horsepower:	115hp @5600rpm
Torque:	113lb-ft @ 4400rpm

*The Cruizer's engine was described as: "A highly efficient 1.6-liter gasoline engine being developed as part of the Chrysler/BMW venture."

Pronto Cruizer specifications.

The text of corporate press releases and comments made by Tom Gale regarding the two-door Cruizer suggested that Chrysler planned to build a production version in the near future. For example, prior to the opening of the Geneva Show, a company representative said: "It had been ten years since Chrysler Corporation introduced a concept car at a European motor show. But when the Geneva Motor Show opens next month, showgoers could be looking into the company's future product window for Europe and around the world."

Gale portrayed the Pronto Cruizer as: "A distinctive and unique combination of the best of American passion for automobiles and the most desired elements of European dynamics and efficiency. It has the same extreme sense of American spirit and daring as the Viper and Prowler, but in a package that could potentially be developed for a much broader market. We think it showcases Chrysler's growing expertise in melding our signature American design to global use and needs."

In retrospect such statements are recognized as thinly disguised diversions, drawing attention away from Chrysler's plans for a production version of the Chrysler Pronto Cruizer. Verbally connecting the dots that joined the PT Cruiser to the Cruizer, Tom Gale later remarked: "We just about hid the idea for such a vehicle in plain sight."

Following the Cruizer's European debut, Chrysler selected the 1999 North American International Auto Show (NAIAS), in Detroit to exhibit its successor, the four-door Chrysler Cruizer AWD. But, except for its drivetrain, this concept car attracted relatively little attention as Chrysler also chose this early January event to introduce the production model Chrysler PT Cruiser, which officially went on sale in March 2000 as a 2001 model.

Speaking at the show on January 3, 1999, DaimlerChrysler Chairman Robert Eaton asserted that Chrysler PT Cruiser

"dramatically changes the profile of the Chrysler brand by expanding the breadth of its product line and the presence of the brand around the world."

Noting that "the Chrysler PT Cruiser is an exceptional addition to the Chrysler brand," Martin R Levine, Vice President of the Chrysler/Plymouth/Jeep Division, added that "because of its distinct design and functionality, it will have universal appeal without regard to traditional demographics. Chrysler PT Cruiser appeals to the emotions of buyers and meets their active lifestyles." With preliminary consumer research indicating that the PT Cruiser was likely to impact Chrysler's brand identity in a fashion similar to what Dodge had experienced after the introduction of the production model Viper in 1992, Levine was on solid analytical ground by adding that the PT Cruiser "will give the Chrysler brand a signature concept-to-production vehicle like no other in the world."

Alluding to DaimlerChrysler's plan to offer the PT Cruiser in over 40 markets around the world, Jim Holden, Executive Vice President, Sales and Marketing for North America, predicted: "With a personality unlike anything on the road today, Chrysler PT Cruiser will be unique in any environment around the world while transcending cultural differences."

During the months spanning January 1999 and March 2000, it seemed that, in spite of DaimlerChrysler's well-crafted publicity program and the media's intense coverage of the PT Cruiser, the public seemed to never get quite enough news and information about the new car to satisfy its interest.

Swiftly moving to maintain this momentum, and virtually global enthusiasm for the PT Cruiser, DaimlerChrysler utilized a variety of media to connect with prospective buyers. By early November, over 225,000 people had requested information about the PT Cruiser, and a PT Cruiser website attracted 35,000 visitors weekly. Building on this internet activity, Chrysler hosted a 60-minute live online discussion

The Chrysler PT Cruiser made its world debut on January 3, 1999 at the North American International Auto Show in Detroit. (Author's collection)

13

on November 18 involving nearly a dozen members of the PT Cruiser team, representing engineers, designers and product planners. Recognizing the popularity of the PT's website, Dan Gliniecki, Chrysler-Plymouth Communications Specialist, explained: "It makes perfect sense that we use this communications medium for direct interaction between our Chrysler PT Cruiser prospects and the people behind its development."

Elaborating on Mr Gliniecki's remarks, the manager of Chrysler-Plymouth Communications, Jay Kuhnie, said: "This

According to Tom Gale, Executive Vice-President for Product Strategy and Design at DaimlerChrysler, the PT Cruiser wasn't influenced by any particular automobile from earlier times. Instead, it was patterned after what he described as the "form vocabulary" of cars from the late 1930s and early 1940s. (Author's collection)

14

These three perspectives of the PT Cruiser were included in a handsome brochure: "The Dream – The Awakening – The Execution –The Realization – The Chrysler PT Cruiser" supplied to anyone requesting advance information on the PT Cruiser in late 1998. The first two sketches were identified respectively as "Early Designer Sketch" and "Developmental Designer Sketch." No caption was provided for the third rendering, and it's not likely that it was missed. (Author's collection)

vehicle's presence in the marketplace and the phenomenal consumer response to it gives us the rare opportunity to try something different with the internet as well as traditional communication channels. We are pushing the boundaries to take full advantage of the Internet's real-time response to build relationships with customers before the Chrysler PT Cruiser goes on sale."

The PT Cruiser website's creative quality earned it many industry awards, including a @dtech Gold Award Automotive Category, the Gold Caddy Award, Interactive/online Category and the Great Lakes Interactive Marketing Association Award in the Non-ecommece Category.

In addition to the PT website and online chat room, this project, known as the PT Cruiser Prospect Management Program, also included communication with potential PT Cruiser owners through e-mail and direct mail. These PT

The 2001 PT Cruiser's 5-door hatchback body style was both stylish and functional. (Author's collection)

Cruiser prospects were given an advance look at its interior features, versatility and color choices. They were also the first public audience to receive advance technical product information through the online chat and direct mailing. In the spring of 2000, everyone participating in this program received an information video and an invitation for a PT Cruiser test drive at their local dealership.

When DaimlerChrysler announced the start of its 2000 model year advertising campaign for Jeep, Plymouth and Chrysler on September 8,1999, the PT Cruiser was still months away from appearing in dealer showrooms. For those having already made up their mind to purchase a new PT Cruiser, this was both the best and the worst of times. On the other hand, it seemed to be just more teasing from Chrysler, a promise that someday, but not just yet, a PT Cruiser would be parked in their driveway.

For those with a higher tolerance for delayed gratification, this was an opportunity to see new images of the PT Cruiser and learn more about features that someday they would experience first-hand.

For Chrysler the PT Cruiser fit perfectly into its new "Driving Passion" advertising topic, which, under the general theme of a passion for cars and driving, emphasized the different personalities of each vehicle. The PT Cruiser made its television debut in a Chrysler brand spot entitled "Soul" on ABC College Football on September 11. Commenting on this advertisement, Jay Kuhnie, said: "The PT Cruiser changes the profile of the Chrysler brand by expanding the breath of the product line. We wanted to show it for the first time in our full-line television ad to raise awareness of this exciting new vehicle."

The PT Cruiser also made pre-production appearances at college football games nationwide as part of the PT Cruiser Tailgate events. By early November 1999, over 200,000 university alumni, students and other PT prospects had attended these affairs.

This creative approach to connecting the PT Cruiser with potential customers, which also gave the Chrysler brand a more contemporary image, was reflected in the content of its print and television advertising. "We set out to create an international look for the PT Cruiser campaign that was more emotional than rational," explained Jay Kuhnie. "To achieve this goal, we used less verbiage, clean lines and stunning photography for a design that can be used anywhere in the world."

Components of the PT Cruiser's print and television advertising included one 60-second, and six 30-second television spots, one 8-page and four 4-page newspaper inserts, 17 print ads and an infomercial.

The 60-second commercial appeared on over 6500 movie screens across the US on April 21. The following day, television advertisements were aired as part of the Greater Greensboro Chrysler Classic Golf Tournament. PT Cruiser ads also appeared during commercial breaks on *Law & Order, ER, Frasier, The Practice, Tonight with Jay Leno, David Letterman, Good Morning America*, and both regular season and championship NBA, NHL and NFL games.

One of the design goals established for the 2001 PT Cruiser was to provide a vehicle whose compact overall exterior length would attract customers in global markets, yet have the space and function of a larger vehicle. Seen here is a PT Cruiser equipped with the Touring Edition package in Inferno Red Tinted Pearl Coat. Its 16in painted aluminum wheels were included in the Touring Group. (Author's collection)

Print ads for the 2001 PT Cruiser were featured in the June 2000 issues of such magazines as *Outside, Men's Journal, Metropolitan Home, Food & Wine, GQ and Vogue,* as well as newspapers including *USA Today* and the *New York Times.* In the July 2000 issue of *Motor Trend,* Editor-In-Chief, C Van Tune, devoted his entire 'right-of-way' column to the PT Cruiser. It was, he wrote: "The $16,000 People Magnet ... Everywhere it stops traffic, turns heads, and generally disrupts normal life like no other car at any price."

Two years earlier, Volkswagen's New Beetle had generated a wave of positive reaction that was seen as the second coming of Beetlemania. "But as it turns out," asserted Van Tune, "that was just a hint at the untamed public response the Cruiser's debut would bring." This reaction prompted Van Tune to wonder whether PT stood for "People Tempting."

Automobile magazine, which added a PT Cruiser to its long-test test fleet after being on an "an interminable waiting list," reported that it had "quickly won admirers as much for its drivability and outstanding packaging as for its head-turning shape."

In July the PT Cruiser was prominently featured in the DaimlerChrysler exhibit at the Republican National Convention, held in Philadelphia. One lucky visitor to the display, located in the Grand Hall of the Train Shed at the Pennsylvania Convention Center, drove away in a new PT Cruiser. To qualify, the entrants had to answer several exhibit-related questions. The winning name was randomly drawn by a company representative at a party themed 'Too Cool ParTy.' In addition, the first 500 partygoers received miniature PT Cruisers. Mini PT Cruisers were also found on ice, ice cream and in frozen drinks. The party also featured music by the group 'The Cruz-zers.'

The 2001 PT Cruiser's steering wheel combined four thick rubberized spokes with a small center hub containing an airbag. The color of the gauge enclosure, and the passenger side airbag door, coordinated with the exterior body color. The Aquamarine Metallic inserts seen here would be used with a Cruiser having an Aquamarine Metallic Clear Coat exterior. (Author's collection)

To assure that the PT Cruiser would meet the demands of a global consumer, much of the initial work on its development took place in Europe. The Cruiser's head-turning look was influenced by the result of a unique form of research known as 'Archetype' that was conducted in France, Germany, Italy, the United Kingdom, and the US. The PT's design team was included in this research process to assist it in better understanding the needs and desires of customers around the world.

The Archetype strategy not only reviewed the choices of a study group but also what previous factors influenced their preferences. In the case of the PT Cruiser, this helped researchers to identify not only who loved or hated it, but also what they did or didn't find appealing. These intense reactions to the PT Cruiser's design was similar to the

responses to the first minivans and the Dodge Ram pickup of 1994. The resulting documentation was of great value in achieving DaimlerChrysler's goal of having the PT Cruiser's design and packaging meet very specific transportation needs in a fashion with broad international appeal.

"Once we settled on an initial design, explained Bryan Nesbitt, Chrysler PT Cruiser exterior designer, "there were folks that absolutely loved PT Cruiser when they saw it. There were others that didn't like it at all but, after taking some time to soak with it, fell for it as well. That tension is what gives a glimpse at how popular this vehicle can eventually be because of the similar spectrums of emotion we've seen with such ground-breakers as the minivan and Ram."

The guiding dictum of the design of the PT, form follows function, wasn't exactly the most original idea in the world, but one that was executed in a very unique, highly original, and as sales quickly indicated, in a very successful fashion. "Using our own 'form follows function' design imperative, PT Cruiser," said Tom Gale, "establishes a new standard for combining design and function in one vehicle. It's this combination that appeals to both the emotional and rational needs of consumers."

The code name assigned to the development of the PT Cruiser's exterior was 'Street Smart', which, said Nesbitt, "summarizes the look and feel of the PT Cruiser. The vehicle has a bold presence coupled with an intelligent use of space to provide an unparalleled degree of fashion and function."

The PT Cruiser's distinctive side profile combined a uniquely proportioned roofline and high beltline. The roof rose to the rear for both aesthetic and functional reasons. Its slant gave the Cruiser a 'hot rod' posture while providing abundant rear passenger headroom as well as a large cargo area. The high beltline was accented by the three side windows. At the same time, the proportions of the bodyside sheet metal and side glass, along with the use of blacked-out B and C-pillars reinforced the Cruiser's hot-rod look. By positioning the PT Cruiser's body inward from the wheels and fenders, designers gave

Two views of the PT Cruiser's front suspension, combining MacPherson struts, coil springs, tubular shock absorbers and an anti-roll bar.
(Author's collection)

This X-ray, overhead view of the PT Cruiser illustrates the positions of its front MacPherson suspension and twist-beam rear suspension.
(Author's collection)

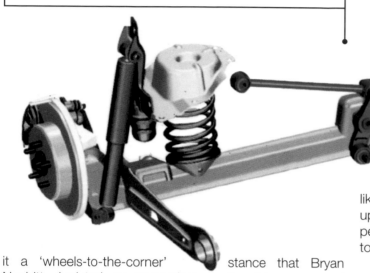

This perspective of the PT Cruiser's rear suspension shows its Watt's linkage in blue. By limiting the twist beam's lateral movement, the linkage limited its undesired side-to-side movement. The rear suspension had 8.5in of travel. (Author's collection)

it a 'wheels-to-the-corner' stance that Bryan Nesbitt depicted as promoting "confidence and durability."

It seemed as if there were endless examples of effective juxtapositioning of components of varying sizes and shapes that accentuated the PT Cruiser's basic 'cool looks.' The front fenders, drawn away from the hood and wrapped tightly around the wheels, made the wheels appear larger. The prominent forms of the front and rear fenders, connected by simulated flared side sills evoked memories of automobiles with running boards and broad-shouldered fenders from an earlier era.

By positioning the headlamps close to the front wheels, again in the style of autos from the past, front overhang was minimized, contributing to the PT Cruiser's trim exterior dimensions.

Compared to the sharply-sloped windshields used on Chrysler's cab-forward models for nearly a decade, the PT Cruiser's was far more upright, giving it an appearance associated with rear-wheel drive cars and trucks. The Cruiser's bullet-shaped tail lights were nostalgic reminders of the style common to many US cars of the 1940s. More than one new PT owner envisioned replaced the stock lenses with units having classic 'blue-dots.'

The use of large front and rear bumpers conveyed a sense of protection and security, while, for those of a certain age, the grille's shape evoked memories of any number of cars from the late '30s and early '40s, including Plymouths, Cadillacs and the Lincoln-Zephyr.

Others, not especially well acquainted with automobiles from those years, were likely, upon seeing a PT Cruiser for the first time, to conjure up visions of a California beach, an endless summer, and perhaps Frankie Avalon and Annette Funicello getting ready to take it for a spin to the downtown soda shop.

It really didn't matter how old or young you were when you saw your PT Cruiser; it cut across age, gender and ethnic lines with disarming ease, justifying Nesbitt's assertion that "the PT Cruiser means a variety of things to everyone who sees it, whether it's a certain era, image or need. You can't avoid its retro, yet still-contemporary cues. But with that there is a feeling of durability and toughness with that stance that resembles a bull dog."

Amplifying Nesbitt's depiction of the PT Cruiser, as well as noting its versatility in everyday use, Tom Gale added that "PT Cruiser has a distinct personality that envelops a variety of eras. [It] can be whatever the individual owner wants it to be. It fits any lifestyle. I may see one era, another may see something else, but one thing is certain ... everyone who sees it has an extremely emotional response to PT Cruiser. Some may see it as a tribute to the classic era; some as a street rod, others as a multi-faceted and functional light truck in a class of its own. There is really nothing like it on the road today."

It was difficult to take issue with Chrysler's assertion that the design of the PT's interior made it the automotive version of the Swiss Army Knife. "It is the exterior of the PT Cruiser that gets the obvious first notice and gawks on the road," said Larry Lyons, Vice President, Small Car Platform Engineering. "However, the element that closes the deal in the minds of those who see it is the incredible functionality that comes from the innovative interior."

This attribute resulted from the efforts of the PT's designers, whose objectives included developing a product

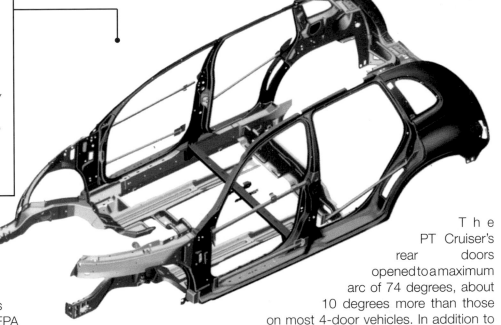

with the overall exterior length of a small car yet having the interior space and function of a much larger vehicle. For example, at 168.8 inches, the overall exterior length of the Cruiser was 5.3 inches shorter than the Ford Focus, yet its EPA interior volume of 120.2 cubic feet rivaled that of a full-size sedan.

Lyons explained that this was achieved by "paying close attention to packaging, and providing a command-of-the-road feel for the driver." By utilizing the PT's distinctive and relatively high roofline, designers had also provided its occupants with abundant head and leg room. Furthermore, the PT's overall 63.0in height, combined with unique front and rear seat configurations (the PT Cruiser's seating could be arranged in more than 25 different configurations), gave owners the ability, in just seconds, to transform their PT Cruiser from a five-seater passenger, into a vehicle having seating for the driver and the cargo capacity of a light truck.

The key to this versatility was the Cruiser's 65/35 rear seats that could be folded to form a flat load-carrying surface. For additional load capacity and flexibility, they could also be removed independently. Three different mechanisms were used to fold, tumble and remove the seats. The design of the quick-release removal latch was exclusive to the PT Cruiser in the US market. No tools were required for seat removal and each seat was fitted with a carrying handle and rollers for relatively easy handling.

The PT Cruiser's rear doors opened to a maximum arc of 74 degrees, about 10 degrees more than those on most 4-door vehicles. In addition to making entry and exit into the rear section more convenient, this feature also aided the removal of the seats and in stowing cargo through the door that otherwise might have to be loaded through the tailgate.

An optional front passenger seat could be folded completely forward for use as a table for the driver or to provide the space to load an eight-foot ladder from the rear of the vehicle. With the rear seat in the upright position, the PT Cruiser had a rear storage compartment with a multi-purpose shelf that could be placed in any one of five positions, or removed completely. One of the shelf's

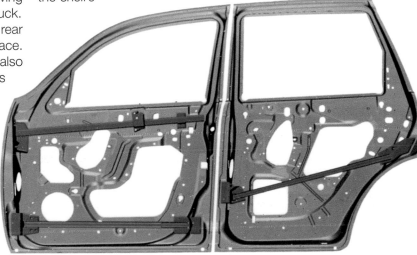

The 2001 PT Cruiser's standard 16in steel wheel had this bolt-on cover. (Author's collection)

This five-spoke, 16in painted aluminum wheel was included in the 2001 PT Cruiser's Touring Group package. It was also optional on the Limited Edition. (Author's collection)

Included with the Limited Edition and available in the Luxury Touring Group was this 16in five-spoke chrome aluminum wheel. (Author's collection)

positions converted it into a table top suitable for a variety of uses, including tailgate picnics.

Referring to the PT Cruiser's versatile mix of seating and cargo space, Tom Edson, Director – Interior Systems Engineering Small Car Platform, explained: "When the PT Cruiser was first shown, some found it easy to try and categorize it as part of a 'retro' movement with the Volkswagen Beetle or Ford's T-Bird. But there's no way you are going to fit everything from an eight-foot ladder to three bicycles in those vehicles. That's what sets the PT Cruiser apart from the crowd; a cool, emotion-inducing exterior with a practical interior of unprecedented proportion ..."

The key that enabled the PT Cruiser's 'Swiss Army Knife' interior to be moved from one configuration to another in a seamless fashion without exceeding cost and weight limits was the design of a multi-articulating forward support for the rear seat. This component was required to support the rear seat in all positions, allow for the easy removal and reinstallation of the seat, and do so reliably over many years of use.

Existing hinges were available, but their bulk made their use in the PT Cruiser impractical. Tom Edson summed up the team's successful solution: "By looking harder at the geometry, specifying high-strength materials held to close tolerances and working closely with the body-in-white

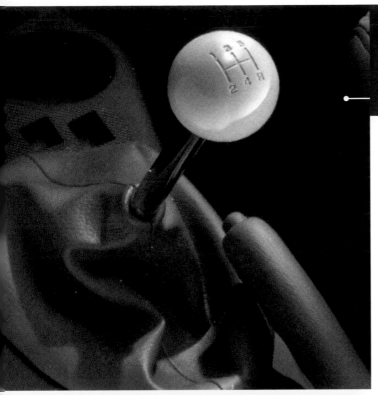

engineers, the team achieved all of their objectives for the pivot hinge and the rear seating position as a whole."

As with the PT's exterior, a unique design was ingrained into the form follows function philosophy of its interior trim and appointments.

Placement of the instrument panel, steering wheel, pedals and seats relative to the front door opening provided entry and exit that, claimed DaimlerChrysler, "was easy as any vehicle on the market."

Using virtual reality technology, PT Cruiser engineers were able to position roof pillars to maximize outward visibility and spaciousness. This technology was also used to achieve the best ergonomics for the instrument panel-mounted controls, the transmission shifter, armrests, window cranks, door release lever and door-mounted switches.

The PT Cruiser interior, said Jeff Godshall, Chrysler PT Cruiser Interior Designer, "blends innovative features and packaging to create a vehicle that has one of the most sophisticated and flexible vehicle designs, regardless of size. The esthetics of Chrysler PT Cruiser's interior fulfills the promise of its exterior design, while adding a new level of function for people with active lifestyles." Examples of this design approach were easy to detect. Harmony with the PT's exterior was created by the use of a symmetrical, browless instrument panel incorporating colored panels that coordinated with the exterior body finish. Use of straightforward bright-ringed circular gauges recessed into the instrument panel reflected, said Chrysler, "the heritage of precision workmanship." Adding a light and airy atmosphere to the interior was the steering wheel's small circular center hubs and spokes, and its Light Neutral/Dark Taupe two-tone trim.

In addition to the steering wheel hub and gauges, the interior's circular motif was incorporated into such normally disparate elements as heater/air conditioning controls,

This storage drawer, installed under the front passenger seat, was added as a 'late availability feature' for the 2001 PT Cruiser Limited Edition and Luxury Touring Group option. As seen here, it could accommodate up to eight CDs or six cassette tapes. (Author's collection)

The 2001 PT Cruiser's center stack contained the climate control knobs, power window switches and the sound system controls. (Author's collection)

horn pad and pad accents, cargo lamp, three power point outlets, their covers, and map pocket accents. Unique to the PT Cruiser were rounded rearview mirror and sun visor-mounted warning labels.

The interior door handles, with the same chrome finish as the exterior handles, incorporated thumb and finger depressions to provide a solid grip for easy closing. Map pockets with "see through" hole patterns were installed in the front and rear doors. A flexible storage bin with a movable tray in the left corner panel allowed objects to be stored either horizontally or vertically. Four cup holders (two front, one center, two rear), were provided. The two front units incorporated a patented letter slot. The rear holders could also be used to store either three CDs or two cassettes. In addition, the center and rear holders accommodated tall drink containers, including juice boxes. A washable, pop-out coin holder designed to contain both North American and European coins was also provided. Air ducts integrated into the rear floor directed heated air to the rear passengers.

Summing up these attributes, Jeff Godshall said: "inside and out, you can't escape the uniqueness of the PT Cruiser. It is a vehicle with purpose, practicality and unmatched style. Most importantly, you're only limited by your imagination, certainly not the vehicle's cavernous, flexible interior."

Tom Edson took a historical perspective in summing up

his thoughts on the virtues of the PT Cruiser. "Years from now, when people talk about this vehicle," he said "there is no doubt the exterior will be listed as the attention grabber. But through some outstanding innovation and teamwork, PT Cruiser also has one of the most innovative and versatile interiors of any vehicle imaginable, with a spectrum of functions offering anything from the comfort and safety of a five-passenger seating to the utility of a small cargo van or truck."

Often overlooked by a public going head-over-heels for the PT Cruiser's combination of contemporary and nostalgic

Fog lamps were included in the Touring Group and Luxury Touring Group packages, and were standard for the 2001 Limited Edition PT Cruiser. (Author's collection)

The power moonroof was included in the Moonroof Group, which was optional for both the Base model and those ordered with the Touring Group. It was standard for the Limited Edition. (Author's collection)

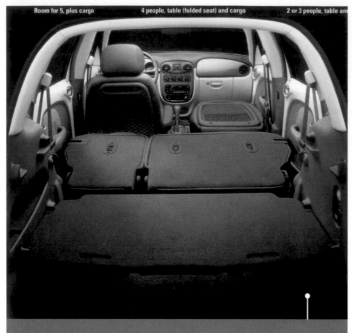

Room for 5, plus cargo   4 people, table (folded seat) and cargo   2 or 3 people, table and

As seen here, by folding the 65/35 split-folding rear seat, adjusting the rear panel to the same height as the back of the seat and utilizing the fold-flat front passenger seat (included in the Touring Group and Limited Edition), the PT Cruiser could accommodate objects up to eight feet long with the liftgate closed! (Author's collection)

Research conducted during the early stages of the PT Cruiser program confirmed that a large, flexible interior was important to consumers. One result was the Cruiser's five-position rear shelf panel. It is seen here in its tailgate position, where it becomes, said Chrysler, "the perfect party platter." (Author's collection)

styling cues, were the highly sophisticated techniques used in its engineering. Dan Knott who served as the Director of Vehicle Development, Small Car Platform Engineering, offered this perspective on the PT Cruiser's development: "There's no question that PT Cruiser's design brought challenges to

The cargo net included in the Touring Group and Limited Edition is seen here in use with the rear shelf to provide a handy and tidy storage area. The net's snap hooks are connected to tie-down loops located on the rear trim panels just behind the rear seat, and on the shelf near the tailgate. (Author's collection)

wiring harnesses were assembled. Combining the E-3-D system with VR enabled the PT Cruiser's developers to start and stop electrical functions as part of the early simulations to validate designs and placements.

Both DMA and VR were used by engineers as design and analysis tools. DMA's three-dimensional computer analysis capability enabled engineers to virtually assemble components and assure proper fit prior to the building of the physical prototype. VP allowed development team members to share in the evaluation of all product designs at every point in time in a three-dimensional computer environment.

In this manner engineers experienced the PT Cruiser from the perspective of its

the engineering and programing staff," he said. "We all loved the mold-breaking design, but had to come up with equally unique ways to package material on the engineering side, while holding true to the product and process efficiencies from a program management perspective."

"PT Cruiser," added Larry Lyons, "has been described using a variety of adjectives. All the accolades would not have been possible had we not developed some equally unique processes to make the vehicle a reality."

These included the most extensive use to date of Computer-Aided Three Dimensional Interactive Application (CATIA), Digital Modeling Assembly (DMA) and Virtual Reality (VR).

CATIA, used first among auto makers by Chrysler (prior to the creation of DaimlerChrysler), linked all major disciplines in the development of a vehicle from concept to job one, including suppliers, design, engineering, and manufacturing from the earliest stages of its development, allowing all participants to keep informed of the latest updates. Building on the experiences of previous platform teams (including the Viper's) the PT Cruiser team utilized CATIA to determine a component's optimal design much more quickly than previously, leaving more time for validation and testing.

A prime example was the use of CATIA-based, rather than manually-designed, wiring on the PT Cruiser. Using E-3-D wiring design software, the CATIA system integrated information stored in a database connected to the wiring harness with the three-dimensional location of the various components. E-3-D was used to determine wire lengths and identify specific device-to-device connections. Suppliers then used this information in a correlated program called Formboard to build manufacturing fixtures on which the

occupants, allowing them to optimize the interior package and related ergonomics. The ability to simulate the interaction of people within the models, prior to an actual PT Cruiser prototype being built, was efficient and cost effective. Don Knott used his opportunity to discuss the role of VR in the PT Cruiser's creation to clarify its relationship to the Neon. "Neon and PT Cruiser are two distinctly different vehicles, and you can't combine or compare the two," he said. "They are of two distinctly different platforms. The reality is, the two vehicles share more in process than parts or design. Much of the early VR technology we used on PT Cruiser came from knowledge we gained on the 2000 Neon program. We were able to solve unique issues because of what we learned, and that early information sharing is what saved so much time."

Specific elements of the PT Cruiser, whose design and function were evaluated by VR, included the following:

❖ Overall interior and exterior appearance
❖ Liftgate function, fit and design
❖ Effect of changes to painted surface visibility in door and liftgate openings
❖ Outward visibility for occupants in a variety of settings and seat positions
❖ Rear window wiper patterns
❖ Instrument cluster and switch patterns
❖ Child safety seat tether hook visibility and placement

Summarizing the benefits of utilizing these advanced technologies in engineering the PT Cruiser, Dan Knott said: "The exterior is such a significant departure from anything on the market. Because the design is so unique, we used CATIA and VR from the beginning to yield higher quality vehicles right from the start. For example, packaging issues were much easier to resolve on screen prior to building actual parts."

Production of the PT Cruiser took place in DaimlerChrysler's Toluca, Mexico, assembly plant. Having built three totally different vehicles (simultaneously), it was also one of the company's most flexible facilities. This versatility made it possible to launch a new vehicle while continuing volume production of other products. In the case of the PT Cruiser, when its production began, the plant continued for a time to turn out the Chrysler Sebring Convertible and Dodge Stratus on the same assembly lines. Toluca had the capacity to produce 40 vehicles per hour, and plans called for a steady increase in PT Cruiser output and a concurrent decline in Sebring and Stratus production.

Toluca was scheduled to reach full PT Cruiser production (about 180,000 units annually), with approximately 3400 workers operating on a two-shift schedule by summer 2000.

From the outset, the PT Cruiser had been designed to accommodate both right- and left-hand systems, and, to prepare the Toluca plant to produce both versions for the world market, additional right-hand drive assembly and testing capabilities were added. These included on-line electrical

In 2001, Chrysler had no difficulty in associating this building with the PT Cruiser. "The Chrysler building," it explained, "in all of its Art Deco glory, is easily the world's most identifiable skyscraper, defining and celebrating an age of substance, prosperity and timeless beauty. It was just this kind of inspiration that went into creating the 2001 Chrysler PT Cruiser. Chrysler designers wanted to create a technologically advanced vehicle that would be a celebration of this classic era ... From its powerful grille, rounded fenders and smooth expressive hood, to its chrome pushbutton door handles, bullet-shaped tail lamps and elegantly sloping liftgate, PT Cruiser is reminiscent of a time-honored era in automotive history." (Author's collection)

Just behind this PT Cruiser on the Toluca, Mexico, assembly line is a Chrysler Sebring Convertible. (Courtesy DaimlerChrysler Media Services)

The production of 40 PT Cruisers per hour at Toluca by mid-July, 2000, enabled the factory to turn out 180,000 units annually. (Courtesy DaimlerChrysler Media Services)

Prior to moving on to the paint shop, this PT Cruiser body has been dipped in primer. On July 10, 2000, DaimlerChrysler reported that on Friday, July 7, the Toluca Assembly Complex achieved its maximum level of PT Cruiser production two weeks ahead of schedule. By improving efficiency, cooperative efforts with suppliers and working some overtime, the plant gained approximately 4000 additional units for the year. (Courtesy DaimlerChrysler Media Services)

system testers, radiator and hose installation processes, chassis dynamometers, wheel alignment equipment, seat installation and tool duplication for all operations that varied between the two configurations.

Training of the Toluca workers began with the earliest concept vehicles at the DaimlerChrysler Tech Center (DCTC) Pilot Plant in Auburn Hills, Michigan. This was the first time worker education had commenced with the start of pilot builds at DCTC, and involved selecting a core team of production line employees who became trainers for their co-workers. Groups of workers rotated to Auburn Hills in six week intervals over a period of eight months. As participants, representing every workstation in the plant, became familiar with specific aspects of PT Cruiser assembly, they also acquired additional expertise in multiple operations. Their training placed special emphasis on the areas of greatest process differences between the PT Cruiser and other products. Ultimately, one assembler per workstation per shift was trained at Auburn Hills before work on the pre-production PT Cruisers began, representing about 25 per cent of the total workforce at Toluca. Each trainer received nearly 500 hours of instruction and was regarded as a crucial part of the refining and evaluation of production processes.

Following the pilot build in Auburn Hills, pre-production vehicles were built on the Toluca assembly line during normal operations. This helped refine production processes, such as

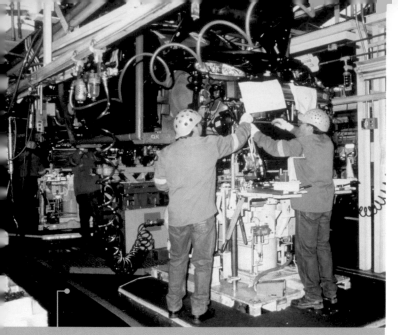

Approximately 3400 workers were employed on two, nine-hour shifts at the Toluca complex in 2000. Seen here are workers installing a PT Cruiser's engine and transaxle as it moved on an overhead carrier. (Courtesy DaimlerChrysler Media Services)

repeatability and standardization, on each station that were essential to assure a quality assembly of the PT Cruiser.

Supporting these efforts were many state-of-the-art quality systems, including:

❖ A metrology lab for checking body panels and assemblies for dimensional accuracy.
❖ A new Quality Alert System (QAS) allowing assemblers to

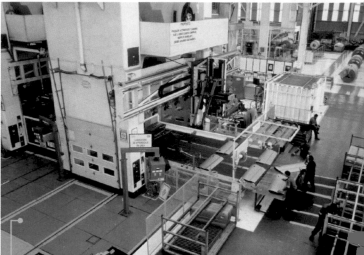

Internal quality measures for the PT Cruiser, as well as the first two months' warranty claims set a new benchmark in quality for a Chrysler production launch of an all-new vehicle. Contributing to this success was the use of protective covering on the PT Cruiser body as it moved along the assembly line. (Courtesy DaimlerChrysler Media Services)

The Toluca plant made extensive use of robotic operations in the production of the PT Cruiser. In addition to being used for crucial dimensional and integrity welding purposes, they were also used, as shown here, for accurately feeding sheet metal into the body panel presses. (Courtesy DaimlerChrysler Media Services)

In addition, computer-generated 'Dimensional Control' templates were used throughout the build process to provide rapid feedback of dimensional data on all body sheet metal systems, from the detailed parts, through body sub-assemblies to the completed bodyshell.

Like other DaimlerChrysler facilities, Toluca included an on site stamping plant to help improve final build quality by placing responsibility for stampings under one management team.

The Toluca plant had a reputation for producing high-quality vehicles at low cost, and was among the plants benchmarked by DaimlerChrysler to develop the core practices for its Operating Principles that were to be followed in all its plants. "Rather than merely a way to assemble vehicles," explained a company representative, "the Operating Principles represent the way the company does business and maintains a team-extended enterprise. It begins with core values and beliefs, the philosophical principles from which decisions are made. From there we look at the 'how', identifying the enablers and subsystems needed to execute our work (like human infrastructure, balanced schedules, value added activities and robust processes). We then identify ways to support those processes, tools for implementation and standardized measurements to gauge effectiveness."

The Operating Principles gave DaimlerChrysler employees a 'big picture' perspective from which to perform their work. At the same time, they provided a work environment of standardized methods and repeatable processes. The effectiveness of this program was evaluated by having all team members contribute to five internal gauges: Safety, Quality, Delivery, Cost and Morale.

Examples of the Operating Principles in practice at Toluca included well-organized workstations, standardized processes, efficient material handling and a balance of high-tech and manual processes.

To ensure that PT Cruiser customers were purchasing a car with world-class quality, the Toluca plant verified parts and processes, as well as fit and finish, at each step of production. Some of Toluca's quality assurance processes resulting from its implementation of the Operating Principles included:

The Chrysler PT Cruiser's exterior designer Bryan Nesbitt described it as "a celebration of automotive heritage coupled with innovation, efficiency and a twist of rebellion. It borrows design cues from classic American automobiles and interprets them with a healthy dose of American fun and freedom." (Courtesy DaimlerChrysler Media Services)

hold or stop the line if a concern arises. The system provided both a visible and a unique audible signal for each work zone to promptly alert support personnel.

❖ A new, more powerful and flexible plant-wide computer network to monitor and record data from plant operations to audit and evaluate progress and performance.

❖ Hand-held testers to program electronic systems and verify their functions to reduce the need for later repairs.

❖ Measuring dimensional accuracy of eight full bodies daily by determining millimeter variances in the x, y and z axis of 2000 points on the body using 5493 charts.

❖ The use of 55 additional robots in the PT Cruiser's dimensional and integrity welding areas, including two framing stations.

❖ Daily weld and sealing audits, performed by ultrasonic weld detection.

A variety of views of the 2001 PT Cruiser interior. "We have applied a circular theme to the interior of the PT Cruiser that allows it to be elegant in its simplicity," said Jeffrey Godshall, chief interior designer. (Author's collection)

❖ Daily body, paint and assembly audits for internal and exterior evaluation.

❖ One hundred per cent electrical and mechanical audits.

❖ One hundred per cent water tests.

❖ Daily customer satisfaction audit.

❖ One hundred per cent road test evaluation on the Toluca proving grounds.

Jeffrey Godshall told a reporter from Automotive News that "we designed the Cruiser to be a duffle bag. A duffle bag can hold one teddy bear. Or it can hold 50." (Author's collection)

The interior of a 2001 PT Cruiser in the United Kingdom. One of the cars journalists in the UK compared to the PT Cruiser was the Renault Megane Scenic. During the PT Cruiser's development, its designers had studied the Renault, particularly its shelf that concealed cargo from curious passersby. "We started to wonder," Godshall explained to Automotive News, "what happens if we could move (the shelf) around?"
(Courtesy DaimlerChrysler Media UK)

The PT Cruiser's front overhang was kept to a minimum by positioning the headlamps as close to the front wheels as possible. (Courtesy DaimlerChrysler Media Services)

In addition to these procedures, the Toluca plant also maintained a lean and efficient operation by having many of its parts and modules delivered via a Sequential Parts Delivery (SPD) process and on a just-in-time schedule. This required the plant to maintain only about a day and a half of inventory. In addition, several suppliers located operations near Toluca in order to improve the quality of their service. Depending on the type and amount of components they supplied, they either delivered to one of several nearby sequencing centers or directly to the plant.

Total startup costs for the PT Cruiser, including design, development, retooling, training, facility improvements, increased automation and pre-production trials totaled less than $600 million. Elaborating on this accomplishment, Gary Henson, DaimlerChrysler's Executive Vice-President of Manufacturing, said: "Bringing the PT Cruiser to market quickly, for relatively low cost, is the result of taking advantage of new technologies in development, implementing best practices throughout launch, cutting waste out of the value

change, and using our Operating Principles to efficiently produce repeatable, reliable world class quality."

But Henson, was keenly aware that, in spite of all the effort, careful planning and best intentions that went into the preparations for producing the PT Cruiser, pivotal to its efficient production at Toluca had been the successful hands-on solution in 1999 of seemingly insurmountable problems encountered by workers assigned the task of installing the PT Cruiser's engine.

"Chrysler PT Cruiser embodies a design that evokes emotion in people all around the world. The distinct personality of the PT Chrysler is unmatched by any vehicle on the road." – Tom Gale. Chrysler planned to market the 2001 PT Cruiser in 39 counties outside the US. In Australia, prospective owners were told that "it's for the Peter Pans of the world, people who have grown up but don't want to admit it." (Author's collection)

Chapter 2 – An entirely new car for a whole new century

The 2001 PT Cruiser

Producing the PT Cruiser involved converging the engine assembly line with the main chassis line. As Gary Henson told Elliot Blair Smith of *USA Today:* "You've got a moving vehicle, you've got a moving engine, and, all of a sudden you start moving the engine vertically. It's kind of like trying to put your shoe on while you're running."

Obviously, fitting the engine was a difficult task at the best of times and under the most ideal conditions. But in the case of the PT Cruiser, it was exacerbated by a design which provided what Smith referred to as only "a tiny 0.6in clearance in which to work, more than a third smaller than the tightest engine tolerance on any previous Chrysler vehicle." The only way the engine could be installed was by having the workers stop both lines and then position the engine in the chassis. "At that pace," wrote Smith, "the PT Cruiser never would be profitable."

Gary Henson had plenty of experience in dealing (successfully) with unforeseen last minute glitches that threatened to de-rail the smooth production launch of key Chrysler vehicles. Just a year earlier he had to cope with front door bolts on the new Chrysler LHS that, being inaccessible to factory tooling, could not be tightened. The solution was to tighten them manually until the tooling could be adjusted.

"But never before the PT Cruiser," wrote Smith, "had Henson experienced a potentially fatal flaw so late in a new model's development."

Working with plant manager Luis Rivas, Henson decided to resolve the crisis in Toluca and not back in Auburn Hills. Smith quoted Henson as telling the workers: "Before we declare we can't build this, here's what I want to do; until I come back in two weeks, I want you to just practise."

To accomplish that, Rivas and his assistants established a practice area in a corner of the plant with color keyed floor sections (green, yellow and red). Each colored section corresponded to a specific step in the assembly process. If the workers, working in teams of five, were unable to complete their specific tasks before the vehicle moved into the next colored zone, they were to pull an emergency alarm that stopped the line.

Before the start of this effort, it took the workers a day to build each car. When Henson returned, the production rate was one PT Cruiser every ten minutes. This was still far from the target production speed, but, as Henson told Smith: "It was a turning point in the launch. Once they saw this huge obstacle they had, and solved it, everything else looked pretty minuscule. I said 'good, I'm coming back again in another two weeks'."

When Henson arrived back at Toluca, PT Cruisers were being produced at a rate of one every four minutes. Eventually, with still more practice, this was improved to a PT Cruiser every eighty seconds.

Plans for the PT Cruiser's second year of production included a goal of reducing this time by twenty-five per cent. The workers at Toluca weren't alone in having their skills honed by this challenge. "Back at Chrysler headquarters", Smith wrote, "Henson says, engineers also improved their factory-simulation skills."

One of the engines that the Toluca factory learned to handle with finesse and ease was the 2.4-liter, dual overhead

PT Cruiser owners were able to select from a wide assortment of accessories from DaimlerChrysler's Mopar Division. This PT Cruiser's distinctive appearance results from the installation of the Ground Effects Package consisting of front and rear air dams, wheel lip moldings and side skirts. Its price, primed and ready to paint was $835. It was also offered in the PT Cruiser's body color for $1255. Also installed on this Cruiser are fog lights integrated into the front fascia openings ($105), and painted cast aluminum wheels that listed for $540. (Author's collection)

cam (dohc), 16-valve engine with counter-rotating balancing shafts that was also used in base models of the Chrysler Cirrus, Dodge Stratus and Plymouth Breeze. It was installed in all PT Cruisers destined for the North American market.

This view of the PT Cruiser with the Ground Effects Package shows that it is also equipped with the $250 rear spoiler. Components of the Ground Effects Package could also be purchased individually. The air dam listed for $250 (primed) or $355 (body color). The Wheel Lips Moldings were priced at $310 (primed) or $480 (body color). The Side Skirts were priced at $290 (primed) or $440 (body color). (Author's collection)

14

This exhaust tip was constructed of heavy-gauge chromed-steel and was secured to the exhaust pipe by a rivet. It was designed to extend beyond the rear bumper. Chrysler promised buyers of this $31.50 item that it would "add extra street smarts to your PT Cruiser." (Author's collection)

Both the PT Cruiser's standard 5-speed manual and optional 4-speed automatic transmissions had seen service in other Chrysler products. For use in the PT Cruiser, the automatic had new final drive gearing for improved acceleration and economical highway cruising. The primary engine for other markets was a 2.0-liter, dohc, 16-valve, 140hp 4-cylinder engine previously used in the Dodge Stratus when equipped with a 5-speed manual transmission.

By National Highway Traffic Safety Administration (NHTSA) standards, the PT Cruiser was classified as a light-duty truck. The 2.4-liter engine with either the manual or automatic transmission met Low Emission Vehicle (LEV) standards and Ultra-Low Emission Vehicle (ULEV) requirements in California, New York, Massachusetts, Vermont and Maine. In Europe, Australia, Japan and other Asian-Pacific markets, the 2.0-liter engine met all necessary Stage 3 regulations.

Both engines had a new catalytic converter technology that, along with DaimlerChrysler's existing emission control technology, helped them to exceed regulations for pollutant output. The system included low-mass exhaust manifolds constructed of lightweight, thin wall cast iron that hastened catalytic converter warm-up by absorbing minimal heat from the exhaust system. The converter, a three-way unit, was also mounted closer to the exhaust manifold, further enabling it to reach operating temperature sooner and thus more efficiently control emissions.

Two views of a PT Cruiser fitted with a Hitch-mounted luggage rack and a Class 1 Hitch Receiver. The latter accessory, priced at $270.25, extended beyond the rear bumper and could handing towing a trailer of up to 1000 pounds gross weight. As seen here, it could also accommodate the luggage rack which installed into the trailer hitch and could handle a load of 75 pounds. Its price was $490. (Author's collection)

This removable roof rack appealed to PT Cruiser owners wishing to transport large recreational/sport items and still be able to utilize the Cruiser's interior space for other purposes. It was lockable, easy to install, remove and store. Priced at $157, it is seen here with a pair of Airport Carriers. It was also designed for use with Bike, Water Sport, Ski and Snowboard Carriers. (Author's collection)

All PT Cruiser catalytic converters used new thin wall 600-cell-per-square-inch substances that reduced catalytic light-off time and increased performance. The cumulative benefit of this technology included a reduction in substance mass, which also allowed quicker operation, and, due to the increased number of cells, more of the exhaust gas stream being exposed to the converter's surface area.

Efforts to have key emission control components reach their optimum operating temperature as soon as possible extended to the PT Cruiser's oxygen sensor. Instead of the traditional 'thimble-style' sensor, a faster responding, more efficient 'planar' unit with lower mass was used. The sensor's electric heating system contributed to its faster emission control time. As the exhaust flow reached normal operation, the heater power was automatically reduced.

To further upgrade emission control in all markets, the on-board refueling vapor recovery (ORVR) system, which was required of all domestic PT Cruisers by federal regulation, was included on all models regardless of their destination. ORVR prevented fuel vapor in the tank from venting to the atmosphere during refueling, as well as during vehicle operation. The vapor was routed to a canister located in the fuel tank and was burned in the engine while driving.

The PT Cruiser was also equipped with a leak detection system that was mounted in this fuel vapor storage canister.

The system included a small air pump that periodically applied light pressure to the entire fuel supply system to check for possible vapor leaks. If a leak occurred, the on-board diagnostic system turned on the 'service engine soon' icon in the instrument panel.

Justifiably proud of the PT Cruiser's leadership role in the field of engine emissions, Walt Battle, Director – Program Management, Small Car Platform, observed, "In addition to the vehicle's obvious design heritage, there are numerous innovations in the PT Cruiser. Ironically, the innovation involved in everything from its design to the new environmentally friendly technology on the vehicle make it a very futuristic product as well."

The PT Cruiser's suspension mounting, body structure stiffness and suspension calibrations were tuned to minimize noise, vibration and harshness, and body lean. The front suspension was attached to the body structure by a stiff crossmember that also supported the steering gear. As explained by Dan Knott, its use contributed to what most critics judged to be a low level of cabin noise under most conditions. "Stiffness, which results in a high natural vibration frequency," he said, "helps limit the transmission of road noise and engine vibration to the interior."

The MacPherson strut front suspension had a high roll-center to enhance steering response while limiting body

Two sizes of Airport Carriers were available for the PT Cruiser. One, measuring 9.25 x 5.5 x 59in when closed, extended up to 87in and listed for $200. The second unit measured 12.5 x 6 x 61in when closed, extended to 67in, and cost $230. (Author's collection)

Seen here is a PT Cruiser fitted with the Removable Roof Rack and the Water Sports Carrier which could transport kayaks, sailboards or surfboards. Its $143 price included latching, push-button nylon strap attachment, front and rear tie-down attachment and a theft-deterring installation tool" -should be directed to the large illustration at the lower left.-the PT with the surfboard on top.

"Wintertime adventures are no problem with the PT Cruiser," promised Chrysler. This PT's roof rack is fitted with the $93 Ski and Snowboard Carrier. This carrier held up to six pairs of skis or four snowboards, or a combination of both. (Author's collection)

lean in brisk cornering. The suspension geometry, labeled 'low lean' by Chrysler, was arranged to provide a taut ride and what Chrysler described as the "desired suspension handling performance," which was to say the PT Cruiser had handling appropriate for its intended purpose as a fun-to-drive, fun-to-be-in vehicle that was not portrayed as a sports car.

At the rear, coil springs supported a twist beam axle. The springs and jounce bumpers were mounted above the beam in line with the wheel centerline to prevent after-shake when a wheel hit a bump. Trailing arms and a Watts linkage respectively provided longitudinal and transverse location of the axle. The Watts linkage included two transverse links pivoting on the body structure at the outer ends and a third link on the inboard ends. The Chrysler Group cited three advantages of the Watts linkage as compared to the more commonly used track bar. It reduced lateral suspension movement relative to the body to help minimize wheel well size, while also inducing less side-to-side variation in handling. Lastly, by distributing transverse loads through two links with four bushings rather

As an alternative to the roof-mounted bike carrier, Mopar offered this $200 Hitch-mount Fold-down Carrier. It held up to two bikes and, as seen here, had a fold-down feature to allow for liftgate opening. This package included carrying clamps with rubber inserts to protect bike surfaces, along with a cable for locking the bikes and an anti-theft bolt that locked the carrier onto the vehicle. For an additional $20, a crossbar adapter was offered to carry bikes without horizontal-style crossbars. (Author's collection)

than one link with two bushings, it substantially increased lateral stiffness for more precise handling. This also reduced body structural stiffness requirements and allowed the use of softer bushings, limiting the transmission of road noise and harshness.

Emphasizing the relationship of the PT Cruiser's body structure's rigid nature to its ride and handling, Ernie Laginess, Director – Body Engineering, Small Car Platform Engineering, explained that "the PT Cruiser's body serves a number of purposes for us. First, the high strength steel assures durability and rigidity for a stable ride and handling. The durability provides a safety element. And the bending and torsional characteristics allow us to meet our aggressive performance criteria for noise, vibration and harshness control."

The PT Cruiser body structure also provided a high level of impact protection. For example, a traverse beam connecting the center pillars and tied into the floorpan at the center tunnel, contributed to side-impact protection and increased body stiffness. The beam was placed directly in line with side-impact loads, helping protect occupants

The major specifications of the PT Cruiser.

Wheelbase:	103.0in (2616mm)
Front and rear track:	58.3in (1481mm)
Overall length:	168.8in (4288mm)
Overall width (at front seat):	67.1in (1705mm)
Overall height (at curb weight):	63.0in (1601mm)
Ground clearance (at curb weight):	6.5in (166mm)
Accommodations	
Seating capacity (F/R)	2/3
Front head room	40.4in (1026mm)
Front leg room	40.6in (1032mm)
Front shoulder room	54.6in (1386mm)
Front hip room	54in (1372mm)
Front SAE volume	51.8cu-ft (1.47cu-m)
Rear head room	39.6in (1006mm)
Rear leg room	40.8in (1038mm)
Rear knee clearance	2.6in (65.8mm)
Rear shoulder room	53,9in (1368.4mm)
Rear hip room	46.8in (1188mm)
Rear SAE volume	49.4cu-ft (1.40cu-m)
Cargo volume (aft of rear seat)	19.0cu-ft (0.538cu-m)
Cargo volume (rear seats removed)	64.2cu-ft (1.82cu-m)
Weight distribution (% F/R)	59/41 (with manual transmission at curb weight
Curb weight:	
2.4-liter engine/manual transmission):	3124lb (1418kg)
2.4-liter engine/automatic transmission):	3187lb (1446kg)
2.0-liter engine1/manual transmission):	3049lb (1383kg)
2.0-liter engine/automatic transmission):	3133lb (1421kg)
Drag coefficient:	0.379
Fuel tank capacity:	15.0gal (57 liters)
Engine [1]	2.4-liter, 4-cylinder, in-line, liquid-cooled
Construction:	Cast iron block, cast iron bedplate, aluminum alloy cylinder head and balance shafts
Displacement:	148.2cu-in (2429cc)
Bore x stroke:	3.44in x 3.98in (87.5mm x 101.0mm)
Valve system:	Belt-driven DOHC, 16 valves, stamped steel roller followers, hydraulic lash adjusters
Fuel injection:	Sequential multiport, electronic
Compression ratio:	9.4:1
Horsepower:	150hp @ 5500rpm, 112kw (62.5hp/liter)
Torque:	162lb-ft 220Nm) @ 4000rpm
Maximum engine speed:	6240rpm (electronically limited)
Fuel requirement:	Unleaded, regular, 87 octane R+ M/2
Oil capacity:	4.3qt (4.3L) plus filter
Coolant capacity:	7.4qt (7.0L)
Emission controls	Three-way catalyst, heated oxygen sensor, internal engines features
EPA fuel economy (MPG city/hwy)	20/26 (manual); 20/25 automatic (for 2002 these were revised to 21/28 (manual), and 20/24 (automatic)
Alternator/battery:	120amp/540amp, Group 26R maintenance-free
Manual transmission:	All-synchromesh, 5-speed, overdrive

Gear ratios: 1st: 3.50; 2nd: 1.96; 3rd 1.36; 4th: 0.971; 5th: 0.811; Reverse: 3.42; Final drive: 3.94; Overall top gear: 3.20

Automatic transmission: Four-speed, overdrive
Gear ratios: 1st: 2.84; 2nd: 1.57; 3rd 1.00; 4th:0.69 Reverse: 2.21; Final drive: 3.91 (2.4 liter engine); 4.07 (2.0 liter engine); Overall top gear: 2.694

(2.4 liter engine); 2.808 (2.0 liter engine)

Suspension
Front: MacPherson struts, asymmetrical lower control arms, coil springs and link-type stabilizer bar
Rear: Trailing arms, twist beam axle with integral tubular stabilizer bar, Watt's linkage, coil springs, gas-charged shock absorbers, and linked stabilizer bar

Steering: Power, rack and pinion
Overall ratio: 18:1
Steering turns (lock-to-lock):   3.0
Turning diameter   With base tires and manual transmission: 36.5ft (11.1m) With 16in tires and automatic transmission: 39.7ft (12.1m)

Wheels:
Standard: Steel disc, 15 x 6.0in
Optional: Cast aluminum, 16 x 6.0in
Tires:
Standard (except Europe and RHD)
Size and type: P195/65R15 All Season Touring
Manufacturer and model: Goodycar Eagle LS
Revs/mile: 835 (519km)
Optional
Size and type: P205/55R16 All Season
Manufacturer and model: Goodyear Eagle LS
Revs/mile: 840 (522km)
Standard Europe and RHD
Size and type: P195/65HR15 All Season Performance
Manufacturer and model: Goodyear NCT5
Revs/mile: 832 (517km)

Optional Europe and RHD
Size and type:P205/55R15 All Season Performance
Manufacturer and model: Goodyear NCT5
Revs/mile: 837 (520km)
Optional Europe and RHD
Size and type:P185/65R15 All Season Performance
Manufacturer and model:Goodyear Eagle Vector
Revs/mile: 854 (531km)

Standard brakes:
Front: 10.94 x 0.9in (278 x 23mm) vented disc with 2.25in single-piston sliding caliper

Swept area: 198.5sq-in (1281sq-cm)
Rear: 8.66 x 1.57in (220 x 40mm) drum
Swept area: 86sq-in (556sq-cm)
Optional:
Front: Same as standard with ABS
Rear: 10.62 x 0.35in (269 x 9mm) solid disc with 1.43in 36mm) single-piston sliding caliper and ABS
Swept area: 173.4sq-in (1119sq-cm)

[1] The 2.0-liter 4-cylinder, in-line, liquid-cooled engine available only for markets outside North America had these specifications:

Construction: Cast iron block, cast iron bedplate, aluminum alloy cylinder head and balance shafts
Displacement: 121.8cu-in (1995cc)
Bore x stroke: 3.44in x 3.27in (87.5mm x 83.0mm)
Valve system:Belt-driven DOHC, 16 valves, stamped steel roller followers, hydraulic lash adjusters
Fuel injection: Sequential multiport, electronic, returnless
Compression ratio: 9.6:1
Horsepower: 140hp @ 5700rpm (70.0hp/liter)
Torque: 139lb-ft @ 4150rpm
Maximum engine speed: 6752rpm (manual transmission); 6720rpm (automatic transmission, electronically limited)
Fuel requirement: Unleaded, 90 octane R+M/2
Oil capacity: 4.0qt (3.8L)
Coolant capacity: 7.4qt (7.0L)
Fuel economy European (Liter/100km, urban/extra-urban): 11.5/7.0 (manual); 13.1/7.9 automatic

The nine exterior colors offered for the PT Cruiser had these identifications:

Color code	Color
PQW	Aquamarine Metallic Clear Coat
PX8	Black Clear Coat
PS2	Bright Silver Metallic Clear Coat
PMT	Deep Cranberry Pearl Coat
PEL	Inferno Red Tinted Pearl Coat
PB7	Patriot Blue Pearl Coat
PGR	Shale Green Metallic Clear Coat
PW1	Stone White Clear Coat
PTK	Taupe Frost Metallic Clear Coat

Both of these PT Cruisers are equipped with a black rear step pad, priced at $24, that was designed to prevent scratching and scuffing of the rear bumper fascia when loading and unloading items. It was made of the same material as the fascia and had the same character lines as the sill trim. It was installed with a 3M adhesive. The Cruiser on the left also has the Molded Cargo Tray, a $67 skid-resistant thermoplastic rubber tray that fit into the cargo tray to protect the carpeting. The other Cruiser has the $107 Adjustable Cargo Tray made of black molded plastic that was designed to protect the cargo area from grease, dirt, grime and spills. It had high walls to limit the movement of loose items, as well as adjustable dividers to keep items firmly in place. (Author's collection)

These are two of the 15in aluminum wheel designs, sold in sets of four, that Mopar offered for the PT Cruiser. The painted wheel on the left was listed for $540. The polished version to its right sold for $780. (Author's collection)

A set of these 16in painted aluminum wheels was priced at $600. A polished version was also available for $720. (Author's collection)

during side-impact collisions. A longitudinal beam in each front door helped distribute crash energy to the center pillar where a die-cast zinc alloy extension, attached to the pillar, accepted the load.

Both the PT Cruiser's driver and front passenger airbags were of a next-generation design. New technology and the PT Cruiser's unique front end impact design allowed the mounting of a driver airbag that was more compact and made of a lighter material than those used in previous DaimlerChrysler vehicles. The bag's reduced bulk enabled it to be positioned beneath the small, circular steering wheel trim cover. In addition, a cleaner burning pyrotechnic propellant permitted the elimination of the filter screens previously needed to trap particulate matter.

The passenger airbag included a hybrid inflator that used a small amount of pyrotechnic propellant to release and heat compressed air stored in a high-pressure cylinder. Supplemental side airbags were included with optional leather-trimmed seats, but otherwise were a stand-alone option, since the PT Cruiser met all side impact regulations without them.

The 2001 PT Cruiser was as available in Base and Limited Edition versions. The Limited was available as a 'Quick Order Package' identified as either 27G for Cruisers ordered with manual transmission or 28G for those with an automatic transmission. The Base PT Cruiser, identified as the PTCH44, had a suggested retail price of $15,450. The Limited Edition listed for $18,620. The PT Cruiser's Destination Charge was $550. The Base model could be upgraded with the Touring Group (option code ADT). Included in the Limited Edition was the Luxury Touring Group which was also available for the Base model as an option (option code ADY).

Effective July 1, 2000, the PT Cruiser's base price was

The features and optional equipment of the PT Cruiser in Base and Limited Edition form.

Feature	Base	Limited Edition
Exterior		
Black B-pillar applique:	S	S
Limited Edition badge:	NA	S
Rear window defroster:	S	S
Bright door handles:	S	S
Front fascia (accent/body color)	S	S
Rear fascia (accent/body color)	S	S
Solar control glass (all windows)	P	S
Deep-tint Sunscreen (rear door, quarter and lift gate windows; Solar Control in windshield and front doors)	S	S
Halogen quad headlamps:	S	S
Backup lamps:	S	S
Fog lamps (included instrument cluster warning indicator)	P	S
Park/turn daytime running lamps (Canada only)	S	S
Bright lock bezels (door and lift gate)	S	S
Mirrors:		
Manual, remote control	S	NA
Power, remote control, heated, fold-away	P	S
Power moonroof (tilt/vent/slide with solar glass, sliding sunshade and one-touch open Feature [1]	P	S
Body color bodyside molding	S	S
Roof rack [2]	O	O
Two-speed windshield wipers with variable		

Feature	Base	Limited Edition
intermittent delay and mist wipe	S	S
Rear window wiper/washer with fixed intermittent delay	S	S
Interior		
Assist handles (4)	P	S
Cargo net	P	S
Passenger and cargo compartment		
Carpeting	S	S
Air conditioning with fluidic instrument panel outlets	S	S
Floor heater outlets – front and rear	S	S
Rear coat hooks (2)	S	S
Dark Taupe/Light Pearl Beige color combination	S	S
Full length floor console [3]	S	S
Overhead console [4]	O	S
Front and rear door trim panels with storage pockets	S	S
Front and rear floor mats	S	NA
Front and rear floor mats, front mats embroidered with PT Cruiser logo	P	S
Locking glove box	S	S
Instrumentation		
Gauges: (speedometer, tachometer, fuel level and engine temperature)	S	S
Digital display: odometer, trip odometer, door ajar and liftgate ajar	S	S
Warning lamps: low fuel, seat belts, brake system, check engine, high beam headlamps, airbags, engine oil pressure, electrical system and engine overheat	S	S
Turn signal indicators	S	S
Lamps:		
Cargo compartment [5]	S	S
Front dome [5]	S	S
Day/night manual rearview mirror	S	S
Day/night manual rearview		

Feature	Base	Limited Edition
mirror with reading lamps	P	NA
Center console 12 volt electrical power outlet	S	S
Fixed, fluted antenna	S	S
AM/FM stereo radio with cassette player and CD changer controls	S	S
AM/FM stereo radio with cassette and CD players	O	O
Speakers – six, premium	S	S
Tilt steering column	S	S
Seat and door trim bolster material:		
Tipton II cloth	S	NA
Leather trimmed seats with preferred suede accents and vinyl door bolsters	NA	S
Front seats:		
Reclining, low-back buckets [6]	S	NA
Reclining, Low-back buckets [7]	NA	S
Fold flat front passenger seat (included seatback tray)	P	S
Driver, Power Height Adjuster (NA with CPOS 2D)	O	S
Rear seats:		
Fold and tumble with 65/35 split		
Cushion and back, and quick release removal system	S	S
Two-way adjustable locking outboard head restraints	P	S
Leather wrapped shift knob (with automatic transmission)	P	S
Speed control [8]	O	S
Molded urethane steering wheel	S	S
Leather wrapped passenger seat underseat storage drawer [9]	P	S
Sliding sun visors with covered mirrors	S	NA
Sliding sunvisors with illuminated vanity mirrors	P	S
Five position removable utility panel	S	S
Power windows front (with one-touch open switches) and rear	S	S
Powertrain and chassis		
2.4-liter engine	S	S
5-speed manual transmission with ball shifter	S	S
4-speed automatic transmission	O	O
Power brakes (front disc/rear drum	S	S
Anti-lock 4-wheel disc (includes low-speed traction-control)	O	O
Engine block heater (standard in Canada)	O	O
Chrome exhaust tip	P	S
Power steering	S	S
Front and rear stabilizer bars	S	S
Normal duty suspension	S	NA
Touring tuned suspension	P	S
Compact spare tire with aluminum wheel	S	S
P195/65R15 BSW all-season touring tires	S	NA
P205/55R16 BSW all-season touring tires	P	S
Bolt-on 15in wheel covers with bright retaining nuts	S	NA
15in x 6.0in steel wheels	S	NA
16in x 6.0in painted aluminum wheels (credit option on Limited Edition)	P	O
16in x 6.0in aluminum, chrome plated	P	S
Remote keyless entry [10]	P	S
Power locks [11]	P	S
Rear door child protection	S	S
Next generation front airbags	S	S
Airbags-supplemental side, front, outboard occupant [12]	O	S
Security alarm [13]	P	S
Sentry key theft deterrent system [14] (standard in Mexico)	P	S
User-ready LATCH child seat anchorage system-lower anchors and tether-ready upper anchors	S	S
Warning chimes: key in ignition, headlamps on, low fuel or front		

Feature	Base	Limited Edition
seat belt not buckled	S	S
28F equipment package [15]	O	NA
Light group [16]	O	S
Luxury touring group [17]	O	S
Moonroof group [18]	O	S
Touring group [19]	O	NA

S Standard
O Optional
NA Not Available
P Package

[1] Optional in Canada for Limited Edition.

[2] Included two continuously adjustable crossbars with side-by-side "Spoiler Appearance" stowage capacity and quick release latches.

[3] Included two front, one center and one rear cup holders; removable coin holder, pencil tray, CD/cassette holder, front storage slot and center storage tray.

[4] Included driver and passenger map/reading lamps with integral on/off switches, compass and outside temperature display with US/metric switch and standard rearview mirror. Not available with CPOS 2D.

[5] Included theatre dimming and automatic time out.

[6] Features consisted of two-way adjustable, locking head restraints, driver inboard pivoting armrest and passenger seatback storage net.

[7] Features consisted of four-way adjustable locking head restraints, driver inboard pivoting armrest, and driver and passenger seatback storage nets.

[8] Included steering column controls and instrument cluster indicator lamp.

[9] Initially noted as 'Late availability during model year', it was listed as a $25.00 option as of July 1, 2000.

[10] Included two transmitters and panic alarm.

[11] Included central locking and customer programmable automatic locking.

[12] Included seatback storage nets and carpet insets. Not available in Mexico.

[13] Included horn pulse, flashing headlamps,and parking lamps, and cluster warning lamps. Standard in Mexico.

[14] The Sentry Key Theft Deterrent System was also included with European equipment Groups and optional in all other markets. It included two keys that operated the system and deterred theft by making it impossible to start the engine without the owner's key. The system included an integrated circuit chip encapsulated in the head of the ignition key and a module mounted on the steering column near the ignition key cylinder. The module only recognized the frequency emitted from the driver's key chip and would not allow the vehicle to run without it. This arrangement met the current European insurance and homologation regulations.

[15] Included Light Group; fold flat front passenger seat; two-way adjustable locking front seat outboard head restraints, cargo net,interior assist handles (4), front passenger underseat storage drawer (late availability); Sunscreen glass; power, heated fold-away mirrors, remote keyless entry, Sentry Key Theft Deterrent System; power locks and security alarm system.

[16] Included sliding sun visors with illuminated vanity mirrors, rearview mirror with reading lamps, (standard mirror used with overhead console), auxiliary 12-volt electric power outlets, and console flood lamp.

[17] Included front floor mats, with embroidered PT Cruiser logo, leather-wrapped shift knob (with automatic transmission), fog lamps, chrome exhaust tip, leather-wrapped steering wheel, Touring Tuned Suspension, P205/55R16 BSW All-Season Touring tires, 16in chrome-plated aluminum wheels, and Touring Edition badge (badge deleted on Limited Edition).

[18] Included power moonroof with one-touch open switch and sliding sunshade, Light Group (with 2-D Package), interior assist handles (with 2-D Package), and overhead console with compass and temperature display.

[19] Included fog lamps, Touring Edition badge, Touring Tuned Suspension, P205/55R16 BSW All-Season Touring tires,and 16in painted aluminum wheels. Not available with Luxury Touring Group.

The prices of the individual options for the 2001 PT Cruiser were as follows:

Option Code	Option	MSRP
27D	Quick Order Package 27D [1]	$0
27F	Quick Order Package 27F [2]	$1140
27G	Quick Order Package 27G [3]	$3170
28D	Quick Order Package 28D [4]	$0
28F	Quick Order Package 28F [5]	$1140
ADA	Light Group [6]	$160
ADT	Touring Group [7]	$590
ADY	Luxury Touring Group [8]	$975
AJA	Moonroof Group [9]	$750
AJA	Moonroof Group [10]	$665
BRT	4-wheel anti lock disc brakes [11]	$595
CGS	Side airbags	$350
CUD	Overhead console with	

	compass and temperature display [12]	$150
DD5	5-speed manual transmission [13]	$0
DGB	4-speed automatic transmission [14]	$825
EDZ	2.4-liter engine	$0
GEG	Deep tinted Sunscreen glass	$275
JPN	Driver's seat power height adjuster	$100
MWG	Roof rack	$140
NHK	Engine block heater	$20
NHM	Speed control	$225
RAZ	AM/FM stereo radio with cassette, CD and equalizer	$225
WNX	16in painted aluminum wheels [15]	($250)

[1] Included vehicle with standard equipment, not available with automatic transmission (DGB), overhead console (CUD), Luxury Touring Group (ADY), power driver seat with height control (JPN), leather and suede bucket seats (GL), and 16in painted aluminum wheels (WNX).

[2] Included interior assist handles, cargo net, deep tint Sunscreen glass, outboard seating rear head restraints, Light Group, console flood lamp, rear view mirror with reading lamps, front and rear auxiliary 12-volt power outlet and illuminated sliding sun visor, power auto central locks, power-heated fold-away mirrors, fold flat front passenger seat, keyless entry system with panic alarm, security alarm and sentry key theft deterrent. Not available with DGB, AJA, and Touring Group (ADT)

[3] Included airbags, Limited Edition badge, interior assist handles, cargo net, deep tint, Sunscreen glass, outboard seating rear head restraints, console flood lamp, rear view mirror with reading lamps, front and rear auxiliary 12-volt power outlet and illuminated sun visor, power auto central locking locks, power heated fold-away mirrors, power height adjuster driver's seat, leather trim seats with preferred suede, fold-flat front passenger's seat, keyless entry system with panic alarm, security alarm, sentry key theft dotorront oyotom, opeed oontrol and power express open moonroof. Not available with DGB, AJA and ADT

[4] Included vehicle with standard equipment. Required 4-speed automatic transmission (DGB). Not available with CUD, ADY, JPN, GL and WNX.

[5] Included interior assist handles, cargo net, deep tint Sunscreen glass, outboard seating rear head restraints, 12-volt power outlet and illuminated sun visor, power auto central locking locks, power heated fold-away mirrors, fold-flat front passenger's seat, keyless entry system with panic alarm, security alarm, sentry key theft deterrent system, speed control and power express open moonroof. Required DGB. Not available with AJA and ADT.

[6] Included console flood lamp, rear view mirror with reading lamps, front and rear auxiliary 12-volt power outlet and illuminated sliding sun visor mirror. Not available with CUD.

[7] Included Touring Edition badge, fog lamps, touring suspension, P205/55R1689T BSW all-season tires, and 16in painted aluminum wheels.

[8] Included Touring Edition badge, fog lamps, touring suspension, P205/55R1689T BSW all-season tires, 16in chrome aluminum wheels, bright exhaust tip, luxury front and rear floor mats, leather-wrapped steering wheel and shift knob.

[9] Included power express open moon roof, interior assist handles, overhead console with compass and outside temperature display, Light Group, console flood lamp. rear view mirror with reading lamps. front and rear 12-volt power outlet and illuminated sliding sun visor mirror. Not available with 27G, 28G, 27F and 28F.

[10] Included power express open moonroof and overhead console with compass and outside temperature display. not available with 27D, 27G, 28D and 28G.

[11] Included traction control.

[12] Included driver and passenger map/reading lights with integral on/off switch, compass, outside temperature readouts, US/metric toggle switch and blue-green display.

[13] Not available with 28D, 28F and 28G.

[14] Included 3.91 axle ratio.

[15] Required 27G or 28G. Not available for 27D, 27F, 28D and 28F.

increased $500 to $15,935. At the same time prices were also adjusted on the following options:

Option	New price	Change
Luxury Touring Group	$1025	+$50
Silver painted 16in aluminum wheels	(-$300)	(-$50)

The painted wheels were a credit option for the Limited. The aluminum chrome wheels were standard for the Limited. Accompanying these developments were a number of revisions. Added to the Limited Edition as a running change were heated driver and front passenger seats with a driver's seat manual lumbar adjuster.

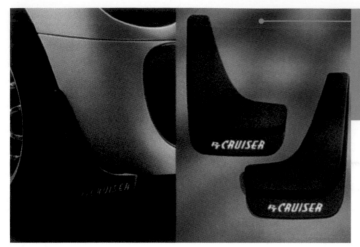

With market researchers reporting that the PT Cruiser was drawing more non-Chrysler owners into Chrysler's showrooms than any of its other products, these price revisions and adjustments were of little consequence to anyone wanting to become a Cruiser owner. Commenting on this situation, analyst Tom Libby said: "It just appeals to everybody across the brands and ages. It's just like a mad rush. Everybody is buying it, whether it's a 25-year old or a 55-year old. I can't see any patterns other than that."

In late September, Chrysler announced that the PT Cruiser would be making its UK première at the October, 1999 London Motor Show held at Earls Court. The Cruiser's display was part of a major effort by Chrysler to expand its presence in the UK under an 'Expect The Extraordinary' theme. This campaign also included a revamped, lower priced Neon with more equipment than when it was first introduced to the UK in 1996, and the availability of a new 5-cylinder, 3.1-liter Turbo Diesel version of the Jeep Grand Cherokee.

"There's no doubt," said Richard McKay, Managing Director of Chrysler Jeep Imports UK, "the PT Cruiser will turn heads at Earls Court next month and on Britain's roads from next summer [production of right-hand drive Cruisers began early in 2000 at the Toluca plant] because it has a stunning look all its own. It has borrowed design cues from classic American cars and interpreted them with an injection of true American fun, freedom and spirit to break down the barriers of conventional car design and function.

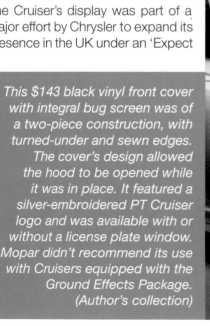

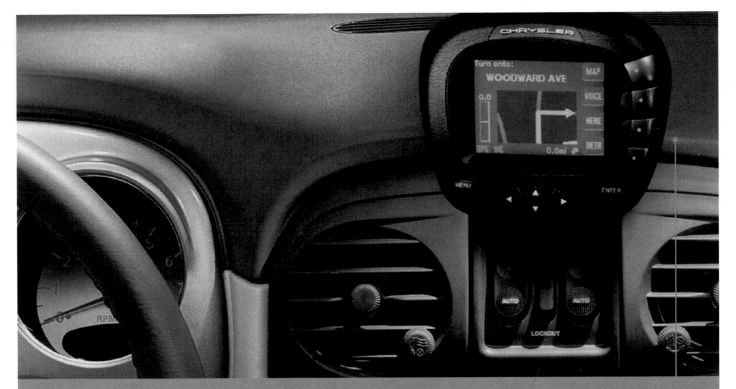

This Mopar Navigation System listed for $1800 and utilized Global Positioning System (GPS) satellite technology and an onboard computer. The system calculated the most efficient route to the driver's destination, provided a visual map display and used voice-command technology to 'talk' the driver through each turn. The system included the purchaser's choice of one of three geographic CDs of the USA. Additional or update geographic CDs were available for $150. (Author's collection)

"Chrysler's design team has brought the entire art form of the automobile to a new level, blending contemporary and nostalgic design ideas to create a look and personality that is unmatched anywhere in the world. There's a hint of a mean and cool American hot rod with the curvaceous styling of the body and the retro touches on the inside. It's unique in many ways – not the least the way it combines versatility and efficiency, wrapped in a distinctly American design blending many characteristics to create an all-new segment in the market."

Virtually from the moment the Cruiser went on display at Earls Court, Chrysler's UK dealers were inundated with inquiries and advance orders. Obviously pleased with this outpouring of enthusiasm, Simon Elliot, Richard McKay's successor as Managing Director of Chrysler and Jeep in the UK, commented: "The PT Cruiser is simply stunning and turns heads everywhere – there is nothing else like it anywhere in the world. But it doesn't just look good – it is immensely practical, comfortable, flexible and versatile. By adhering to a strict design philosophy of 'form follows function', it delivers a highly practical solution to the changing standards of motorists."

Chrysler had been making slow but steady progress in the UK automotive market with the arrival of the Neon in 1996, followed by the Voyager and the Viper (badged as a Chrysler in the UK). Reviewing these developments and his expectations for the PT Cruiser, Simon Elliott explained: "We have a strong foundation in the UK built upon several years of selling highly-praised vehicles and a determination to deliver customer satisfaction at every stage of the purchase and ownership experience. The launch of the eagerly waited PT Cruiser takes us onto a new plane, allowing us to grow by targeting another sector of the market and a new customer base."

The enthusiastic reception given the PT Cruiser by show goers at Earls Court gave free rein to Elliot's optimism about its prospects in the UK: "I expect us to sell our entire allocation of 2600 cars during this year and then we're hoping for an allocation of 6000 cars in our first full year of sales in 2001."

Independence. Today.

Chrysler PT Cruiser from £14,995.

CHRYSLER

Chrysler followed the PT Cruiser's introduction in the UK with a new advertising campaign in June 2001 highlighting its base £14,995 price. Even with 4500 having been sold since July 2000, customer research indicated that the PT Cruiser was consistently perceived as a £20,000 automobile. (Courtesy UK DaimlerChrysler Media Services)

When the PT became available for UK customers, it was offered in three trim levels: Classic, Touring and Limited. "I expect ..." said Elliot, " ... the model mix to be split approximately ten per cent for the Classic, thirty per cent for Touring and sixty per cent for the Limited." Initially, all three versions were powered by the 1996cc 2.0-liter engine. Towards the end of 2001, a 2.2-liter turbo diesel became available. Depicting the 2.0-liter PT Cruiser with its standard 5-speed manual as a blend of lively performance and impressive fuel economy, Chrysler claimed it accelerated from zero to 60mph in 9.6 seconds, and reached a top speed of 118mph. It returned 40.4mpg on the extra urban cycle and a combined cycle figure of 32.5. With the optional 4-speed automatic transmission, the PT Cruiser was credited with a zero to 60mph time of 12.4 seconds and a 103mph maximum speed.

The fuel economy* of the automatic and manual transmission versions of the PT Cruisers were as follows:

Cycle:	Combined	Extra Urban	Urban
Manual	33.6mpg	40.9mpg	26.2mpg
Automatic	28.8mpg	35.8mpg	21.6mpg

*Over time, the official fuel consumption figures released by the government's Department for Transport (DFT) aroused a good deal of controversy in the UK. For example, in 2005, one popular magazine, *Auto Express*, cited statistics indicating that they might be as much as 20 per cent beyond what most motorists might expect from their automobiles. *Auto Express* compared fuel consumption figures provided by automotive manufacturers with the results from what was depicted as a government-approved test covering a mix of driving in town, country and on motorways. In contrast, "the official test", explained David Johns, the editor of *Auto*

The three PT Cruisers had these major equipment specifications:

Item	Classic	Touring	Limited
Driver and front passenger front and side airbags	S	S	S
Four-wheel disc brakes with ABS	NA	S	S
Fog lights	NA	S	S
Traction control	NA	S	S
15 x 6in steel wheels	S	NA	NA
15 x 6in alloy wheels	NA	S	NA
16 x 6in chrome finish alloy wheels	NA	NA	S
Six-speaker AM/FM radio/ cassette/CD player	S	S	S
Air conditioning	S	S	S
Removable rear panel shelf	S	S	S
Cruise control	NA	S	S
Leather wrapped steering wheel	NA	S	S
Leather wrapped gear knob (automatic only)	NA	S	S
Mini overhead console	NA	S	S
Leather/suede seats	NA	NA	S

Express, "is carried out on a mechanical rolling road and bears no comparison to real-life driving on UK roads."

Even before the American versions of the PT Cruiser went on sale officially in March (PT Cruiser sales in Japan and Europe began in May. Chrysler dealers in the UK began selling Cruisers in early July 2000), DaimlerChrysler, recognizing the merits of Raymond Lowey's modus operandi

On November 2, 1999, Tom Gale introduced the GT Cruiser show truck, along with the Howler concept vehicle at the 1999 SEMA show in Las Vegas, Nevada. DaimlerChrysler created a 1950s drive-in theater setting for the Howler/GT Cruiser press conference. The event included classic Chrysler cars, lawn chairs and a concession stand. (Courtesy DaimlerChrysler Media Services)

of never leaving well enough alone, displayed the 'GT Cruiser Concept Show Truck' (subsequently identified as the 'Chrysler GT Cruiser concept vehicle') at the November 1999 Specialty Equipment Market Association's (SEMA) Show in Las Vegas. Tom Gale was on hand to give it a solid send-off. "PT Cruiser is already difficult to categorize," he said. "With GT Cruiser we're showing the SEMA show participants – who are all about customizing and tuning – how we would take PT Cruiser to the next level, with subtle modifications and added power.

"With GT Cruiser we explore just one of the many ways the new Chrysler PT Cruiser can be personalized, and created a customized performance concept."

Also on hand at the show was Kenneth Carlson, Senior Designer at DaimlerChrysler, who was responsible for the GT Cruiser. "We followed traditional customizing guidelines," he said. "However, we applied a distinct modern design vocabulary to the modifications. Lowering the vehicle by one inch, while widening the track by two inches, gives it a mildly 'slammed' impression.

"We also removed the badges from the hood and deck and integrated the bumpers in the fascias. On GT Cruiser, the badges are incorporated in the grille and rear license plate brow, as you would see on a classic hot rod."

Adding to the GT Cruiser's sporty appearance were its dual chrome exhaust pipes, chrome 17in wheels, 215/50 tires and flared fender wheels.

Powering the GT Cruiser was a 2.4-liter turbocharged engine with 200hp @ 6000rpm and 225lb-ft of torque @ 4000rpm. A 5-speed American Club Racing (ACR) manual transmission was used. The lowered suspension incorporated ACR Koni/Mopar struts and upgraded sway bars.

The GT Cruiser made an encore appearance at the 2000 North American International Auto Show (NAIAS), where another PT Cruiser-based concept, the Panel Cruiser, was introduced on January 11. The Panel Cruiser had the same engine/transmission/suspension and revised height and track as the GT Cruiser. Its exterior, with bumpers integrated into the fascias, and lacking hood and deck badges was almost identical to the GT Cruiser's. But there were many,

Although derived from the PT Cruiser, the GT Cruiser had many unique features. Evident here is the absence of a hood badge, the corresponding incorporation of an identification badge into the grille, and the integration of the front bumper into the fascia. (Courtesy DaimlerChrysler Media Services)

Powering the GT Cruiser was a 2.4-liter turbocharged engine with ratings of 200hp @ 6000rpm and 225lb-ft of torque @ 4000rpm. (Courtesy DaimlerChrysler Media Services)

The GT Cruiser's flared fender wells accommodated 17in wheels and 215/45 tires.
(Courtesy DaimlerChrysler Media Services)

easily detectable differences, the most sensational being a wood floor with bright skid strips, and side quarter panels fitted with wood bars and cargo straps.

"Through its siblings, the PT Cruiser and the GT Cruiser show vehicle, The Panel Cruiser show truck," explained Tom Gale, "borrows design cues from classic American panel trucks and combines them with the power, handling and fun of a sports sedan. This concept is a good example of how we're approaching new styles while staying true to the heritage of the Chrysler brand. We've developed a versatile, yet stylish and exciting vehicle to drive."

Focusing on specific attributes of the PT Panel, Kenneth Carlson, Design Manager at DaimlerChrysler, said that "by replacing the rear doors and windows with panels and the rear seat with a wood floor, we've created a versatile rear cargo space that could be used as a light delivery truck or an individual lifestyle vehicle, the possibilities are endless."

As the summer of 2000 came to an end, three additional special edition PT Cruisers were introduced in NYC at the fifth annual Louis Vuitton Classic held at Rockefeller Center in New York City. These three PT Cruisers, along with the PT Panel and GT Cruiser graphically depicted a not-too-distant future when thousands of PT Cruisers would be customized across a nearly boundless plain of self-expression by their owners. The ease with which both independent and DaimlerChrysler designers had transformed an already uniquely designed and proportioned car into a platform for self-expression and individuality made it almost a certainty that the PT Cruiser was about to earn recognition as one of the greatest 'head-turning' automobiles of modern times.

In addition to a Louis Vuitton version, the other special edition PT Cruisers exhibited in New York were created by TAG Heuer and Meguiar's. These were three very different organizations, each having a reputation for the very distinctive

Seen here are Brian Setzer and Michael Castiglione, the Design Manager of DaimlerChrysler's Pacifica Advanced Product Design Center displaying a rendering of Setzer's Vavoom! Cruizer. (Courtesy DaimlerChrysler Media Services)

The Vavoom! Setzer Cruizer was unveiled on October 30, 2000, the eve of the 2000 SEMA show in Las Vegas, Nevada. (Courtesy DaimlerChrysler Media Services)

style of their products. A DaimlerChrysler representative explained that each firm had "seen the PT Cruiser as a marvelous palette upon which to make their own statement through the addition of subtle features mixed with unique colors and fabrics."

Clearly pleased with the results, Tom Gale, who was joined by Trevor Creed who was on hand for the display's September 21 opening, declared that "the PT Cruiser can be whatever the individual owner wants it to be. It fits any lifestyle: some may see it as a tribute to the classic era – a street rod – others as a multi-faceted and functional light truck in a class of its own. Or some as simply a cool set of wheels. You can love it for what it is, or fashion your own statement on this retro-yet-modern vehicle. And the latter is just what we did in concert with our partners at Louis Vuitton, TAG Heuer and Maguiar's."

Luggage provider, Louis Vuitton, which sponsored classic car concours d'elegance events in both North America and Europe, had a long association with the automotive industry. In 1897, its founder, George Vuitton, created what is regarded as the first automotive trunk. This item was, as the name indicated, a trunk designed to be attached to an automobile. Even after storage capacity became an integral part of the automobile, it continued to be identified as 'the trunk'.

The PT Cruiser Louis Vuitton Edition had an Aquamarine metallic paint exterior, 16in chrome wheels, and a chrome exhaust tip. The front door carried a 'PT Cruiser by Louis Vuitton' identification.

Interior features included a 'Louis Vuitton Classic 2000' sun shade, Louis Vuitton 'LV' fabric inserts on the doors and seats, and saddle leather accents on the door pull handles and steering wheel. Naturally, the PT Cruiser's cargo area was fitted with tailor-made Louis Vuitton luggage. Trevor Creed

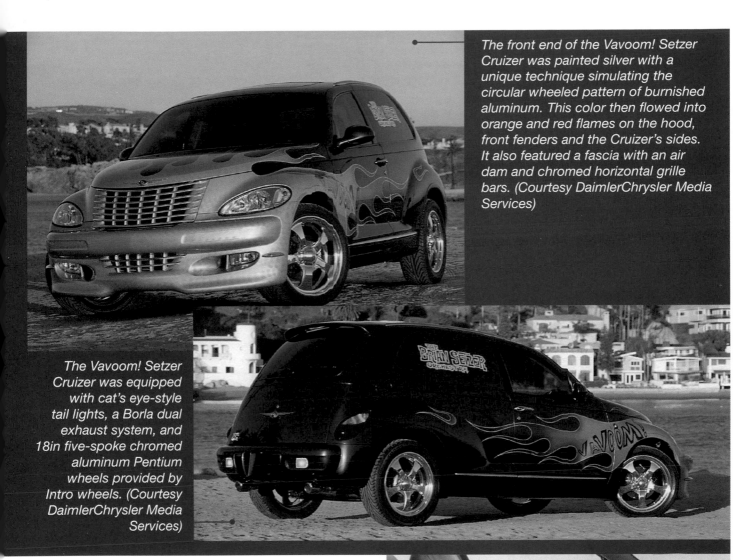

The front end of the Vavoom! Setzer Cruizer was painted silver with a unique technique simulating the circular wheeled pattern of burnished aluminum. This color then flowed into orange and red flames on the hood, front fenders and the Cruizer's sides. It also featured a fascia with an air dam and chromed horizontal grille bars. (Courtesy DaimlerChrysler Media Services)

The Vavoom! Setzer Cruizer was equipped with cat's eye-style tail lights, a Borla dual exhaust system, and 18in five-spoke chromed aluminum Pentium wheels provided by Intro wheels. (Courtesy DaimlerChrysler Media Services)

asserted that the "PT Cruiser Louis Vuitton Edition embodies the attributes valued by both companies: quality and style, tradition and innovation, functionality and creativity."

The TAG Heuer Edition of the PT Cruiser was finished in a Bright Silver Pearl paint, evocative of the cases used for the firm's sport watches. Addtional exterior features included silver TAG Heuer lettering on the front doors, polished, 16in multi-spoked wheels, a chrome exhaust tip and a full-vehicle ground-effects package. The interior was ergonomically-

The Vavoom! Setzer Cruizer's interior reflected the design themes of its exterior. Red leather seat inserts resembled the sounding board of Brian Setzer's classic Gretsch guitar. The seat beading, a flexible neon cable, lit up when the doors were opened. (Courtesy DaimlerChrysler Media Services)

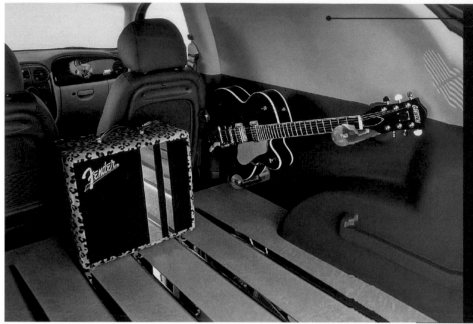

The cargo area behind the Vavoom! Setzer Cruizer's front seats was redesigned with a classic, high-gloss, bird's eye wood truck bed flooring with chrome rub strips. Michael Castiglione called it "the Setzer Swing Dance Floor." A holster for Setzer's guitar was provided for the panel behind the passenger seat, and a combination Fender amplifier and speaker system was mounted on the panel behind the driver. "Setzer can plug his guitar into the amplifier and play it through the system when he's parked at the beach or any time the spirit moves him," said Castiglione. (Courtesy DaimlerChrysler Media Services)

designed with metallic seat and door-trim inserts and bright silver pearl accents on the instrument panel.

Meguiar's had produced quality waxes for automotive surfaces since 1901, and its PT Cruiser was finished in Black Pearl with a 'one-of-a-kind' flame treatment in Maguiar's signature red and yellow. It was also equipped with five-spoke chrome wheels.

Clearly pleased with the outcome of this project, which had been coordinated by several members of DaimlerChrysler's Product Design Office, Creed was willing to lift the curtain just a bit on DaimlerChrysler's future plans for the PT Cruiser. "These special editions," he explained, "are the next design and styling exercises based on this vehicle. Earlier this year we showed the GT Cruiser and Panel Cruiser as the first variations and we will continue to create special editions, either with partners as Louis Vuitton, TAG Hauer and Meguiar's, or as projects by our own design staff. In addition, we know many owners will customize their PT Cruiser based on their impression of just what kind of vehicle it is."

When the GT Cruiser was displayed at the

This 'Futuristic Woody' seen at the 2000 SEMA show was a harbinger of PT Cruisers to come from DaimlerChrysler. (Courtesy DaimlerChrysler Media Services)

1999 SEMA show, Tom Gale had offered a challenge to SEMA's members. After reminding them that "the distinct personality of the Chrysler PT Cruiser is unmatched by any vehicle on the road," he turned his attention to the GT Cruiser, which, he noted, "also borrows design cues from classic American automobiles, but shows how this design can be individualized to suit anyone's taste. With GT Cruiser we're showing the SEMA show participants – who are all about customizing and tuning – how we would take PT Cruiser to the next level: lowered, with subtle modifications and added power. Now it's up to the specialty equipment market to follow our lead."

His call to action was well taken and, at the 2000 SEMA show, displays of highly-modified PT Cruisers were among the most popular exhibits. This extravaganza began on the eve of the Show (October 30, 2000) when the Vavoom! Selzer Cruzier debuted to answer the rhetorical question posed by DaimlerChrysler: "What do Chrysler designers get when they blend big band sound with hot rod attitude, an electric guitar, red hot flames and a grammy-winning artist?"

The grammy winner was Brian Setzer, who, aside from his multi-platinum recording successes was also a custom car aficionado. He had been attracted by the PT Cruiser's appearance and proposed customizing a PT Cruiser that he could take on tour to promote his new album Vavoom!,

an eclectic collection of classic swing, boogie, rock-a-billy and jump blues. Setzer collaborated with DaimlerChrysler's Pacifica Advanced Product Design Center in Carlsbad, California, where he met twice with its Design Manager, Michael Castiglione. "The entire design of the vehicle," said Castiglione, "reflects his latest album Vavoom!, and the street rod cruiser mystique. The brilliant Oriental Blue color, highly stylized flames, and 18in wheel design that recalls the muscle cars of the '50s and '60s were all 'must haves' according to Brian."

Castiglione was responsible for numerous details of the Vavoom! Setzer Cruiser, including a rear spoiler that flowed from the roof over the rear door, a front fascia with an integral air dam, chromed horizontal grille bars, and taillights suggestive of the cat's eye lenses popular with hot rodders in the 1950s.

The Vavoom! Setzer Cruizer was constructed by Gaffoglio Family Metalcrafters, a Fountain Valley, California automotive prototyping specialty house that builds concept vehicles for DaimlerChrysler.

But even the most standard of PT Cruisers was a stand-out vehicle, whether parked on Main Street or at the mall. Cruiser sightings were no longer media events, but the PT Cruiser's ability to turn heads and prompt second looks remained as strong as ever.

With its PT Bruiser, Performance West graphically demonstrated how, by using aftermarket parts, a stock PT Cruiser could be transformed into a strikingly attractive and unique automobile. Under its hood was a supercharged, intercooled engine that was rated at 271hp. With its nitrous-oxide injection system output could be increased to as much as 325hp. It was displayed at the 2000 SEMA show. (Courtesy DaimlerChrysler Media Services)

Law enforcement officers among the visitors to the 2000 SEMA show undoubtedly had visions of enjoying an eight-hour shift of highway patrolling behind the wheel of the Paddy Cruiser. (Courtesy DaimlerChrysler Media Services)

The PT Rodder by BlackByrd Design had overtones of the look and style of the elegant Lincoln-Zephyrs of the late 1930s. (Courtesy DaimlerChrysler Media Services)

Chapter 3 – Cruiser mania

On January 8, 2001, nearly a year after Robert Eaton's announcement at the 2000 North American International Auto Show that the 2001 Chrysler PT Cruiser's starting price would be $16,000, it was named the the 2001 North American Car of The Year at the 2001 Show. The PT Cruiser was selected for this recognition from a group of over twenty new cars by a panel of nearly 50 automotive journalists representing a variety of Canadian and American newspaper, radio, television, magazine and internet news outlets. One of the participants, Denise McCluggage, who in addition to her motor sports journalistic career, was a well known and very successful sports car driver in the 1950s and 1960s, was a charter member of the jury when it was formed in 1992.

The journalists were charged with selecting a vehicle that had set new standards or benchmarks in its class, while considering aspects, such as general design, safety, fuel economy, handling, general roadworthiness, performance, functionality, technical innovation, driver satisfaction and price. The award was open to both new or significantly revamped vehicles that were available in North America during 2001.

For 2001, the three finalists for the North American Car of the Year award were the PT Cruiser, the Honda Insight and the Toyota Prius. In that context, the jurors had first voted in

Chrysler Group President Dieter Zetsche accepted the North American Car of the Year Award for the Chrysler PT Cruiser on January 8, 2001, at the North American International Auto Show. (Courtesy DaimlerChrysler Media Services)

"From Times Square and Sunset Boulevard to the Champs D'Elysee and Potsdamer Platz," said Jim Holden, DaimlerChrysler President, "PT mania is sweeping the globe." (Courtesy DaimlerChrysler Media Services)

one of the three finalists had been the Chrysler 300M), Dieter Zetsche, President and Chief Executive Officer of the Chrysler Group, said: "The Chrysler PT Cruiser is the latest example of innovation from the company that has consistently invented new vehicle segments. That's a tradition we fully intend to preserve. The PT Cruiser demonstrates that you can have head-turning style, practicality and value all in one package."

In addition to the North American Car of the Year Award, the PT Cruiser was also recognized at the show as the *African Americans On Wheels* magazine Car of the Year. It also received two awards from *American Women Road & Travel*: "Car of the Year: Most Likely to Succeed," and "Classic: Most Likely to be Remembered."

On the last day of calendar year 2000, Britain's biggest selling newspaper, *The Sun*, recognized the PT Cruiser as its Car of the Year. Its motoring correspondence, Ken Gibson, declared: "The bold and decidedly different Cruiser was the most refreshing breath of fresh air to hit the motoring scene for years, a family car that turned heads in a way usually reserved for Ferraris."

Responding to Gibson's enthusiastic summation of the Cruiser's appeal, Simon Elliott remarked: "We have always believed the PT Cruiser was a winner from the day we first introduced it to Britain. But to have that belief backed by a publication as big and influential as *The Sun* is very pleasing indeed." As 2001 began, almost every PT Cruiser that Chrysler had brought into the UK had been sold, resulting in a waiting list that extended early into the new year.

During its model run, the 2001 PT Cruiser amassed a long list of awards from a wide spectrum of publications, as this representative sampling indicates:

Source . .. . .Award
AAA .. ..Top Car
Austria Automobile Press 2000. .. .. . Bronze Award
*Automobile Journalists Association
of Canada (AJAC)* .. .. Best New Family Sedan
Under $25,000
Autoweek .. .. America's Best
Business Week. .. .. Products to Watch
Car and Driver.. .. ..10 Best
Consumers Digest.. .. .. Best Buy
Edmund's.com. .. .. Most Significant Vehicle: 2001

Production of right-hand drive PT Cruisers began at the Eurostar factory at Graz, Austria, in mid-July, 2001. The Eurostar plant had the capacity to produce 50,000 PT Cruisers annually. Participants in the July 21, 2001 'Job One' ceremony marking the first day that customer-ready Cruisers began rolling off the assembly line included Eurostar Managing Director Gary Cash, Herbert Paierl, Minister of Economy & Finance of the state of Steiermark, Alfred Stingl, Mayor of Graz, and hundreds of Eurostar employees. (Courtesy UK DaimlerChrysler Media Services)

Just a month after the closing of the 2001 North American Auto Show the PT Cruiser received two additional awards. The first, a Drivers' Choice Award, recognizing the PT Cruiser as the 'Best Cross-Over Vehicle' was presented by the television automotive magazine *Motorweek* on February 8, 2001.

The selection of the winners of the 12 categories established by *Motorweek* was based on superior performance, technology, practicality and dollar value, but the host of *Motorweek* and its executive producer, John Davis, also characterized the PT Cruiser as "the most talked about vehicle of our time."

Whereas the winners of *Motorweek's* Drivers' Choice awards were selected by a team of 17 judges, comprising journalists, staff and crew of *Motorweek*, the recipients of awards presented by the German magazine *auto motor und sport*, for the 'best cars of 2001,' were determined by the results of a poll involving 127,223 people. For vehicles exported to Europe, the Jeep Grand Cherokee finished first in the Off-Road category, with the PT Cruiser the winner in the Van segment.

"This is a special award," commented Dieter Zetsche, "since readers, the people who buy and drive their vehicles for an extended period of time get to chose their favorites in each category. This is quite an honor when you consider the number of readers who participated in this survey and the fact

The Eurostar plant produced both right- and left-hand drive versions of the PT Cruiser for Europe, Asia-Pacific and Africa. (Courtesy UK DaimlerChrysler Media Services)

which soon became known as 'Cruiser mania,' by increasing the availability of PT Cruisers in both North America and Europe. On March 20, 2000, when it had already received over 300,000 requests for information about the PT Cruiser and had already taken many orders, it announced that "in response to unprecedented worldwide demand," it was supplementing production at the Toluca plant by, beginning in the summer of 2001, using its Eurostar facility in Graz, Austria to produce European and 'rest-of-the-world versions' of the PT Cruiser. This was expected to add about 50,000 left- and right-hand drive units of the PT Cruiser annually, for a total of approximately 230,000 worldwide.

"From Times Square and Trafalgar Square," said Jim Holden, DaimlerChrysler Corporation President, "PT mania is sweeping the globe. The phenomenal interest for this vehicle helps underscore the potential growth for the Chrysler brand worldwide.

"The arrival of the Chrysler PT Cruiser has again demonstrated that DaimlerChrysler knows very well how to rewrite the rules in today's incredibly competitive auto industry. In literally inventing a new segment with the PT Cruiser, which is 'too cool to categorize,' we see the overwhelming opportunity to give our customers more of what they want with less wait. The PT Cruiser will take the Chrysler brand to the next level in Europe where it is already sold out for the first year allocation. In addition, this incremental increase in production volume will allow more PT Cruisers to be sold in the North American market."

The utilization of the Eurostar plant, which also produced the Chrysler Voyager for Europe and other international markets, to assemble the PT Cruiser was welcome news for Chrysler's corporate leaders in Europe who had been unable to satisfy increasing demand for the PT Cruiser under the existing production limitations. For example, Simon Elliot, who early on had recognized the PT Cruiser's sales potential in the UK market, commented: "Demand is already very high for PT Cruiser and it shows the level of interest this remarkable car is attracting. I am absolutely delighted that this further commitment has been shown to us in Europe and there is every indication that future capacity for right-hand drive cars could be increased."

The Eurostar plant had been in operation for about ten years and, said, Gary Henson: "Has the capacity, track record and location to best support Europe and rest-of-world markets with the PT Cruiser. In order to react quickly to the demands of our customers, we need the ability to maximize opportunity among our worldwide operations."

Just over a month later, on June 30, 2000, when the PT Cruiser had been on sale for only a short time, DaimlerChrysler reported that the Toluca plant was running at its maximum

that there was representation from 15 European countries. All of us at the Chrysler Group are extremely proud to receive recognition from this prestigious publication."

Arguably the best known Car of the Year (COTY) award had been presented to the PT Cruiser by *Motor Trend* magazine. In its January, 2001 issue, *Motor Trend* set the stage for selecting the PT Cruiser as its 2001 COTY by dismissing cynics who believed that by definition fun cars must be high priced, were convinced there's never anything really new, and that by definition inexpensive cars are dull looking and uninspiring to drive, as people who "have never seen, driven, or enjoyed Chrysler's amazing '01 PT Cruiser."

Against that backdrop *Motor Trend* had no difficulty in singling out the PT Cruiser from a field of 21 vehicles as the car most worthy of being its 2001 COTY. In particular, *Motor Trend* cited the PT's high marks in five of the criteria established for the COTY competition: Design, Daily livability, Value, Special features,and Fun factor.

"People's biggest challenge with the PT," said *Motor Trend* in summing up its impressions and evaluation of the PT Cruiser, "is trying to categorize it. Is it a heritage-design inspired economy car? Ultra-cool, compact wagon? High-value family hauler? Affordable hot rod? Call Chrysler's innovatively conceived, smashingly styled, intelligently packaged, inexpensive, fun-to-drive, ultra-practical, positively segment-busting PT Cruiser anything you want. We call it *Motor Trend's* 2001 Car of the Year." By the time the January 2001 issue of *Motor Trend* reached the newsstands and the mailboxes of its subscribers, it was hard to imagine anyone over the age of twelve who hadn't seen a PT Cruiser. From its market introduction in March 2000, to mid-April 2001, over 175,000 had been sold in fifty-eight countries worldwide.

DaimlerChrysler had reacted quickly to this demand,

The Chrysler Group introduced this PT Cruiser Convertible Styling Study at an April 11 press conference held at the Chrysler stand at the 2001 New York International Auto Show. (Courtesy DaimlerChrysler Media Services)

daily rate of 40 vehicles per hour. This was achieved two weeks ahead of schedule and represented a gain of 4000 units for the year.

DaimlerChrysler also announced that there were fourteen Eurostar engineers at Toluca 'bench marking' the plant's best practices in preparation for PT Cruiser production in Graz.

Even these efforts proved inadequate to meet demand and, on April 23, 2001, DaimlerChrysler announced that it would invest $300 million to increase production at Toluca by 80,000 units annually beginning in the autumn of 2002. Commenting on this decision, Dieter Zetsche said: "Among the many scenarios we studied to gain incremental volume of PT Cruiser, this was the best business decision."

Product Design Vice President Trevor Creed portrayed the Convertible Styling Study, along with the earlier GT Cruiser and Panel Cruiser designs, as examples of the PT Cruiser's multi-faceted personality. (Courtesy DaimlerChrysler Media Services)

While DaimlerChrysler was scrambling to crank up the supply of PT Cruisers to meet demand, various publications and professorial organizations continued to acknowledge the PT Cruiser's innovative design. On June 29, 2001, the Chrysler Group was the only automotive manufacturer to receive Gold Awards from the 2001 Industrial Design Excellence Awards (IDEA) Competition, an annual contest sponsored by the Industrial Designers Society of America (IDSA) and *Business*

Week magazine. Chrysler was the recipient of two Gold Awards, one for the PT Cruiser in the Transportation category; the second, in the Design Explorations competition, for the Jeep Willys concept vehicle. "It's an honor," remarked Dieter Zetsche, "to receive awards for the PT Cruiser – a success story we have on the road right now – and the Jeep Willys, a concept vehicle that we unveiled earlier this year. We have a proud heritage of bringing concepts to reality and it's gratifying for our company to be recognized for what we have in our dealerships now and for what could be available in the future."

A record number of entries, 1260, were received for the 2001 competition from locations around the world, including South Korea, Germany (the Mercedes-Benz C-Class won a Transportation Bronze Award), France, Japan, Italy, Britain, Canada, Singapore, and the Netherlands. There were 44 gold winners, as well as 63 silver and 82 bronze prizes.

Following its media debut, Trevor Creed unveiled the PT Cruiser Convertible Styling Study to the general public at the NY Auto Show. Its appearance was highlighted by a lowered header and roof, 19in wheels, and resculptured rear wheel flares. (Courtesy DaimlerChrysler Media Services)

The selection process for the Gold Awards was conducted by a jury of 18 non-affiliated designers who reviewed all entries during two-and-a-half days of evaluation and debate. "For sheer emotional appeal," wrote *Business Week* in its June 25, 2001 issue, highlighting all the Gold Award winners, "the PT Cruiser is a grabber. Its retro design from the 1940s makes for a crossover hot rod – one that has a sensible four-cylinder price and lots of interior space."

All the winners were later honored at a gala celebration closing the 2001 IDSA National Convention at the Berklee Performance Center in Boston, Massachusetts. The winners were also featured in a Design Gallery running through the convention in the Park Plaza Castle as well as on the IDSA's website, www.idsa.org.

On the same day, the IDEA awards were announced, *Autoweek* magazine released the results of its 13th annual reader survey. *Autoweek* had a weekly circulation of 340,000 and the survey had been sent to a one per cent random sampling of its readers. Included in the survey's list of the top ten 'Best American Cars' were the Dodge Viper, Chrysler 300M and the PT Cruiser.

The PT Cruiser received yet another award when the research firm Strategic Visions announced on July 3, 2001 that it was the winner in the Compact Car segment of its 2001 Total Quality Index (TQI) survey. Strategic Vision had assessed new vehicle owner satisfaction and calculated TQI annually since 1995. It was a detailed measure of the new car owner experience, including the owner's emotional response to the vehicle. Owners participating in this study had purchased their vehicles in October, November and December of 2000. They were surveyed after they had had at least 90 days to experience their car or truck.

Joining the PT Cruiser as TQI segment winners from DaimlerChrysler was the Dodge Dakota, Chrysler Town & Country and Chrysler LHS. Regarding the PT Cruiser's first place finish, Strategic Vision commented: "Style, craftsmanship, ease of use, thoughtfulness and innovation get especially high marks, delivering strong emotions of freedom, esteem and harmony. This is a smart choice that's fun to drive and gives its owners great delight."

In response, Richard Schaum, DaimlerChrysler's Executive Vice President of Product Development and Quality, had this to say: "When it comes to quality, consumers want to get information from credible, prestigious third party organizations such as Strategic Visions. That's why we're extremely honored to finish first in every one of these critical segments. We're also pleased that Strategic Visions named Chrysler the most improved brand in the study."

During 2001, with sales booming and the Toluca plant

After calling the Convertible "drop-top gorgeous" at the 2001 New York Auto Show, DaimlerChrysler played the role of the party wet fish by declining to announce any plans for its production. (Courtesy DaimlerChrysler Media Services)

Major aspects of transforming a 4-door PT Cruiser into a 2-door convertible included lowering the header and roof, utilizing a special windshield, one inch shorter than on the production model, resculpting the rear fender flares, and, to accommodate the longer doors, the use of a new rear panel. The operating convertible top originated as a Chrysler Sebring unit.

Giving the convertible added distinction were body-colored bumpers and a chrome-accented grille. In addition, the vehicle was lowered by 1.5in (38mm). New York-themed 'Empire' 19in cast aluminum wheels were used along with custom made BF Goodrich 225/35ZR19 tires. The Convertible powertrain was identical to the production model PT Cruiser's.

Design Director, Lance Wagner, provided additional details of the Convertible's creation and identity. "Based on the regular production Chrysler PT Cruiser, the convertible's design," he said, "emphasizes its free-spirited attitude. We

working at maximum capacity to meet demand, Chrysler didn't miss a beat as it kept public interest in the PT Cruiser at a fever pitch. On April 11, at the 2001 New York International Auto Show, Trevor Creed's designers showed off their latest design study, a PT Cruiser Convertible. Later in the year, on October 24, the Convertible was shown in Japan for the first time at the Tokyo Auto Show.

"The PT Cruiser Convertible is a natural," asserted Creed. "In the same tradition as the Chrysler GT Cruiser and PT Panel Cruiser styling studies, this vehicle shows yet another personality for PT Cruiser. Once again we want to demonstrate the tremendous potential of PT Cruiser."

Later, in October 2001, the Convertible Styling Study made its Asian debut at the Tokyo Auto Show. Its Deep-Shadow-Blue Pearl exterior was joined by a interior featuring a Dark Taupe and Light Pearl Beige color scheme, with Cognac and body-color Blue accents. (Courtesy DaimlerChrysler Media Services)

created a more simplified form. For example, the bodyside molding recesses were filled in to strengthen its contemporary clean lines. There's purity in the convertible's design that respects the original styling. While its fresh appearance embodies a totally new character, it still retains and builds on the excitement of the PT Cruiser."

As a derivative of the PT Cruiser, the convertible's appearance exhibited both modern and classic styling themes. Its powered 'fastback' top was singled out by Creed as a prime example of this design duality. "Many will say," he began, "that the Chrysler PT Cruiser Convertible is two vehicles in one. It has a certain modern look when the top is down with its sport bar and long passenger compartment. Yet when up, the top has a slammed-forward retro-position, much like a '30s custom chopped coupé, emulating the tension of an archer's bow being drawn back."

Taking this opportunity to give his audience a hint of what DaimlerChrysler had in store for the PT Cruiser, Creed added that "... the PT Cruiser Convertible styling study is the latest example of the sort of fun we can have with PT Cruiser. And there's more to come."

The Convertible's exterior was finished in Deep-Shadow-Blue Pearl Coat, while the interior had a Dark Taupe and Light Pearl Beige color scheme with cognac and body-color blue accents. Seating was provided for four passengers, with the rear seat occupants sitting higher than those in the front for what Chrysler described as a "command-of-the-road experience."

As Senior Design Manager, Jeff Godshall, who was responsible for the convertible's interior pointed out, this feature minimized the impact upon interior space of a slight reduction in roof height as compared to the production model. "Even though the convertible roof was lowered by an inch (25.4mm)," he explained, "the rear passenger compartment provides ample room and comfort."

Godshall also commented on other unique aspects of the convertible's interior: "Utility and convenience are added to the interior with a speaker and a mesh storage pocket completing the longer front door trim panels, and a recessed arm rest and courtesy light in each quarter panel. Equally practical, the rear and front passenger seats fold down for easy storage, providing pass-through for such things as golf clubs, skis, or surf boards."

As part of the events associated with the 2001 New York International Auto Show, *Road & Track* sponsored an evening charity 'Tailgate Party' to benefit the East Side House Settlement. Displayed along with a Ford Thunderbird Convertible was the Chrysler PT Cruiser Convertible.

Later, in mid-August, PT Cruiser owners were invited to join with Plymouth Prowler owners in the 'Woodward Dream Cruise' a run down Detroit's Woodward Avenue with the reputation as one of North America's most famous 'cruise strips.' The Dream Cruise was held annually on the third Saturday of August and was described as "the world's largest one day show celebrating the cars that made Detroit and the cruising era so special," attracted over 1.5 million visitors and over 30,000 muscle cars, street rods, custom, collector and special interest vehicles. Seeming to be taking a cue from this enthusiastic, easy-on-the eyes celebration of automotive passion that blended the best of the past with today's newest hot commodity, Chrysler announced on August 15 that it would be adding two new offerings to the PT Cruiser lineup in 2002: the Dream Series 1 and the Woodie edition.

"Without question," said Tom Marinelli, Vice President-Chrysler/Jeep Global Brand Center, "Chrysler PT Cruiser has become an icon for the Chrysler brand. By offering two

A massive gathering of PT Cruisers and Plymouth Prowlers at the August 2001 Woodward Dream Cruise down Detroit's Woodward Avenue. (Courtesy DaimlerChrysler Media Services)

"You're not dreaming. This is a reality," said Chrysler, as the Dream Cruiser Series 1 made its debut. Clearly pressing all the right buttons on the Cruiser Mania keypad, it reported that it was the first in a line of factory-customized Dream Cruisers to be introduced yearly. The Inca Gold paint color was exclusive to the Dream Cruiser 1. (Author's collection).

new models, we're broadening the appeal for PT Cruiser while keeping the brand and nameplate fresh in consumers' minds."

In the case of the Dream Cruiser, which arrived in dealer showrooms in February, 2002, (Dream Cruiser production began on January 7, 2002, and only 7500 were built in North America), it was identified by Chrysler as "the first in a series of factory-customized Dream Cruisers to be introduced on an annual basis." The Dream Cruiser's MSRP, effective August 15, 2001, was $23,170 with manual transmission and $23,995 with the automatic transaxle, including a $565 destination charge.

Linking the Dream Cruiser to an important development in PT Cruiser history was its Inca Gold exterior. This was an evolution of the color first shown on the Chrysler Pronto Cruizer when it debuted at the 1998 Salon de l'Automobile in Geneva. This chrome-yellow gold color with its metallic spark was exclusive to the Dream Cruiser. Trevor Creed was pleased with this color and the exterior appointments that accompanied its use. "Visually, the Inca Gold monochromatic appearance unifies the Chrysler PT Cruiser's dramatic form," he said. "With its unique color-keyed grille, bumpers and bodyside moldings, the vehicle takes on more of a customized look."

Special Inca Gold trim was used on the Dream Cruiser 1's doors and seats. Matrix leather was installed on the seat cushions, seatback inserts, steering wheel and automatic transmission shift knob.
(Author's collection)

The Dream Cruiser 1 was equipped with these 16in Mopar chrome wheels with a customized gold center cap and a bright PT Cruiser graphic.
(Author's collection).

As Dream Cruisers were produced, they were numbered sequentially, and a plaque on the dash told owners which of the 7500 manufactured was theirs.
(Author's collection)

The driver of this 2002 Dream Cruiser Series 1 undoubtedly was warmly welcomed by the Street Cruiser club that gathered at this diner every Wednesday night. The Dream Cruiser Series 1 was available beginning in February 2002. (Courtesy DaimlerChrysler Media Services)

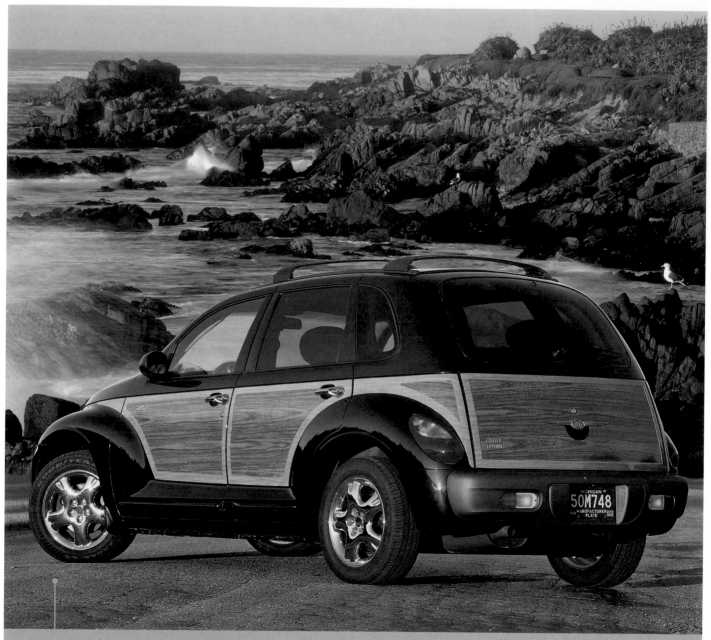

Long-time Chrysler enthusiasts easily saw the influence of the 1941 and 1942 Chrysler Town & Country models in the 'Woodie' accent option (officially identified as the Woodgrain Exterior Accents Package) for the 2002 PT Cruiser. (Courtesy DaimlerChrysler Media Services)

Additional exterior features of the Dream Cruiser consisted of a 'Dream Cruiser Series 1 chrome badge on the liftgate, body color roof molding, 16in MOPAR chrome wheels with customized gold center caps, and bright PT Cruiser graphics.

Inca Gold-colored accents were key elements of the Dream Cruiser's interior, positioned on key elements including instrument panel and cluster, bezel and passenger-side airbag. Door bolsters were finished in a matching gold grain vinyl. The seats were upholstered in a Dark Taupe/Light Pearl Beige combination with Inca Gold half-moon inserts. A unique 'Matrix' textured leather was used for the seat

This Touring Edition PT Cruiser's Patriot Blue Pearl Coat finish makes a handsome contrast with the Woodgrain Exterior Accents' natural appearance. Chrysler, happy to associate the Woodgrain's appearance with the best of the past, noted that "it hearkens back to Chrysler's strong wood-body car heritage, and recreates the carefree fun of 1960s California surf wagons." The Woodgrain graphics could be applied to any color PT Cruiser. (Author's collection)

cushion, seat back inserts, steering wheel, and, on models with automatic transmission, the shift knob.

Integrated into the Dream Cruiser's instrument panel was a plaque reading 'Dream Cruiser Series 1' that also marked the vehicle 1-7500, indicating its position in the production run. In addition, 'Dream Cruiser' lettering was embroidered with Inca floor mats.

The Dream Cruiser was also equipped with Anti-Lock 4-wheel disc brakes with traction control, heated front seats, an AM/FM radio with cassette and CD. Except for the automatic transmission, there were no options offered for the Dream Cruiser Series 1.

Far less expensive than the Dream Cruiser, with an $895 MSRP, the visual impact of the Woodie option was also less startling since many aftermarket companies began offering wood panel applications for the PT Cruiser almost as soon as it became available in early 2000. One such aftermarket package was developed by Auto-Tech Plastics of Mt Clements, Michigan. Its president, Ron Schuman, asserted that Auto-Tech had carefully duplicated the look of the Marine Teak and Sara Rosa Oak that had been used by many of the manufacturers of woodie models in the 1930s and '40s. "We have very carefully duplicated the look of those materials using modern polymers and advanced manufacturing processes," Schuman explained. "It's not at all uncommon for people to ask us whether these panels are 'real' wood."

Chrysler avoided being stigmatized as a copycat of these products by linking the PT Woodie with vehicles from its past. "For the Chrysler PT Cruiser 'Woodie' Edition," a media representative explained, "Chrysler designers reached back to the brand's strong wood-body car heritage which was established in 1941 through 1950 with the Chrysler Town & Country series. Later, in 1968, Chrysler introduced simulated wood-panel design applications on its stationwagons, and most recently on its best-selling Chrysler and Dodge minivans in the 1980s and Jeep Grand Cherokee in the early 1990s."

Concerning himself with the challenge designers faced in creating a fresh interpretation of this heritage for use on the PT Cruiser, Trevor Creed remarked, "... we wanted a design execution that recreated the carefree fun of the popular 1960s California surf wagons. We wanted a clean, elegant execution that flowed with the lines of the car as well as a professional factory-level look currently not available in the aftermarket."

The Woodie option was available, beginning in November 2001, for all three PT Cruiser models and consisted of a graphic that was applied to the doors, quarter panels and liftgate. The graphic was a linear Medium Oak woodgrain framed with Light Ash surround moldings.

This Deep Cranberry PT Cruiser with Fading Blue-to-Cranberry flames was displayed at the June 7, 2001 'What's New for 02' presentation at DaimlerChrysler's Chelsea, Michigan Proving Grounds. (Courtesy DaimlerChrysler Media Services)

Chrysler predicted that the 2002 PT Cruiser, with its new flame accents, would "heat things up" in 2002. (Courtesy DaimlerChrysler Media Services)

When Tom Marinelli participated in the introduction of the Dream Cruiser 1 and the Woodie option, he indicated that Chrysler wouldn't need any prodding to make the most of a great idea. "Look for Chrysler," he said, "to continue to launch models similar to these into the marketplace."

PT Cruiser fans had only to wait for the June 7, 2001, "What's New for '02" presentation at DaimlerChrysler's Chelsa, Michigan Proving Grounds for the next installment of Cruiser mania. Calling it "the hottest vehicle on the road," Chrysler said the PT Cruiser would be heating things up in 2002 with a new Flames option. Seemingly inspired by the contents of a mid-fifties *Hot Rod* magazine, DaimlerChrysler reported that the new option made it possible for customers to order a 2002 PT Cruiser with "subtle tone-on-tone flames rippling over the hood and front fenders."

Tom Marinelli needed little coaxing to take the Flames story beyond this point. "The PT Cruiser has been enthusiastically received in the custom car community," he began. "The optional flames are a great way to extend that excitement to our entire PT Cruiser customer base. The PT cruiser is rejuvenating America's love affair with the automobile. For those who love customized cars, this is a great way to rekindle that spirit. There's an entire customer base that has never personalized a vehicle and this is a fun way to start."

The coordinating flames were available in four exterior colors:

❖ Fading Orange-to-Red flames with Inferno Tinted Pearl Coat.
❖ Fading Blue-to-Cranberry flames with Deep Cranberry Pearl Coat.
❖ Fading Dark Silver-to-Bright Silver with Bright Silver Metallic.
❖ Fading Deep Magenta-to-Black flames highlighted by a Blue border.

In its second model year the PT Cruiser, having no direct competitors in the North American market, was cross-shopped against luxury sedans, sport utility vehicles and minivans. When the PT Cruiser was equipped with the optional Flames Accent package, it was all "down-hill" for those competitors. (Courtesy DaimlerChrysler Media Services)

A Black 2002 PT Cruiser with the Flames option. Its six-spoke 16in chrome-clad wheels were a late availability option for 2002. They were available only for Touring and Limited Edition models in Bright Silver, Inferno Red, Deep Cranberry and Black. (Courtesy DaimlerChrysler Media Services)

The vinyl flames were applied after the PT Cruiser left the Toluca paint shop and, like the Woodie trim, were covered under Chrysler's three-year/36,000 mile warranty. The MSRP for the flame accents was was $495. They were available for all 2002 PT Cruiser models except the Dream Cruiser Series 1.

Asserting that "no other car maker is bold enough to offer such an option," Tom Marinelli added that "... on no other vehicle would it be so appropriate. That's what makes PT Cruiser so special."

Chrysler didn't need any additional help in making the PT Cruiser one of the most talked about cars since the 1947 Studebakers, but it received it anyway at the November 2001 SEMA show where Decoma International displayed its PT/10 Lifestyle Cruiser, a 500hp Viper-powered pickup based on the PT Cruiser. Decoma International was the world's largest supplier of high-volume production exterior parts for automakers. The workmanship of the PT/10 exemplified

Decoma's international reputation for also creating high quality low production and one-off speciality vehicles.

In the case of the PT/10, the replacement of the PT Cruiser's rear doors and hatch with a pickup box was so effective and aesthetically pleasing that some industry observers envisioned it as a forerunner of a production version. That didn't happen, but even in the rarefied atmosphere of the SEMA show, where the audacious was commonplace, it was one of the event's most popular attractions. Its 500hp Viper RT/10 V10 engine was part of a powertrain/suspension system that, supported by a custom tube frame, included a 6-speed manual transmission, a side exhaust system, BBS wheels, Wilwood Venter disc brakes, Michelin high-performance tires, and a combination of Viper and Air Lift Company suspension components.

The Lifestyle Cruiser's pickup box was protected by a stainless steel tonneau cover. Highlighting its front end appearance was a unique grille and fascia. Additional

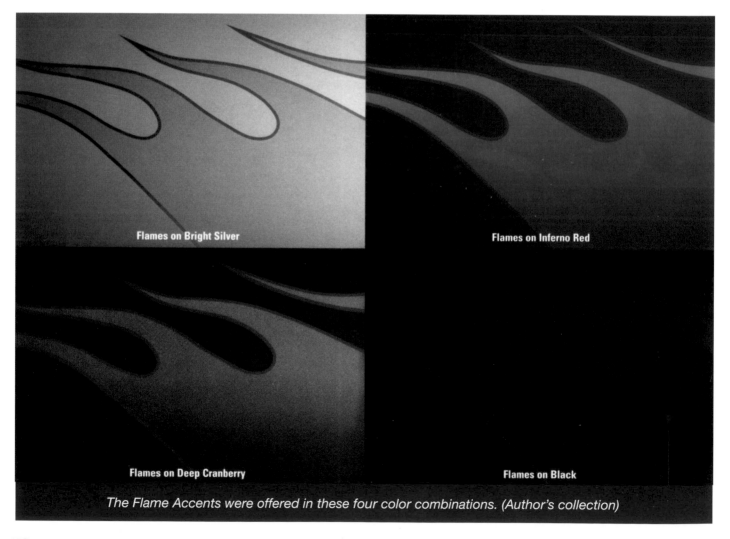

The Flame Accents were offered in these four color combinations. (Author's collection)

The Decoma PT/10 Lifestyle Vehicle as seen at the 2001 SEMA Show in Las Vegas. DaimlerChrysler noted that it "nears the limits of PT extremism." (Courtesy DaimlerChrysler Media Services)

distinctive features included custom taillights, rear roll pan and a bed spoiler.

Dieter Zetsche, making his first visit to a SEMA show, announced on October 31, that DaimlerChrysler was awarding its SEMA 2001 Design Excellence Award to Decoma for the PT/10. Chrysler based its Design Excellence Award on design achievement, craftsmanship, market significance, technical execution, attention to detail and overall lifestyle focus and relevance.

Also receiving recognition in the form of a Chrysler Brand Application Excellence Award for its performance hood application for the PT Cruiser was the PTeaser Corporation. Joining PTeaser as recipients of this award were Kamanari

(Performance Hood Application for Neon), AMP Research (Retractable Step Assist for Dodge truck) and Maggiolina (Roof Mounted Tent Structure for Jeep). They were evaluated on standards very similar to those used to select the winner of the Design Excellence Award, including design achievement, overall quality, technical execution, attention to detail and conceptual relevance.

The entries for both awards were judged by the Chrysler Group's Image Team, consisting of four cross-functional teams representing Engineering, Design, Product Planning and Marketing. Its leader, Dennis Myles, DaimlerChrysler's Senior Design Manager, explained the importance of these programs to DaimlerChrysler. "Through the Design Excellence

A view of the 500hp Viper V10 nestled in the PT/10's engine bay. (Courtesy DaimlerChrysler Media Services)

and Application Excellence Awards," he said, "we recognize the outstanding innovation, creativity and craftsmanship of SEMA members and their contribution to a growing speciality market that is now more than $24 billion strong. These awards are a reflection of the growing relationship we've developed with the speciality manufacturers."

For the 2002 model year, the PT Cruiser's three Equipment Groups were replaced by three models ranked according to their ascending prices:

Model	MSRP Effective June 1, 2001	MSRP Effective March 9, 2002
Base	$16,200	$16,400
Touring	$17,915	$18,115
Limited	$20,265	$20,465

The PT Cruiser's Destination Charge for June 1, 2001 was $565. It was increased to $590 for March 9, 2002.

Standard on all models was the front passenger underseat storage bin. Also included on all 2002 PT Cruisers was a new front passenger seat inboard armrest. The outboard head restraints for the rear seats on the Touring and Limited Edition models had a new 'Low Profile' design. Improved seat cushion lateral support was provided for the Limited Edition's front seats. All models had a new emergency seat back release handle that was accessible from the rear

cargo area. Chrome-plated 16in aluminum wheels were now optional for the Touring Edition. Previously, they had been available only with the Luxury Touring Group.

Deleted from the PT Cruiser's exterior color selection was Aquamarine and Shale Green. Two new colors, Light Almond Pearl Metallic Clear Coat (Code PKJ), and Steel Blue Pearl Coat (Code PBQ), joined these colors carried over from 2001: Black Clear Coat, Bright Silver Metallic Clear Coat, Deep Cranberry Pearl Coat, Inferno Red Tinted Pearl Coat (available at additional cost of $200), Patriot Blue Pearl Coat, Stone White Clear Coat and Taupe Frost Metallic Clear Coat.

As the following chart indicates, a change in the axle ratio from 3.94 to 3.45 for 2002 resulted in new overall gear ratios for 5-speed manual PT Cruisers.

Overall gear ratios	2001	2002
1st	13.79	12.075
2nd	7.726	6.762
3rd	5.358	1.36
4th	3.825	4.692
5th	1.974	2.797
Reverse:	13.474	11.799
Final drive:	3.94	3.45
Overall top gear:	3.20	2.8

No changes were made in the gearing of the optional 4-speed automatic transmission.

As a current production model, the 2002 PT Cruiser was not regarded as a competitor for the industry's wide range of Car-Of-The-Year-related awards. It did, however, receive the Reader's Choice Award: Crossover Vehicle from Woman Motorist.com. Also, as Tom Marinelli explained, the

Standard and optional features of the three PT Cruiser models.

Feature	Base	Touring	Limited
Exterior black center-pillar applique	S	S	S
Rear window defroster	S	S	S
Bright door handles	S	S	S
Front and rear fascias (accent/body color)	S	S	S
Fog lamps (included instrument cluster warning)	NA	S	S
Solar glass (all windows)	S	S	S
Deep-tint sunscreen in rear door, quarter and liftgate windows, solar control in windshield and front doors	O	S	S
Halogen headlamps	S	S	S
Bright door and liftgate lock bezels	S	S	S
Mirrors:			
Manual, remote control	S	NA	NA
Power, heated foldaway [1]	P	S	S
Power Moonroof (tilt/vent/slide with solar glass, sliding sunshade and one-touch open feature	O	O	S
Body color side molding	S	S	S
Roof rack (included two continuously adjustable cross bars with "side-by-side spoiler" appearance, and			

Feature	Base	Touring	Limited
quick release latches	Q	Q	Q
Two-speed windshield wipers with variable intermittent delay and mist cycle	S	S	S
Rear window wiper with intermittent delay	S	S	S
Interior			
Assist handles [2]	P	S	S
Cargo net	NA	S	S
Carpet (passenger and cargo compartment)	S	S	S
Air conditioning (with fluidic instrument panel outlets	S	S	S
Floor heater outlets (front and rear)	S	S	S
Rear coat hooks (two)	S	S	S
Full length floor console (included two front, one center and one rear cup holder; removable coin holder; pencil tray; CD/cassette holder; front storage slot; center storage tray	S	S	S
Overhead console (included driver and passenger map/reading lamps with integral on/off switches, compass and outside temperature display with U.S/metric switch, standard rearview mirror [2]	P	S	S
Door trim panel and bolster material: Tipton II cloth	S	S	NA
Preferred Suede	NA	NA	S
Door trim storage pockets (front and rear)	S	S	S
Carpeted floor mats (front and rear)	S	S	S
Locking glove box	S	S	S
Instrument cluster: Digital display, odometer, trip odometer, door ajar and liftgate ajar	S	S	S
Gauges: 120mph (200km/hr) speedometer, 6000rpm tachometer, fuel level and engine temperature	S	S	S
Turn signal indicators	S	S	S
High-gloss instrument cluster			

Feature	Base	Touring	Limited
bezel and passenger airbag door, color-keyed to selected exterior colors; accent color with all others	S	S	S
Console flood lamp [2]	P	S	S
Front dome and cargo compartment lamps (included theatre dimming and automatic time out)	S	S	S
Manual day/night rearview mirror	S	S	S
Power outlets (12-volt):			
Instrument panel and cargo area [2]	P	S	S
Center console	S	S	S
Radios:			
Fixed antenna	S	S	S
AM/FM stereo with CD player and changer controls	S	S	S
AM/FM stereo with cassette and CD players	O	O	O
Premium speakers (six)	S	S	S
Tilt steering column	S	S	S
Seat material:			
Tiplon II cloth	S	S	NA
Royale leather with preferred suede accents, vinyl side facings and vinyl rear center insert	NA	NA	S
Front seats:			
Reclining low-back buckets with adjustable locking head restraints and passenger inboard pivoting armrests and passenger seat back map pocket	S	S	S
Driver manual lumbar support	NA	NA	S
Heated driver and front passenger seats	NA	NA	S
Fold flat front passenger seat with seat back tray and driver seat back storage pocket	NA	S	S
Diver seat power height adjuster	NA	O	S
Fold and tumble rear seats with 65/35 split cushion and back and quick release removal	S	S	S
Removable five-position			

Feature	Base	Touring	Limited
shelf panel	S	S	S
Leather-wrapped shift knob (automatic transmission only)	NA	NA	S
Speed control	O	O	S
Steering wheel with molded urethane rim	S	S	NA
Leather-wrapped steering wheel	NA	NA	S
Under seat storage drawer	S	S	S
Sliding sun visors with covered mirrors with illuminated mirrors [2]	P	S	S
Power windows	S	S	S
Powertrain and chassis:			
2.4-liter engine	S	S	S
Five-speed manual transmission	S	S	S
Four-speed automatic transmission	O	O	O
Power brakes: front disc/rear drum)	S	S	S
Engine block heater	O	O	O
Chrome exhaust tip	NA	S	S
Normal duty suspension	S	NA	NA
Touring tuned suspension	NA	S	S
Compact spare tire	S	S	S
P195/65R15 BSW All-season touring tires	S	NA	NA
P205/55R16 BSW All-season touring	NA	S	S
Bolt-on wheel covers with bright retaining nuts and 15 x 6in steel wheels	S	NA	NA
Chrome plated 16 x 6in aluminum wheels	NA	O	S
Painted (silver) 16 x 6in aluminum wheels	NA	S	NA
Safety and security:			
Accident response illumination system	S	S	S
Brake-shift and park-ignition inter locks (auto.trans only)	S	S	S
Clutch-ignition interlock (manual transmission only)	S	S	S
Outboard rear seat, low profile head restraints, two way adjustable, locking	NA	S	S

Feature	Base	Touring	Limited
Remote Keyless Entry (includes two transmitters and panic alarm [3]	P	S	S
Power locks (included central locking and customer programmable automatic operation) [3]	P	S	S
Rear door child protection	S	S	S
Next-generation driver and front passenger airbags	S	S	S
Restraint system (front outboard occupant supplemental side airbags [4]	O	O	S
Height-adjustable seat belts	S	S	S
Rear seat trapped occupant release handle	S	S	S
Security alarm [5]	NA	S	S
Sentry Key theft-deterrent system	NA	S	S
User-ready LATCH child seat anchorage system	S	S	S
Warning chimes (key in ignition, headlamps on, low fuel or front seat belt not buckled)	S	S	S
Equipment Package Groups			
ABS Traction Group (included 4-wheel disc, anti-lock brakes and traction control)	O	O	O
Light Group (included overhead console with compass and temperature display, sliding sun visors with illuminated vanity mirrors, auxiliary 12-volt power outlets, four interior assist handles and console flood lamp)	O	NA	NA
Power Convenience Group (included power door locks with central locking and programmable automatic operation, power heated foldaway exterior mirrors and remote Keyless Entry System)	O	NA	NA

[1] Inc. in Base PT Cruiser's Power Convenience Group, which was a new option for the Base model.
[2] Included in Base model's Light Group.
[3] Included in Base model's Power Convenience Group.

⁴ Included passenger seat back map pocket and carpet inserts on Base and Touring, and dual seat back map pockets on Limited.

⁵ Included horn pulse, flashing headlamps and park lamps, and instrument cluster warning lamp.

Options available for the 2002 PT Cruiser.

Option Code	Option	MSRP
DGL	4-speed automatic transmission	$825.00
ADA	Light Group (Base)	$250.00
AJP	Convenience Group (Base)	$570.00
AJA	Moonroof:	
	Base	$845.00
	Touring	$595.00
BRT	anti-lock braking system	$595.00
GEG	deep tinted rear glass (Base)	$275.00
NHK	engine block heater	$35.00
MWG	luggage rack	$175.00
RAZ	AM/FM stereo radio with CD and cassette/equalizer	$100.00
CGS	restraint system	$350.00
NHM	speed control	$235.00
PEL	Inferno Red Tinted Pearl Coat	$200.00
	Vinyl Flames	$495.00
	Woodie applique (available after November, 2001)	$895
CMA	Heater front seats	$250.00
JPN	Power driver's seat adjuster	$100.00
WD6	Chrome aluminum wheels	$600.00

PT Cruiser played a major role in Chrysler's 'Drive-Love' advertising theme for its 2002 product line. "This theme," he said, "really underscores in a very direct yet effective way what the Chrysler brand is all about. We have focused on the Chrysler brand to appeal to customers who are confident, creative and extroverted. They are people who don't want basic transportation but a vehicle that expresses their individuality. In other words, a vehicle they can fall in love with. The best example is the PT Cruiser which is arguably one of the biggest product successes in recent times. Our new campaign communicates this relationship with advertising that is fun and appealing."

Credited with creating the 'Drive-Love' tag line, as well as developing all the television and prints ads was Pentamark Worldwide of Troy, Michigan, a full-service global marketing communications agency. For DaimlerChrysler, it provided advertising, marketing, media planning and buying.

The emphasis of the 'Drive' component of the campaign which began on September 10, 2001 with two spots on *Monday Night Football*, emphasized engineering and performance, while the 'Love' aspect focused on the emotional connection between car and owner. "Together," said Tom Marinelli, "Drive-Love acknowledges the fact that love is a powerful emotion that can lift the driving experience from the mundane to the passionate. That's a tough sell

At least 518 PT Cruisers from the United States and Canada gathered at 'Cruisin' The Falls II' held on the Canadian side of Niagara Falls in June 2002. DaimlerChrysler supported this event by displaying its collection of PT Cruiser concept vehicles, including the Pronto Cruizer and the Hot Wheels Cruiser. The 2003 model year Turbo and Chrome Edition PT Cruisers were also on display for the first time in Canada. (Author's collection)

for 'Plain Jane' cars – but it's a natural for Chrysler's head-turning vehicles."

The PT Cruiser got to show off its ability to turn heads in most of the campaign's TV ads that had a light-hearted approach to the different forms of love – love-at-first-sight, true love, the power of love – and how each finds fulfillment in a Chrysler vehicle. In one 30-second ad, *Boy Meets Girl*, a young man is behind the wheel of a PT Cruiser. Next to him is a young woman. Upon arriving at her home they passionately embrace at the front door, but the woman really has her eye on something else. So she lifts the keys from her date's pocket and drives off in the PT Cruiser, the real source of her passion.

This ad was later followed by two additional spots; the first, entitled *Tram*, featured the driver of a parking lot tram who can't help stopping and staring at four Chrysler vehicles parked along his route – a Sebring convertible, 300M, Town & Country minivan and a PT Cruiser. At each vehicle the driver stopped so suddenly that passengers were jerked forward into the seats in front of them, some spilling their soft drinks. Eventually, however, the passengers, join the driver in staring at and photographing the Chryslers, and don't mind the unscheduled stops.

In the third ad, *Pursue Your Passion*, a truck with a mirror strapped to one side attracts three drivers – one in a PT Cruiser, another in a 300M and the third in a Sebring Convertible. Each driver, obviously enjoying the new Chrysler, pulls alongside the moving mirror to admire their cars.

The success of this campaign motivated to Chrysler launch a multi-media 'Heartline' advertising campaign sequel in early February, 2002 that, said Chrysler, was intended to "sweeten up Valentine's Day."

"The romance of Valentine' Day," explained Jay Kuhnie, Chrysler/Jeep Director of Communications, "is the perfect time for Chrysler customers to share the love they have for each other and their vehicles."

To help matters along, Chrysler provided eleven free Valentine's Day e-cards at the Chrysler brand website. Seven were media enhanced with moving graphics, the others had a static format. Titles included 'Flying Hearts,' 'Kiss Me' and 'Heartlight.' The campaign also involved partnering with *Entertainment Weekly* magazine in hosting 10 preview screening of *40 Days and 40 Nights*, a romantic comedy about a bachelor who accepts a bet to remain celibate for 40 days and nights, and his challenges when he meets the love of his life.

From February 7 through Valentine's Day, February 14, 2002 'Heartline' advertisements appeared in *Entertainment Weekly*, *Newsweek*, *Fortune*, *Business Week*, *U.S. News & World Report*, *People*, *Time* and *W*.

While the Heartline logo was an overhead photo of a Chrysler Sebring Convertible whose headlights formed a heart-shaped beam of light in front of the vehicle, for PT Cruiser owners and enthusiasts the high point of this promotion was a redo of the Drive-Love *Boy Meets Girl* TV commercial. As in the original version, the couple, in a PT Cruiser, arrive at the young lady's residence after a date. After an embrace at the front door, she lifts the keys to the Cruiser from her date's pocket and drives off. Pentamark Worldwide created two new versions of the ad. Through February 13, *Boy Meets Girl*, ended with a heart covering everything except the girl's mouth, which had a rosy hue. White lettering reminded viewers to "send e-valentines from Chrysler.com." On February 14, the message changed to "Happy Valentine's Day."

Just two days earlier, on February 12, 2002, Chrysler gave its 92 dealers in the UK a valentines of sorts by announcing that "the next stage in the development of Chrysler's popular PT Cruiser range has arrived, bringing with it new colors, equipment and technology, but without losing any style or elegance." Steel Blue and Light Almond were new exterior color choices, and an engine identification badge was now positioned on the Cruiser's rear deck. All models (three versions – Touring, Classic and Limited were offered in the UK) now had body-colored bumpers, seats with improved lateral support, an armrest for the front passenger seat, and a carbon particulate air filter. 'AutoStick,' Chrysler's clutchless electronic gear shifting system was now optional for the Touring and Limited models at a price of £800. AutoStick allowed the driver to manually select the next ratio sequentially by tapping the lever to the left to shift down and to the right to change up. The shift range (P, R, N, D), or gear range (1, 2, 3, 4), currently in use was displayed in the instrument cluster. Also added to the Cruiser's list of options was an electric sunroof (£500) and Special paint (£230) for the Touring and Limited PT Cruisers. All models with automatic transmission had a new shift lever and instrument panel clusters.

Summing up the anticipated impact of these developments upon the its popularity, Simon Elliott said: "The PT Cruiser has already shown what a stylish car and value-for-money package it can be, and these new improvements will make the car an even more attractive proposition for our customers. The interior changes are significant and useful, and the two new colors give the range a whole new dimension."

In February 2002, collectors of PT Cruiser memorabilia took notice of a PT Cruiser concept car displayed at the 2002 Canadian International Auto Show in Toronto. There had been hundreds of scale model PT Cruisers produced

Model	On the road price [1]
Classic	£14,995
Touring	£15,995
Touring CRD	£17,495
Limited	£17,395
Limited CRD	£18,895

[1] This price included a 12-month Road Fund License, currently £155 annually, and, if applicable, a First Registration fee of £25.

Model Feature	Classic	Touring	Limited
Front side airbags	S	S	S
Headlamp leveling system	S	S	S
Four wheel disc brakes with ABS	NA	S	S
Fog lights	NA	S	S
Traction control	NA	S	S
Body-color side moldings	S	S	S
Chrome plated exhaust pipe	S	S	S
15 x 6in steel wheels	S	NA	NA
16 x 6in alloy wheels	NA	S	NA
16 x 6in chrome finish alloy wheels	NA	NA	S
6-speaker AM/FM radio/cassette/CD	S	S	S
Air conditioning	S	S	S
Removable rear panel shelf	S	S	S
Cruise control	NA	S	S
Leather-wrapped steering wheel	NA	S	S
Leather-wrapped gear knob (automatic only)	NA	S	S
Mini overhead console	NA	S	S
Leather/suede seats	NA	NA	S

since its introduction, and one of these, manufactured by Hot Wheels, featured in an attention-grabbing 'Hot Wheels' PT Cruiser advertisement, shown on Canadian television, was the inspiration for this PT Cruiser 'Hot Wheels' Edition.

Typically, Hot Wheels models exemplified free-spirited expressions of speed, horsepower, high performance and individuality, and this full-sized version was no exception. It featured a custom Tangerine Metallic exterior and interior accents, 'Hot Wheels Cruiser Edition' badges, a 'Roman Chariot' grille, flush front and rear fascias, and Goodyear Eagle 225/40ZR-18 HP Ultra Plus tires mounted on 18 x 18.5in aluminum wheels. The Cruiser's engine, equipped with a Whipple supercharger and a custom Dynamax dual exhaust system was credited with over 200 horsepower. The use of H & R Stage 2 Sport Lowering Springs lowered the car 1.4in at the front and 1.3in at the rear.

As expected, both DaimlerChrysler and Mattel, the manufacturer of Hot Wheels, were pleased with this PT Cruiser. "The 'Hot Wheels' Edition, is drawing a lot of attention," observed Pearl Davies, Chrysler/Jeep Brand Manager for DaimlerChrysler Canada. "It's especially popular with showgoers big and small, young and old who enjoyed playing with their prized 'Hot Wheels' toy."

Carson Lev, Director of Design and Licensing, Collector and Racing Products, Mattel Hot Wheels, was equally enthusiastic. "The 'Hot Wheels' Edition," he said, "is an exciting culmination of two very popular brands. We've successfully transformed a Hot Wheels car into reality."

Although output at the Toluca assembly plant wasn't scheduled to begin until the first quarter of 2004, the Chrysler Group selected the 2002 Geneva Auto Show to announce, on March 4, its intention to manufacture a production version of the PT Cruiser Convertible Styling Study. Recalling its debut at the 2001 New York Auto Show, Dieter Zetsche said: "We were overwhelmed by the positive consumer and media response when we took the wraps off the original Convertible Styling Study. In fact, an internet poll taken immediately after the unveiling showed that almost 90 per cent loved the vehicle and begged us to build it."

Zetsche also depicted the soft top as an example of DaimlerChrysler's ability to react quickly to changes in consumer interests. "Announcing production of the Chrysler PT Cruiser Convertible," he said, "demonstrates yet again the company's dedication to bringing great new products to our customers. This is further proof that we are, and will continue to be, aggressive in our product offensive, not only with the Chrysler PT Cruiser, but with all of our products across all of our brands."

The Convertible, known in Europe as the Cabrio, was entering a market that had been growing rapidly since the late nineties. In the US, Chrysler, with its Sebring Convertible model had a 15 per cent share of the soft top market, and, said Tom Marinelli, "the PT Cruiser Convertible will further expand our reach in this part of the market."

Since 1997, sales in the convertible segment of the Western Europe automotive market had grown to exceed

The PT Cruiser Convertible as it appeared at the 72nd Geneva Motor Show in March 2002, where Dieter Zetsche announced plans to build a production version in 2004. (Courtesy DaimlerChrysler Media Services)

150,000 units in 2001. "We want to take advantage of this growing market," commented Thomas Hausch, Executive Director of International Sales and Marketing, Chrysler Group, "by expanding our Chrysler PT Cruiser family to now offer the PT Cruiser Cabrio."

The Cabrio benefited both from its attractiveness to open-air motoring enthusiasts and the popularity of the current PT Cruiser, whose sales had exceeded 39,000. Of that total, Germany was the market leader with 10,700 units sold.

Also debuting at the Geneva Show was the European version of the Dream Cruiser Series 1, identified as the Street Cruiser Series 1. It became available in Chrysler's European dealerships in the spring. Like its North American counterpart, it was depicted as the first in a series of factory-customized PT Cruisers to be introduced annually. Its Inca Gold finish was the same as that of the Dream Cruiser. The European model had a 'Street Cruiser Series 1' shield-shaped liftgate badge in Inca Gold, with a chrome outer edge and chrome lettering.

Displayed along with the PT Cruiser Convertible at the 2002 Geneva show was the Inca Gold PT Street Cruiser. It was powered by the 2.0-liter 4-cylinder engine, and was available with either manual or automatic transmission. It began arriving in DaimlerChrysler's European dealerships in spring 2002.
(Courtesy DaimlerChrysler Media Services)

The Street Cruiser's seats combined Light Pearl Beige leather with Inca Gold half-moon inserts of 'Alvis' perforated leather for the seat cushion and seat back. The door bolsters were a matching gold 'Royale' leather and the floor mats were embroidered with special 'Street Cruiser' badging in gold thread. A unique Matrix textured leather was utilized for the steering wheel and shift knob on automatic transmission models. The Street Cruiser's standard equipment matched that of the PT Cruiser Limited version. "PT Cruiser has already become something of an icon on British roads," said Simon Elliott, "and with the introduction of Street Cruiser, the appeal for PT Cruiser will be broadened further while keeping the brand and nameplate fresh in people's minds. This is just Series 1. There are lots more exciting developments on PT Cruiser to come."

Echoing the remarks Tom Marinelli had made regarding future special edition PT models when he introduced the

Dream Cruiser 1, Tom Hausch, Executive Director of Sales and Marketing, Chrysler International, suggested that his audience should "look to the Chrysler brand to continue to launch models similar to these in the future."

Also on hand for the Street Cruiser's debut was Trevor Creed, who summed up its attributes in this fashion: "Visually, the Inca Gold monochromatic appearance unifies the Chrysler PT Cruiser's dramatic form. With the color-keyed grille, bumpers and bodyside mouldings, the vehicle takes on more of a customized look."

With the debut of the Street Cruiser with its standard 16-valve, 2.0-liter engine, PT Cruisers were available in a range of four different models for the European market: 1.6-liter gasoline, and 2.2-liter Common Rail Diesel (CRD) for the PT Cruiser and the 2.0-liter gasoline engine for both the PT Cruiser and Street Cruiser.

After the world première of the PT Cruiser with the 2.2 CRD engine at the Brussels Motor Show in January 2002, and its availability beginning in March 2002, it had quickly

The Street Cruiser had an identification badge on its liftgate. (Courtesy DaimlerChrysler Media Services)

Cherokee and Jeep Grand Cherokee in the Chrysler Group's range of models available with CRD engines.

Anticipating the impact of this strategy upon PT Cruiser sales, Thomas Hausch, said: "The Chrysler PT Cruiser has been one of the hottest cars on the planet since its launch ... and now it's become even more attractive with this excellent, new common rail diesel engine that adds further excitement and practicality to an already expressive yet practical car. Every buyer needs to have rational, as well as emotional

been perceived as an appealing niche vehicle, blending the uniqueness of the PT Cruiser with the economy and power of a diesel engine. Officially identified as the OM664 engine, the 2.2 CRD was jointly developed by Chrysler and Mercedes-Benz engineers, using an existing Mercedes-Benz diesel as a starting point. The new engine shared such essential features as its base engine block, key cylinder head elements and fuel injection system with the older engine. Its operation was enhanced by the addition of balance shafts.

Utilizing proven Mercedes-Benz common-rail technology, including direct injection and an IHI turbocharger with a mixed flow turbine, the four-cylinder engine, which was manufactured in Stuttgart-Untertuerkheim, Germany, had these specifications, joined by those of the 2.0-liter gasoline engine, when appropriate:

The availability of the CRD PT Cruiser was a key element in DaimlerChrysler's plan to make its Jeeps and Chryslers more competitive in the international automotive market. With its introduction, it joined the Chrysler Voyager, Jeep

Engine type:	Direct injection, four-cylinder, turbocharged and intercooled.
Construction:	Deep skirt, cast iron block, aluminum alloy cylinder head, balance shafts.
Valve train:	Chain driven, dohc,16 valves, bucket tappets, hydraulic lash adjusters.
Displacement:	2148cc.
Bore x stroke:	88mm x 88.3mm.
Compression ratio:	18:1.
Fuel injection:	Common rail, high pressure.
Maximum power:	89kW (121hp) @ 4200rpm.
Maximum torque:	300Nm (221lb-ft), produced from 1600-2600rpm).
Transmission:	Five-speed manual.

Ratios:	2.2 CRD Getrag G288	2.0 Gasoline NVG T350
1st	3.923	3.500
2nd	2.208	1.960
3rd	1.458	1.360
4th	1.114	0.971
5th	0.881	0.811
Reverse	3.624	3.240
Final drive ratio	3.290	3.940
Overall top gear	2.586	2.800

Clutch	
2.2 CRD	Hydraulically operated, dual mass flywheel, dry clutch
2.0 gasoline	Hydraulically operated, single plate, dry clutch

Performance:	
0-62mph (0-100km/h):	12.1sec.
40-60mph:	5.4sec.
50-70mph:	7.0sec.
Top speed:	183km/h (114mph)

Fuel economy:	
Combined cycle:	40.9mpg
Combined CO2:	185gl/km

reasons to buy a car. While its great looks give buyers many emotional reasons to buy PT Cruiser, this practical, economical and high performance engine will give our customers all the rational reasons they need to confirm their choice. PT Cruiser offers a unique combination of outstanding design and practicality."

Adding to this perspective, Simon Elliott commented: "We now have a fantastic range of CRD engines for our vehicles – those engines are fitted to our most successful cars, such as Chrysler Voyager, and the Jeep Cherokee and Grand Cherokee. And I am delighted that a CRD has been fitted to the PT Cruiser. We know that many of our customers have been waiting for a diesel-powered PT Cruiser and now they have it. We expect this car to be very popular indeed."

The Street Cruiser was equipped with 16in chrome wheels with chrome outer edges and chrome lettering. (Courtesy DaimlerChrysler Media Services)

Indicating both the PT Cruiser's popularity and the major advances made by the Chrysler Group in the quality of its vehicles, was Strategic Vision's July 18, 2002 announcement that for the second consecutive year the PT Cruiser ranked number one in the Compact Car category of its Total Quality Index (TQI) survey. Topping the list of competitors in the Compact Pickup division for the fourth straight year was the Dodge Dakota.

The 2002 version of the study asked 46,900 owners of 2002 model-year vehicles about the overall quality of their ownership experiences, including factors such as the vehicle's performance and handling. The 75-question survey, measuring the entire experience of buying, owning and driving a new vehicle, was given to buyers ninety days after they had purchased their new car or truck. "At the core," explained the President of Strategic Visions, Dr Darrel Edwards, "are the values and feelings that drive decision-making."

The PT Cruiser's creators had to be ecstatic when they learned of Strategic Vision's opinion of the 2002 model. The Chrysler PT Cruiser, it said: "Blows away the competition not only in styling, but also on room and innovation. This truly capable and very individual vehicle strongly delivers on esteem and harmony issues."

Don Dees, Vice-President – Quality at the Chrysler Group, offered this explanation of the popularity of the Dakota and PT Cruiser: "Our top ranking demonstrates the Chrysler Group's ability to create vehicles that evoke a positive emotional response, yet deliver on the quality and reliability side of the equation."

Even though the PT Cruiser had been on the market for only a short time, Tom Marinelli had no difficulty in viewing this achievement in the perspective of that phenomenally successful history. "The Chrysler PT Cruiser," he said, " has always appealed to the emotions of buyers who wanted to personalize their transportation. This latest study shows that the vehicle continues to elicit that same response two years after its launch, a fact we continue to support with an entire lineup of factory-customized PT Cruisers."

Two months later, in early September, the PT Cruiser was again the recipient of a major award. This time the honor came from the BBC's *Top Gear* automotive show, whose 2002 Motoring Survey involving over 37,000 motorists, was the largest of its type conducted in the UK, and covered most aspects of modern-day motoring, including reliability, running costs, and treatment from dealers. After scoring more points than any other car in the 'Small MPVs' and 'Large MPVs' categories, the PT Cruiser was described by *Top Gear* as "One of the freshest cars to make an appearance

... service received from dealers, mechanical reliability and spaciousness are excellent."

Whether sold in the UK or the US, the PT Cruiser arrived at its new owner's residence replete with an impressive warranty. In the UK the package provided three years/60,000 mile coverage plus seven years/unlimited mileage anti-corrosion warranty and three years roadside emergency protection. In the United States the Chrysler Group had earlier announced a new seven year/70,000 mile limited powertrain warranty for all Chrysler, Jeep and Dodge vehicles purchased after July 9, 2002. Referring to this warranty, Dieter Zetsche cited the contribution quality had made to the success of products such as the PT Cruiser. "Simply stated," he said, "our overall quality levels have improved substantially, while warranty costs have dropped 20 per cent in the latest model year, and have been cut in half since 1996. Our entire management group has a mind set of making quality the top priority, and this program is yet another one in our 'disciplined pizzazz' approach."

As Zetsche spoke, new 2003 PT Cruisers with even more pizzazz and enhanced performance were arriving at Chrysler dealerships. Just how well disciplined their owners would be in displaying enthusiasm for their new Cruisers was a foregone conclusion.

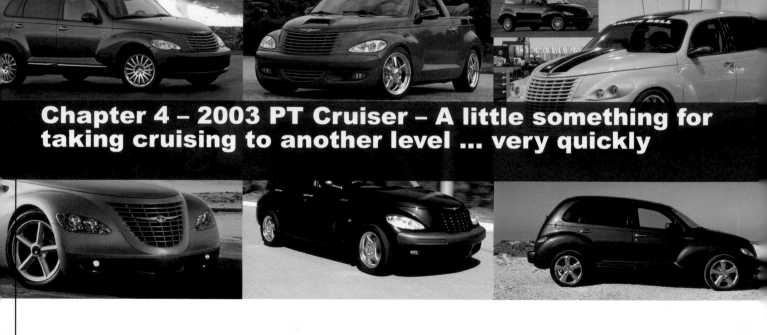

Chapter 4 – 2003 PT Cruiser – A little something for taking cruising to another level ... very quickly

Chrysler selected the March, 2002 New York Auto Show to continue its parade of exciting, and often unconventional, new model announcements, events and debuts. This media blitz had started three weeks earlier at the Geneva Show, in Switzerland, with the announcement that Chrysler would be manufacturing a PT Cruiser Convertible.

At the New York Show on March 27, 2002, Chrysler suggested that anyone urgently needing to get somewhere in "a New York minute" need not wait long for an automobile that might be helpful, a turbocharged PT Cruiser would soon be available as a 2003 model. Eager to capitalize on the PT Cruiser's inherent hot rod character, Chrysler promised that "with 215 horses under its hood and styling cues to prove it, the new 2003 Chrysler PT Turbo has performance backed by attitude."

Tom Marinelli, as Vice-President of the Chrysler/Jeep Global Brand Center, was familiar with the role special models had played in the PT Cruiser's success. "The Chrysler PT Turbo," he said, "is the perfect vehicle for customers seeking added performance along with too-cool-to-categorize styling. With that powerful combination, we're offering yet another choice in the PT Cruiser lineup. This shows our commitment to keeping the Chrysler PT Cruiser exciting, and extends it into a whole new class. The Chrysler PT Turbo gives us a tremendous opportunity to expand our customer base to performance-minded buyers looking to share in the optimism and spirit that the Chrysler PT Cruiser evokes. This new model will take the Chrysler PT Cruiser nameplate to yet another level."

Heading its development group was Larry Lyons, Vice-President, Small Vehicle Product Team Engineering. He began his review of the Turbo's creation by reminding his audience that "just two years ago we launched the Chrysler PT Cruiser and created a new category of transportation. Now, we're giving that whole new category a boost – literally. Now, our customers will not only have more than enough room for all the 2x4s and tools they'll buy at the hardware store, they'll also be the fastest getting there and back."

Intent on dispelling any perceptions of the latest PT Cruiser as a quick and easy setup in response to market demand, Lyons added that "we didn't just bolt on a turbo off the shelf and close the hood. This engine was created as a 200-plus horsepower motor for the PT Turbo from the beginning. This allowed us to make significant reliability improvements over turbo engines of the past."

Among these improvements was the Turbo's aluminum cylinder block with cast-iron liners, which replaced the standard engine's cast iron block, and a redesigned cylinder head assembly and crankshaft. Additional changes included the use of all-new pistons, and forged steel connecting rods.

Oil and water cooling for the turbocharger was optimized from the start of development, adding to the engine's reliability and durability. In place of the standard engine's 4.5qt (4.3L) oil pan, a larger oil pan with a 5qt (4.75L) capacity was used. The Turbo engine's coolant capacity was also greater than that of the 150hp engine as it used an 8qt (7.6L) radiator rather than the standard 7.4qt (7.0L) unit. Racing-style oil squirting lubricating mechanisms helped cool the pistons. Precise calibration of the turbo's wastegate and integrated

The PT Turbo's engine had 215hp @ 4950rpm and 245lb-ft of torque at 3600rpm, with 90 per cent of peak torque on tap from 2300 to 5000rpm. (Courtesy DaimlerChrysler Media Services)

The PT Turbo debuted at the New York International Auto Show in March 2002. This example is finished in Electric Blue Metallic. (Courtesy DaimlerChrysler Media Services)

Prospective owners of the 2003 PT Turbo were assured by Chrysler that "when the PT Turbo is standing still as required at red lights, others will be able to read the bright graphics." (Courtesy DaimlerChrysler Media Services)

2.4L TURBO

The 2003 PT Turbo was fitted with standard 205/50R-17 93H Goodyear Eagle RSA All-Season Performance tires. Seen here, left-to-right, are examples of its optional 17in chrome-plated aluminum wheels and standard 17in silver painted, five-spoke aluminum wheels. (Author's collection)

turbo/exhaust manifold resulted in quicker boost, while providing better control of the turbo for reduced emissions and improved reliability. Special acoustic dampeners, installed on the turbo's intake manifold, virtually eliminated the whine historically associated with many turbocharged engines.

The PT Turbo's standard transmission was a heavy-duty 5-speed Getrag manual. Having been used in the past on many Chrysler vehicles powered by turbocharged engines, Getrag transmissions were well-known by the marque's performance fans. Larry Lyons was confident about this transmission's quality as well as its popularity among PT Turbo buyers. "The new Getrag transaxle has been proven reliable in Europe for years," he said. "We're sure Chrysler PT Turbo owners interested in performance driving will be just as pleased with the precision feel and fun this manual transaxle offers."

Sharing Lyon's optimism, Tom Marinelli added that "so many of our Chrysler PT Cruiser customers, and especially those looking at a PT Turbo, are interested in a fun driving experience. With the new combination of our High Output Turbo engine and the Getrag manual transaxle, we look for our manual-equiped PT Turbo vehicles to reach 25 per cent of PT Turbo sales, compared with the 15 per cent we typically see for naturally-aspirated PT Cruisers."

PT Turbos for the North American market were also available with a four-speed automatic transmission fitted with Chrysler's AutoStick system. AutoStick's versatility prompted a Chrysler spokesperson to remark that "for the first time, performance-minded PT Cruiser drivers in North America will enjoy the feel of a manual transaxle with the convenience of an automatic."

The three transmissions offered for the PT Cruiser had significantly different gear ratios:

Transmission:	Automatic	NVG T350 5-speed	Getrag G288 5-speed
Gear ratios			
1st	2.84	3.50	3.923
2nd	1.57	1.96	2.208
3rd	1.00	1.36	1.458

The shift knob for the PT Turbo's standard 5-speed Getrag manual transmission had a Satin Silver finish. (Author's collection)

4th	0.69	0.971	1.114
5th	----	0.811	0.881
Reverse	2.21	3.42	3.624
Effective final drive	3.91	3.45	3.29
Overall top gear	2.694	2.80	

The Turbo's approximate curb weight with manual transmission was 3304lb (1502kg). The automatic version was slightly heavier at 3311lb (1505kb). The 5-speed Turbo had a measurable acceleration advantage over those vehicles fitted with automatic transmission. Chrysler reported that engineering estimates showed Getrag-equipped vehicles were capable of zero to 60mph in approximately 7.5 seconds, about a half-second quicker than the automatic PT Turbos. The manual was also faster in the quarter-mile, with an estimated time of 15.8 seconds, versus 16.5 seconds for the automatic version.

All PT Turbos were equipped with a specially-tuned suspension system, an exhaust system with a large diameter chrome exhaust tip, performance 4-wheel disc brakes, ABS, 17in Blade Silver painted five-spoke cast aluminum wheels, and Goodyear Eagle LS P205/50HR17 93H All-Season Performance tires.

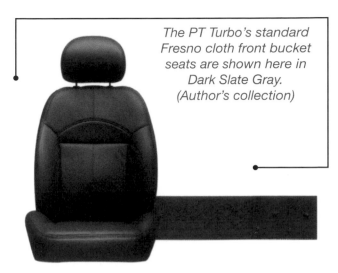

The PT Turbo's standard Fresno cloth front bucket seats are shown here in Dark Slate Gray. (Author's collection)

The PT Turbo was equipped with a large diameter chrome exhaust tip. Chrysler sparked customer interest by reporting that the Turbo had "a pronounced exhaust note," that added "to the vehicle's sporty character." (Author's collection)

The Dark Slate Gray interior of a 2003 PT Turbo equipped with the optional Capeli leather trim and perforated Axis seat inserts. (Author's collection)

Engine:	High output turbocharged, intercooled 2.4-liter dohc, 16-valves	Brakes:	Performance ABS four-wheel disc with traction control
Displacement:	146.5cu-in	Front	280mm x 28mm, vented, Colette 2+ caliper, 57mm diameter piston
Construction:	Iron block and bedplate, aluminum alloy cylinder head, structural aluminum oil pan, oil-cooled pistons	Rear:	270mm x 12mm, solid, standard caliper, 36mm diameter
Compression ratio:	8.1:1	Standard transmission:	Getrag 288S electronic heavy-duty 5-speed manual
Horsepower (SAE net):	215 @ 5000rpm		
Torque:(SAE net)	245lb-ft @ 3600rpm, (over 90 per cent of peak torque available from 2300 to 5000rpm)	Ratios	
		1st:	3.92
		2nd	2.21
		3rd:	1.46
		4th	1.11
Maximum engine speed:	6240rpm	5th	0.88
Fuel requirement:	Recommended: unleaded premium gasoline, 91 octane (R + M)/2	Final drive ratio:	3.29
Estimated EPA fuel economy, mpg (City/ Hwy):	20/26: manual transmission; 19/25: automatic transmission	Optional:	AutoStick 4-speed automatic
		Ratios	
Suspension:		1st:	2.84
Front and rear:	Performance-tuned strut and coil assemblies	2nd	1.57
		3rd:	1.0
Front coil rate:	160lb/in	4th	0.69
Rear coil rate:	140lb/in	Final drive ratio:	3.91

PT Turbo specifications.

The PT Turbo's front fascia had a body-color monotone finish and enlarged lower opening designed to provide an ample air flow to the turbo intercooler. The rear fascia also had a body-color monotone surface and a larger than standard exhaust opening. The bodyside molding color matched that of the body. A 'GT' badge was positioned on the left side of the Turbo's liftgate. It was joined by a '2.4L Turbo' badge on the right. The GT identification resulted in many people referring to this model as the GT Cruiser, a term that, as noted in Chapter Two, Chrysler had previously used to identify the turbocharged 'GT Cruiser Concept Show Truck' displayed at the November 1999 SEMA show. Later, this vehicle was identified as the 'Chrysler GT Cruiser concept vehicle.'

The Turbo's seats were finished in a Dark Slate Gray Fresno cloth that was unique to the Turbo model. As an option, 'Capeli' leather trim with 'Axis' perforated inserts was available. Chrysler promised that the 'performance' front seats provided thigh and lumbar support equivalent to the Turbo's level of performance. A manual lumbar adjuster was provided for the driver.

The dash panel had unique accents, silver-faced cluster gauges, a 140mph/220kph speedometer and '2.4L Turbo' badging for the tachometer. The shift knob on all models had a Satin Silver finish. 'GT' embroidered front floor mats were also installed.

Details of the PT Turbo's major specifications (see accompanying table) further illustrate its role as the performance leader of the PT Cruiser model line.

The MSRP for the manual Chrysler PT Turbo was $22,415. The PT Turbo with AutoStick had a MSRP of $22,855. Both models had an additional $590 destination charge. Commenting on these prices, Tom Marinelli said: "For just over $22,000, performance-minded customers may own the quickest model in the PT Cruiser garage, with all of the same hallmark versatility and customization appeal that the PT Cruiser is known for."

In October 2002, Chrysler launched the first of sixty 'PT Studios,' showcasing 84 emerging young fashion designers, independent short filmmakers, musical performers, DJs, and visual artists at Splashlight Studios in NYC. These nightlife events, subsequently held in Los Angeles, Miami, San Francisco, Chicago and Austin were intended to introduce the PT Turbo to audiences of 25-35 year olds regarded as influential members of their communities. Before the program ended, over 25,000 people attended these events. (Courtesy DaimlerChrysler Media Services)

Chrysler supported the launch of the PT Turbo with a 'PT Studios' entertainment-based program that was intended to introduce the Turbo to 25-35 year-olds in six major cities. Explaining the rationale of this project, Bonita K Coleman, Director, Chrysler Marketing, said "The original PT Cruiser became a hit largely because of the Baby Boomer generation. The new Chrysler PT Turbo, with its more powerful engine, has the kind of performance that appeals to a younger audience. PT Studio is an innovative way to tell that audience about the Chrysler PT Turbo on their terms and in their environment."

That environment, at least as far as PT Studios was concerned, involved a series of nightlife happenings showcasing 84 emerging fashion designers, independent film producers, musicians, and visual artists from around the United States. Over 25,000 people attended these sixty events produced by Gen Art, a national arts organization dedicated to supporting young up-and-coming talent.

The PT Studios, with guests situated in a 'lounge environment,' began on September 12 at the Ivar Project in Los Angeles. Other launch locations and dates were Miami (September 13), San Francisco (October 2), Chicago (October 3), New York (October 8), and Austin, Texas (October 9). A PT Studios mini-site, available at www.chrysler.com, offered on-line registration for the events, an event calendar and an interactive video mixer allowing users to design their own PT Turbo video.

Preceding the launch of the PT Studios, Chrysler, in mid-June, had put the automotive world on notice that "the chrome look was back," by taking the wraps off a new Chrome Accents Package for the 2003 PT Cruiser Touring and Limited Edition models. In spite of its June 12, 2002 announcement, the Chrome package was listed as a "late availability item" when the 2003 models were subsequently introduced in September.

Chrysler carefully avoided associating the new PT

The Base and Touring Edition PT Cruisers for 2003 had this Metro II cloth seating surface as standard equipment. Their front bucket seats are seen here in Dark Taupe. They were also available in Dark Slate Gray. (Author's collection)

In addition to having a Satin Silver painted shift knob, PT Turbos with AutoStick also had a Satin Silver shifter bezel. Pushing the button on top of the shifter ball moved the transmission into manual mode. (Author's collection)

Appropriate identification was provided on the speedometers of PT Turbos equipped with the AutoStick transmission. The speedometer on Turbo models read to 140mph. The maximum on other 2003 PT Cruisers was 120mph. (Author's collection)

package with the excesses of American styling studios in the late fifties, that once prompted AMC's styling vice-president, Richard Teague, to observe: "This was the age of 'gorp.'" Rather than mounting a defense or criticism of the cars that Mr Teague disdainfully described, a media representative diplomatically observed that "in the 1950s, chrome was used widely to accent the entire vehicle, inside and out. Today, chrome accents are used more sparingly to distinguish a vehicle's natural character lines."

Skipping over the 1950s, Chrysler was comfortable in citing two models from the '20s and '30s as representative of the Chrome Package's design heritage. The first was a 1927 Chrysler Imperial, that was depicted as illustrating the use of chrome trim to accentuate rather than draw attention away from its basic form. The second was the 1934 Chrysler Airflow with its signature chrome 'waterfall' grille.

Obliquely referring to the chrome laden cars of an earlier age, Tom Marinelli asserted that "chrome is like jewelry. Tastefully applied, it captures attention. Over-applied, it looks gaudy. With the PT Cruiser Chrome Accents package, we struck the right balance for the brand and for this unique vehicle."

The content of the Chrome Package, when it was announced as the Chrome Accents Group, was as follows:

Exterior:
❖ Body color, monotone grille with chrome horizontal bars.

❖ Monotone body-color front fascia with horizontal chrome bars on the lower opening.
❖ Full surround chrome molding on the entire circumference of vehicle.
❖ Lower chrome bodyside molding.
❖ Chrome-plated billet-look fuel filler door.
❖ 16in chrome-clad wheels.
❖ Bright exhaust tip.
Interior:
❖ Brushed silver front door scuff plates engraved with a bright 'PT Cruiser' graphic.
❖ Chrome shift bezel on models with automatic transmission.
❖ Chrome shaft gear shift lever with satin silver shift knob.
❖ Chrome door locks and handles.

❖ Leather-wrapped steering wheel.

The Chrome Accents option was available on 2003 PT Cruiser Touring and Limited Edition models sold in North American and International markets. The MSRP of the package was $1270 on the Touring Edition and $595 on the Limited. The higher cost of the option for the Touring Edition was due to the inclusion of the 16in wheels, bright exhaust tip and leather-wrapped steering wheel as additional package equipment. These same items were already standard on the Limited Edition.

In late 2000, Auto-Tech Plastics, which had established itself as one of the leading manufacturers of aftermarket products for the PT Cruiser, had anticipated the Chrome Accents Package by offering chrome grille and chrome beltline kits for the PT Cruiser.

Both the Touring and Limited Edition Cruisers were also available with a Tuned Chrome Package that listed for $1360, but "in a special introductory offer," was priced at $655. This option, which could not be combined with either the the Woodie or Flame packages, consisted of 16in chrome-clad aluminum wheels, chrome bodyside moldings, chrome fuel filler door, chromed grille accents, chrome tailpipe, bright sill scuff pads, a silver-look shift knob and a six-disc CD changer. A chrome PRNDL bezel was added to models with automatic transmission.

Production of the 2003 PT Cruisers began in July, 2002. Dealers were advised they could place orders for the 2003 models beginning on June 1, 2002. Although the Turbo was the focus model when the latest PT Cruisers were officially announced on September 1, 2002, there were also many revisions setting them apart from previous models.

As in 2002, the PT Cruiser was available in Base, Touring Edition and Limited Edition versions. Two new exterior Pearl Coat colors, Electric Blue and Onyx Green were introduced. Taupe Frost Metallic Clear Coat was no longer offered.

This 1927 Locke Touralette Chrysler Imperial was cited as representative of the brand heritage inspiring the Chrome Accent Package for the 2003 PT Cruiser. (Courtesy DaimlerChrysler Media Services)

Exterior colors carried over from 2002 were Black Clear Coat, Bright Silver Metallic Clear Coat, Deep Cranberry Pearl Coat, Inferno Red Tinted Pearl Coat ($200 extra cost), Light Almond Pearl Metallic Clear Coat, Patriot Blue Pearl Coat, and Stone White Clear Coat.

Commenting on the availability of Electric Blue for 2003, Margaret Hackstedde, Director of the Chrysler Group's Color, Fabric and Mastering Design, noted that while "one out of every four vehicles that we sell is silver, blue, along with a variety of blue shades, emerges as a popular color choice for 2003."

Formulating exterior colors for the PT Cruiser and other Chrysler automobiles was the mission of a staff solely dedicated to developing new color ideas. Working with a two-to-three year timeframe for bringing new vehicles such as the PT Cruiser to market, Hackstedde explained that "we refer to industry color forecasts, including the Color Marketing Group and the International Color Authority in order to validate our color direction. We have our fingers on the pulse of what colors would be popular in the future."

As an alternative to Taupe/Pearl Beige, the PT Cruiser's interior was now also available in Dark Slate Gray. Cruisers with this interior in combination with Light Almond, Bright Silver, Black and Stone White exteriors had a new Bright Silver Metallic instrument panel cluster and passenger side airbag door.

New 15in bolt-on wheel covers with bright lug nut caps were standard on the entry-level PT Cruiser. Also standard were new accent color bodyside moldings. Now included in the base model's interior appointments was a fold-flat front passenger seat and rear seat head restraints. Replacing the

The popularity of the 1934 Airflow didn't even remotely approach the PT Cruiser's. But both automobiles exemplified Chrysler's willingness to step outside prevailing design boundaries and lead, rather than follow, the competition. The 1934 Airflow was a favorite of designers advocating a streamlined appearance. It is seen here next to one of the popular streamliner trains of the time, the Union Pacific's M-10,000, also known as the City of Salina, which was completed in 1934. (Courtesy DaimlerChrysler Media Services)

Included in the Chrome Accents Package were many distinctive interior appointments. The brushed silver front door scuff plates were engraved with a bright 'PT Cruiser' graphic. (Courtesy DaimlerChrysler Media Services)

A view of the chrome shaft shift lever and satin silver shift knob included in the Chrome Accents Package. They are seen here on a 2003 PT Cruiser with a Dark Slate Gray interior. (Courtesy DaimlerChrysler Media Services)

A full-surround chrome A-line molding, along with a chrome-plated fuel-filler door, make it easy to identify this 2003 PT Cruiser as being equipped with the Chrome Accents Package. (Courtesy DaimlerChrysler Media Services)

Seen here are several other exterior features of the Chrome Accents Package, including a body-color grille with chrome horizontal bars, a monotone, body-color front fascia with horizontal chrome bars on the lower opening, and 16in chrome-clad wheels. (Courtesy DaimlerChrysler Media Services)

2002 Base model's heated, fold-away exterior mirrors were fixed, non-heated units. Traction control and the moonroof feature were dropped from the Base model's option list. Speed control was added to the Base model's Power Convenience Group Option. Previously, it had been a stand-alone option.

Sixteen-inch, painted cast aluminum wheels were now standard for the Touring model, as were new body-color monotone front and rear fascias, speed control and an AM/FM radio with cassette and CD player, which, in 2002, had been a $100 option. The chrome exhaust pipe included on the 2002 Touring Edition was deleted for 2003. An AM/

A 2003 Touring Edition PT Cruiser equipped with the Tuned Chrome Package. (Author's collection)

FM stereo radio with integrated six-disc CD changer was optional on all 2003 models.

Earlier introduced as a running change during the 2002 model year were the Limited Edition's 16in chrome-clad aluminum wheels. Touring models could be ordered with these wheels at extra cost.

On August 13, 2002, coinciding with Detroit's annual Woodward Dream Cruise, Chrysler announced that, early in 2003 an updated version of the Dream Cruiser Series 1 would be available with an exclusive Tangerine Pearl Coat finish. Noting that this new Series 2 model was "similar to the Inca Gold Dream Cruiser Series 1 that we introduced last year," Tom Marinelli depicted it as "an exclusive vehicle for the customer who wants to make a splash on the street."

Adding that "the Tangerine Dream Cruiser Series 2 is yet another flavor of the Chrysler PT Cruiser," he predicted that it would "satisfy the desires of PT Cruiser owners who want to customize their vehicles and really pull away from the crowd."

Production of the Series 2 model began in January 2003, and was limited to 7500 units for North America and 2000 units for international markets where it was identified as the Chrysler PT Street Cruiser Series 2.

In addition to its unique exterior paint, the Dream Cruiser Series 2 had chrome bodyside moldings, body-color rear spoiler, 17in chrome wheels with Tangerine-colored center caps, and a liftgate-mounted 'Dream Cruiser Series 2' badge with Tangerine accents.

A 'Dream Cruiser Series 2' plaque with the vehicle's unique production sequence number was mounted on the instrument panel center stack. The interior was finished in Dark Slate in combination with Tangerine-colored door bolsters, passenger airbag door, and cluster bezel. The performance seats had Tangerine perforated 'Radar' leather inserts. Additional interior appointments included Tangerine-colored floor mats embroidered with a Dream Cruiser logo, a leather-wrapped steering wheel with perforated 'Radar' leather inserts, and a center horn area with an integrated Chrysler winged badge. A chrome shift bezel was installed on models with automatic transmission. All Dream Cruisers had a chrome shaft lever, satin silver shift knob and special door lock knobs. The MSRP for the Dream Cruiser 2 was

Continued on page 110.

The Touring Edition's standard 16in painted aluminum wheel was restyled for 2003. (Author's collection)

Also redesigned for 2003 was the Base model's 15in bolt-on wheel cover. (Author's collection)

This 16in chrome-clad aluminum wheel was standard for the Limited Edition, and optional for the Touring. It was introduced in 2002 as a running change. (Author's collection)

The full range of features available for the four PT Cruiser models offered in 2003.

Model	Base Edition	Touring Edition	Limited	PT Turbo
Exterior				
Black center pillar applique	S	S	S	S
Front license plate bracket	S	S	S	S
Rear window defroster	S	S	S	S
Bright door handles	S	S	S	S
Fascias – front and rear accent/body-color	S	S	S	NA
Fascias – front and rear – body-color	NA	NA	S	NA
Fog lamps (with instrument cluster warning indicator)	NA	S	S	S
Solar Control glass (all windows)	S	S	S	NA
Deep-tint sunscreen in rear door, quarter and liftgate windows, solar control in windshield and front doors	O	S	S	S
Halogen quad headlamps	S	S	S	S
Bright door and liftgate lock bezels (left-front door only when equipped with remote keyless entry)	S	S	S	S
Manual remote control exterior mirrors	S	NA	NA	NA
Power remote control exterior mirrors [1]	P	S	S	S
Power moonroof [2]	P	O	S	P
Bodyside molding, accent color (Dark Gray Metallic matching front fascia accents nerfs)	S	NA	NA	NA
Bodyside molding (body-color)	NA	NA	S	S

Model	Base Edition	Touring Edition	Limited	PT Turbo
Roof rack [3]	O	O	O	NA
Two-speed windshield wipers/washer with variable intermittent delay and mist wipe	S	S	S	S
Rear window wiper/washer with fixed intermittent delay	S	S	S	S
Interior assist handles (4) [4]	P	S	S	S
Passenger and cargo department carpeting	S	S	S	S
Air conditioning with fluidic instrument panel outlets	S	S	S	S
Heater floor outlets, front and rear	S	S	S	S
Coat hooks (2), rear	S	S	S	S
Full-length floor console [5]	S	S	S	S
Overhead console [6]	P	S	S	S
Metro II cloth door trim panel	S	S	NA	NA
Preferred suede cloth door trim panel	NA	NA	S	NA
Fresno cloth door trim panel	NA	NA	NA	S
Caprice vinyl door trim panel [7]	NA	NA	NA	P
Front seats, reclining, low back buckets [8]	S	S	S	NA
Front seats, reclining, low back buckets [9]	NA	NA	NA	S
Driver manual lumbar support	NA	NA	S	S
Heated driver and front passenger seats [10]	NA	NA	NA	P
Fold-flat front passenger seat	S	S	S	S
Power height adjuster [11]	NA	O	S	P
Fold and tumble rear seats with 65/35 split cushion and back and quick removal system	S	S	S	S
Removable, five-position				
shelf panel	S	S	S	S
Speed control [12]	P	S	S	S
Tipton II cloth seats	S	S	NA	NA
Royale leather with preferred suede accents, vinyl side facings and vinyl rear center insert	NA	NA	S	NA
Fresno cloth	NA	NA	NA	S
Leather with 'Axis' perforated leather inserts [13]	NA	NA	NA	P
Front and rear door trim panel storage pockets	S	S	S	S
Front and rear carpeted floor mats	S	S	S	S
Locking glove box	S	S	S	S
Instrument cluster [14]	S	S	S	S
Console flood lamp [15]	P	S	S	S
Front dome and cargo compartment lamps [16]	S	S	S	S
Day/night manual rearview mirror	S	S	S	S
12-volt power outlets [17]	S	S	S	S
Steering wheel with molded urethane rim	S	S	NA	NA
Steering wheel, leather-wrapped	NA	NA	S	S
Steering wheel leather-wrapped with perforated leather pieces on upper and lower rim [18]	NA	NA	NA	P
Under front passenger seat storage drawer	S	S	S	S
Sliding sun visors with covered mirrors	S	NA	NA	NA
Sliding sun visors with illuminated mirrors [19]	P	S	S	S
Front and rear power windows	S	S	S	S
Fixed, fluted radio antenna	S	S	S	S
AM/FM stereo radio				

Model	Base Edition	Touring Edition	Limited	PT Turbo
with CD player and changer controls	S	S	NA	S
AM/FM stereo radio with cassette player and CD players [20]	O	O	S	O/P
AM/FM Stereo radio with six-disc in-dash CD changer	O	O	O	O
Six premium speakers	S	S	S	S
Tilt steering column	S	S	S	S
Five-speed manual transmission with white cue ball shifter	S	S	S	NA
Heavy-duty five-speed manual transmission with Satin Silver cue ball shifter	NA	NA	NA	S
Four-speed automatic transmission	O	O	O	NA
Four-speed automatic transmission with AutoStick	NA	NA	NA	S
Power brakes: front disc/rear drum	S	S	S	NA
ABS with four wheel disc brakes	O	O	O	NA
Performance four-wheel disc brakes (includes ABS)	NA	NA	NA	S
Engine block heater	O	O	O	O
Chrome exhaust tip	NA	NA	S	S
Normal duty suspension	S	NA	NA	NA
Touring tuned suspension	NA	S	S	NA
Sport tuned suspension	NA	NA	NA	S
Low-speed traction control (required ABS)	O	O	O	S
Compact spare tire	S	S	S	S
P185/65R15 BSW All-Season Touring tires	S	NA	NA	NA
P205/55R16 BSW All-Season Touring tires	NA	S	S	NA
P205/50HR17 BSW				
All-Season Performance tires	NA	NA	NA	S
15in bolt-on wheel covers with bright lug nut caps	S	NA	`NA	NA
16in Silver painted aluminum wheels	NA	S	NA	NA
16in six-spoke chrome-clad aluminum wheels [21]	NA	O	S	NA
17in Blade painted aluminum wheels	NA	NA	NA	S
17in Blade chrome aluminum wheels [22]	NA	NA	NA	O/P
17in chrome aluminum wheels with Tangerine center cap [23]	NA	NA	NA	P
Accident Response Illumination System	S	S	S	S
Automatic transmission brake shift and park-ignition interlock	S	S	S	S
Low profile rear seat outboard head restraints, two-way, locking	S	S	S	S
Remote Keyless Entry [24]	P	S	S	S
Power door locks [25]	P	S	S	S
Rear door child protection	S	S	S	S
Next-generation driver and front passenger airbags	S	S	S	S
Supplemental side front airbags [26]	O	O	S	O
Front and rear seat belts	S	S	S	S
Rear seat trapped occupant release handle	S	S	S	S
Security alarm [27]	P	S	S	S
Sentry Key theft deterrent system	P	S	S	S
Child seat anchor system	S	S	S	S
Warning chimes (key-				

Model	Base Edition	Touring Edition	Limited	PT Turbo
in-ignition, headlamps on, low fuel or seat belt not buckled)	S	S	S	S
Equipment groups and packages				
Chrome Accents Group (Late availability)	NA	O	O	NA
Flame Exterior Accents [28]	O	O	O	NA
Light Group [29]	O	S	S	S
moonroof Group [30]	NA	O	S	O
Power Convenience Group [31]	O	NA	NA	NA
Woodgrain Exterior Accents [32]	O	O	`O	NA
CPOS R Package [33]	NA	NA	NA	O

Chrysler said the Tuned Chrome Package's chrome tailpipe gave the PT Cruiser "a street-smart look." (Author's collection)

Legend:
S = Standard, O = Optional, alone or in a group option. P = Available only in a Package option, NA = Not available.

[1] Included in Base model's Power Convenience Group option.

[2] The moonroof was fitted with Solar Glass and had tilt, vent, slide and one-touch open features. This option contained the Light Group when ordered for the Base model. It was included in the PT Turbo R package.

[3] Included two continuously adjustable crossbars with side-by-side 'spoiler appearance' stowage capability and quick-release latches.

[4] Included in Base Light Group.

[5] Included two front, one center and one rear cup holders, removable coin holder, pencil tray, CD/cassette holder, front storage slot, center storage

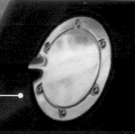

The chrome fuel filler cap of the Tuned Chrome Package. (Author's collection)

tray, and 12 volt auxiliary power outlet.

[6] Included driver and passenger map/reading lamps with integral on/off switches, compass and outside temperature display with US/metric switch and standard rearview mirror; included in Base model's Light Group.

[7] Included in PT Turbo R package.

[8] Equipped with two-way adjustable, locking head restraints, driver and passenger inboard pivoting armrests and driver seat back map pocket.

[9] Equipped with two-way adjustable, locking head restraints, enhanced lateral seat support, driver and passenger inboard pivoting armrests and seat back map pockets; available in Dark Slate Gray only.

[10] Included in Leather Interior Group.

[11] Included in R package on PT Turbo.

[12] Included in Base Power Convenience Group.

[13] Included in PT Turbo R package; available in Dark Slate Gray only.

[14] Digital display included odometer, trip odometer, door ajar and liftgate ajar. Speedometer read to 120mph/ 200kph on Base, Touring and Limited; to 140mph/ 220kph on PT Turbo. All had a 0-6000rpm tachometer and gauges for fuel level and engine coolant temperature.

[15] Included in Base Light Group.

[16] Included theatre dimming and automatic time out.

[17] Positioned on instrument panel and cargo area; included in Base Light Group.

[18] Included in PT Turbo R Package.

[19] Included in Base Light Group.

[20] Included in PT Turbo R package.

[21] Included in Chrome Accents Group and optional with Touring F -Package.

[22] Included in CPOS (Customer Preferred Ordering System) R Package for PT Turbo.

[23] Included in Dream Cruiser Series 2 Group (late availability).

[24] Included two transmitters and panic alarm; included in Base Power Convenience Group.

[25] Included central locking and programmable

automatic operation; included in Base Power Convenience Group.

[26] Included passenger seat back map pocket and carpet inserts on Base and Touring, and dual seat back map pockets on Limited.

[27] Included horn pulse, flashing headlamps and park lamps and instrument cluster warning lamp.

[28] Included tonal decals on front fascia outboard of grille, outside edges of hood, front fenders and doors, tone-on-tone flame decals on front fascia, hood, front fenders and doors; restricted to four exterior colors: Black, Silver Metallic, Deep Cranberry and Inferno Red.

[29] Included overhead console with compass and temperature display, sliding sun visors with illuminated vanity mirrors, auxiliary 12 volt electrical outlets front (center stack battery fed), and rear (cargo area, ignition fed), interior assist handles (four), and console flood lamp.

[30] Included Light Group and power moonroof with express open.

[31] Included power door locks with central locking and programmable automatic operation, power heated foldaway exterior mirrors, remote keyless entry system and speed control.

[32] This included Medium Oak woodgrain trim on front and rear doors, rear quarter panels and liftgate framed by dimensional Light Ash rail moldings. The front fenders featured rail moldings without Medium Oak woodgrain (not available with Chrome Accents Group).

[33] This CPOS (Customer Preferred Ordering System) Package contained leather-trimmed performance seats with perforated leather inserts, unique leather-wrapped steering wheel, supplemental side airbags, driver seat power height adjuster, power moon roof, AM/FM stereo radio with cassette and CD and 17in chrome aluminum wheels.

This provocative artwork was used by Mopar to promote its Body Kit for the 2003 PT Cruiser. The package was available for both turbo and non-turbo models, and included front and rear fascia accents, flared side sills, and flush door trim pieces. These components were available in Black, Bright Silver and Inferno Red, as well as primed ready for painting.
(Author's collection)

Get a
Hot Body Package
for Chrysler PT Cruiser

MOPAR.

Mopar's PT Cruiser body kit raises the art of cruisin' to a whole new level.

PT Cruiser Body Kit accents the entire lower body, creating a sleek and aggressive profile.

"The great American pastime of cruising is more popular than ever," said Mopar, and this 2003 PT Cruiser, decked out with the Mopar Body Kit, fog lights and chrome wheels was just about perfect for "Cruisin' USA." (Author's collection)

Mopar offered three Flame Accent Kits for the 2003 PT Cruiser. Seen here is the 'Out of Control' kit, a combination of Yellow, Orange and Red flames. It was intended, said Mopar, "to give the look of a classic hot rod." Also available were kits of Blue/Purple and Red/Orange that were identical to the production decals. (Author's collection)

The PT Cruiser's prices, effective May 13, 2003, were:
ModelMSRP (including Destination Charge of $590)

Model	MSRP
PT Cruiser	$17,720
PT Cruiser Touring	$19,665
PT Cruiser Limited	$21,905
PT Turbo	$23,430

The prices and availability of the major options offered in the US for the 2003 PT Cruisers were:

Option	Price
Power Convenience Group [1]	$820
Light Group [2]	$300
Supplemental front side airbags (Base, Touring, GT)	$390
Anti-lock 4-wheel disc brakes (Base, Touring, Limited)	$595
Flame Exterior Accents [3] (Base, Touring, Limited, GT)	$495
Woodgrain Exterior Accents Group [4] (Base, Touring, Limited)	$895
Chrome Accents Group (Touring, Limited)	$5355
Deep-tinted sunscreen glass on rear windows (Base model)	$275
Black roof rack with adjustable crossbars, 150lb capacity (Base, Touring, Limited)	$175
AM/FM stereo radio with cassette and CD player and six premium speakers (Base, Touring, GT)	$100
AM/FM stereo radio with in-dash 6-disc CD player and six premium speakers (Base, Touring, Limited, GT)	$2506
4-speed automatic transmission:	$8757
Power moonroof with one-touch-open feature and sliding sunshade (Touring, GT)	$695
Driver seat power height adjuster (Touring, GT)	$100
Quick Order Package 2-R (GT)	$21308
Heated front seats (Limited, GT)	$250
Low speed traction control (Touring and Limited) [9]	$175
16in chrome-clad six-spoke wheels (Touring)	$600
17in chrome five-spoke aluminum wheels	

A view of the standard Capeli leather-trimmed seats of a 2003 PT Cruiser Limited in Dark Taupe with Preferred Suede accents. (Author's collection)

The 2003 PT Cruiser Touring shared this Metro II cloth interior, seen here in Dark Taupe, with the Base model. (Author's collection)

paint colors (Black, Bright Silver, Deep Cranberry and Inferno Red).

4 Not available on Touring in combination with Chrome Accent Group.

5 When announced on June 12, 2002, the MSRP of the package was $1270 for the Touring Edition and $595 for the Limited. The reason for this price differential was due to the Limited already being equipped with many features of the package, including its 16in chrome-clad wheels, bright exhaust tip and leather-wrapped steering wheel as standard equipment.

6 Price for Limited and GT ordered with Quick Order Package 2-R was $150.

7 Price listed was for Base, Touring and Limited models; when ordered for the GT, the price was $250.

8 Price listed was "Manufacturer's Discount Price" for GT with manual transmission. If ordered with automatic, the price was $2280. Package content consisted of front side airbags, AutoStick (with automatic transmission), leather upholstery, power moonroof, AM/FM stereo radio with six disc CD player, driver-seat height adjuster and 17in chrome aluminum wheels.

9 Required ABS brakes.

This power moonroof with a sliding sunshade was standard on the 2003 PT Cruiser Limited Edition. (Author's collection)

| (GT) | $600 |
| Engine block heater | $35 |

1 For Base models, included speed control, remote keyless entry, two transmitters, panic alarm, power mirrors and power door locks with central locking.

2 For Base models, included overhead console with dual map lamps, digital compass and outside temperature display, illuminated vanity visor mirrors, four assist handles, instrument panel and cargo area-mounted power outlets.

3 Applique coordinated to accent specific exterior

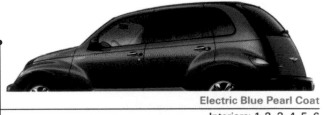

Electric Blue Pearl Coat
Interiors: 1, 2, 3, 4, 5, 6

Electric Blue Pearl coat was one of ten exterior colors for 2003. (Author's collection)

Instrument panel
in Deep Cranberry

Instrument panel
in Inferno Red

Instrument panel
in Steel Blue

Instrument panel
in Patriot Blue

Instrument panel
in Onyx Green

Instrument panel
in Electric Blue

Instrument panel
in Bright Silver

Instrument panel
in Light Pewter

Turbo Instrument panel
in Shadow Dot

Depending on the exterior color, the 2003 PT Cruiser's passenger airbag door was available in this selection of interior colors. Bright Silver Metallic was a new color for 2003. It was used in conjunction with a Dark Slate Gray interior. (Author's collection)

Not every PT Turbo owner was happy that special acoustic dampeners on the turbo engine's intake system had virtually eliminated the whine historically associated with turbocharged engines. (Author's collection)

Production of the 2003 Street Cruiser 2 began in January 2003. It was available for sale in Europe in the spring of 2003. Chrysler announced that production would be limited to 2000 units. (Courtesy DaimlerChrysler Media Services)

The Tangerine Pearl Clear Coat exterior of the 2003 Street Cruiser Series 2 was accentuated by its chrome bodyside moldings, body-color rear spoiler and 16in aluminum painted wheels with Tangerine-colored center caps. (Courtesy DaimlerChrysler Media Services)

A Tangerine-accented identification badge was installed on the liftgate of the Street Cruiser Series 2. (Courtesy DaimlerChrysler Media Services)

The Dream Cruiser 2 interior was finished in what Chrysler described as "a punchy combination of Tangerine and Dark Slate." (Author's collection)

The driver and front passenger seats in the Dream Cruiser 2 were heated, and had Tangerine perforated Radar leather inserts. (Courtesy DaimlerChrysler Media Services)

$26,475 when equipped with the standard 5-speed Getrag heavy-duty manual transmission, and $26,915 if ordered with the AutoStick automatic transmission.

Standard equipment for the Dream Cruiser included a power moonroof with express open feature, heated driver and passenger seats, and a factory-installed Sirius satellite radio system with a customer-activated one-year broadcast subscription. The Sirius radio offered US customers 100 coast-to-coast radio channels, 60 of which were commercial-free music channels. News, sports and entertainment were included in the remaining 40 channels.

Additional standard equipment included a performance-tuned suspension, four-wheel disc brakes, ABS with traction control and a large diameter chrome exhaust tip. Except for the transmission choice, there were no other options offered for the Dream Cruiser Series 2.

Dream Cruisers for North America were powered by the 215hp High Output turbocharged engine. The European Street Cruiser 2 version, which debuted at the Mondial del'Automobile in Paris on September 26, was equipped with the 2.2-liter common-rail turbo diesel and a 5-speed manual transmission in Europe, and with the 2.0-liter gasoline engine (with either the 5-speed manual or 4-speed automatic), for right-hand drive markets.

Regardless of market, collectors of limited edition PT Cruisers found the Street Cruiser 2 a rare commodity. For example, only 47 were destined to be shipped to Australia where they were base priced at $44,890 (Australian).

As with the Series 1 models, there were other differences between the Dream and Street Cruiser 2 models. 'Street Cruiser Series 2' badging was applied to the European model's tailgate, and its front floor mats were embroidered with Street Cruiser logo. The power moonroof was optional, as were the heated driver and passenger seats.

Chrysler also announced at the Paris Show that the Street Cruiser 2, along with the other 2003 PT Cruisers available for the European market (Classic Edition, Touring Edition and Limited Edition), would have four-wheel disc brakes, ABS and supplemental side airbags as standard equipment. In addition, traction control became standard for the Limited Edition and optional for the Touring and Classic Editions.

Making the most of the Dream Cruiser 2's exclusive exterior color and turbocharged engine, Chrysler noted that it "packs a lot of juice under the hood." (Courtesy DaimlerChrysler Media Services)

The Tangerine accents of the Dream Cruiser 2's interior included the 'Dream Cruiser Series 2' plaque with the vehicle's unique production sequence number mounted on the instrument panel center stack. (Courtesy DaimlerChrysler Media Services)

Included in the Tangerine-colored interior appointments of the Street Cruiser Series 2 were its seat inserts, passenger side airbag door, and instrument cluster bezel. (Courtesy DaimlerChrysler Media Services)

Chrysler introduced several changes for the UK market PT Cruisers for 2003. Models powered by the 2.2 CRD engine were offered in the entry level Classic trim level with a £16,495 price. Both gasoline and diesel Classic models had new wheel covers. Limited models had a new chrome look that included chrome accents on horizontal grille bars and bodyside moldings. The filler cap, door lock knobs and gear knob also had the chrome treatment. ABS was standard on all models, a new Deep Cranberry exterior was offered, and a cue ball design shift knob was added to automatic cars. (Courtesy Chrysler Media UK)

This limited edition (only 200 were available), PT Cruiser Electric model was introduced to the UK market in the latter part of June 12, 2003, just as Chrysler's UK dealers were celebrating the sale of their 12,000th Cruiser. Based on the 2.0-liter/5-speed manual Classic model, the Electric had 16in alloy wheels, a bright 'Electric Blue' exterior, and unique 'PT Cruiser Electric' badging. It was priced at £13,500. (Courtesy Chrysler Media UK)

Seen here is Nadahl Shocair, Chief Executive of DeTeWe, a UK telecommunications company, receiving the keys to a fleet of 23 PT Cruiser Classic models powered by the 2.2-liter CRD engine from Tony Golder of Cannon Lane Chrysler and Jeep, and Clive Lloyd, Manager of Corporate Sales for DaimlerChrysler. This sale had a retail value of over £326,000, and surpassed the previous fleet sale record of 19 PTs that had been completed in November 2002. (Courtesy (Chrysler Media UK)

These two views of the Chrysler California Cruiser were displayed at a dinner honoring the judges and organizers of the 52nd Pebble Beach Concours d'Elegance in August 2002. (Courtesy DaimlerChrysler Media Services)

A month before the Paris Show, on August 19, 2002, at the traditional dinner honoring the judges and organizers of the 52nd Pebble Beach Concours d'Elegance, Chrysler previewed the Chrysler California Cruiser, which it described as "the first vehicle in its next wave of trendsetting concept cars."

With the California Cruiser's world debut scheduled for the Paris Auto Show, comments on its design by top Chrysler officials at Pebble Beach were limited in scope. "With PT Cruiser, we created a whole new segment and virtually redefined the blend of design and versatility in the small vehicle market," said Jim Schroer, Executive Vice President Chrysler Group Global Sales and Marketing. "That vehicle anticipated new consumer demands and expectations around the world. Now, we bring you a concept of what might be next, the Chrysler California Cruiser."

Calling attention to the California Cruiser's relationship to recent Chrysler production models, Trevor Creed noted: "This concept introduces the new face of Chrysler to the PT Cruiser. California Cruiser's scalloped headlamps, chrome accented grille and integrated bumper reflect a direction that we started with the Chrysler Crossfire and Pacifica. The more crisp and precise styling themes of those vehicles also influenced the profile and rear design of the Chrysler California Cruiser."

A great deal of prescience wasn't needed to anticipate that, upon the California Cruiser's September 26 debut in Paris, Chrysler would associate its creation with California's legendary surfing lifestyle. "Those on the west coast of the

The California Cruiser was inspired by the sun, sand and waves of the mid-sixties surfing culture. These beach-goers were happily heeding Chrysler's advise to "Be True To Your Cool." (Courtesy DaimlerChrysler Media Services)

United States," explained a media representative, "will tell you that if you catch a wave, you'll be sitting on top of the world. But the designers in the Chrysler Group Design Studio will tell you that if you catch the Next Wave, you just may be sitting in the Chrysler California Cruiser concept – and on the leading edge of true coolness ... The California Cruiser is all-new, and builds on the unique blend of style and practicality seen in the production models of the successful PT Cruiser, proving that the possibilities are endless as summer."

Unlike the production PT Cruiser with its four doors and capacity for five passengers, the California Cruiser had two large side doors and an interior intended for just four occupants. But, as Jim Schroer, who was on hand for the California Cruiser's debut, explained, it "redefines both the look and the interior functionality of a 'Surf Wagon,' with ample space and comfort for four people, every imaginable extreme sports toy, and even the ability to convert to a hotel room for two."

The key to this versatility was an extended load floor with all seats having a 'fold-flat' design that included head restraints that retracted into the seat backs. Reinforcing the belief of Jeff Godshall, Senior Manager of Exterior/Interior Design, that those modular seats exuded 'cool/hip images' was the 'boom box' integrated into the Cruiser's liftgate and its center column-mounted navigation system.

The interior's theme, identified as "linear design" by Godshall, was linked to an exterior that Jim Schroer described as "totally drop-dead gorgeous – a new interpretation of Chrysler Design magic." Along with a 'chopped roof' profile, suggestive of the classic surf wagon, the California Cruiser's

Although the California Cruiser's basic form stayed true to the landmark design of the PT Cruiser, Chrysler noted that its two large doors, unique rear hatch and "chopped roof" profile "amplified what owners love about their PT Cruiser." (Courtesy DaimlerChrysler Media Services)

major styling elements consisted of a fully retractable sunroof, dual projector headlamps, dual chrome exhaust tips, 19in billet aluminum machined wheels, and "hi-tech" clear tail lamps. Fog lamps were incorporated into the grille, which had a chrome Chrysler winged badge and chiseled satin-chrome horizontal bars.

Just two days after the California Cruiser's Paris première, Chrysler demonstrated its awareness that the bedrock of the PT Cruiser's popularity was rooted in middle-America by sponsoring a free "Block Party" for PT owners at Six Flags Great America in Gurnee, Illinois. Previewing the day's wild

The California Cruiser was fitted with clear tail lamps. (Courtesy DaimlerChrysler Media Services)

The satin silver body applique used for the California Cruiser was seen as a contemporary interpretation of the Woodie theme of an earlier age. (Courtesy DaimlerChrysler Media Services)

rides, car exhibits, and live musical entertainment for those planning to attend, Tom Marinelli said: "If you're a PT Cruiser owner and devotee, this is a dream come true. This will be a wonderful day packed with events and activities specifically about PT Cruisers. It is our way of saying thank-you, and it is only available to PT owners and their families.

"The PT Block Party is a unique event celebrating a unique vehicle. We wanted to capture the enthusiasm and passion that people share for the Chrysler PT Cruiser. This is the car that has been described as the vehicle that's 'too-cool-to-categorize,' which is one of the reasons people are so attracted to it."

In addition to having the opportunity to experience the theme park's wide assortment of rides, the approximately 10,000 attendees (who drove over 3000 PT Cruisers to the event), strolled through displays of concept PT Cruisers, the full line of Chrysler vehicles, and had opportunities to test drive several models.

The 'Speed Shop,' a special customization area was staffed by representatives from professional aftermarket accessory companies who held workshops and performed demonstrations showing PT Cruiser owners numerous ways to individualize their car's engines, hoods, grilles, headlights, and taillights.

Equally popular were several round table discussions where PT owners met with PT Cruiser engineers and designers where participants shared customizing ideas and vehicle use experiences. Company employees also encouraged owner input regarding features they hoped would appear on future PT Cruisers.

Not surprisingly, the Block Party's music theme was the nostalgic sounds of the '50s and '60s, with a grand finale concert emceed by radio personality Casey Kasem. This musical extravaganza featured the music of Chuck Berry (*Johnny B. Goode, Maybellene*), The Shirelles (*Dedicated to the One I Love, Soldier Boy*), The Countours (*Do You Love Me?*), The Tokens (*The Lion Sleeps Tonight*), and Little Anthony & the Imperials (*Tears on My Pillow*).

Several 'from mild-to wild' modified PT Cruisers were among the Chrysler, Jeep and Dodge vehicles displayed at the annual SEMA show held in Las Vegas in early November 2002, where the Chrysler Group was the 'manufacturer of show.' In addition to the unique PT Cruisers crafted by SEMA members, both the Chrysler Group's new Vehicle Excitement Team (VXT), consisting of four cross-functional groups representing Engineering, Design, Product Planning and Marketing, and the Mopar Parts and Accessories parts brand exhibited customized versions of the PT Cruiser. Overall, there were over 100 Chrysler Group cars and trucks at the SEMA show, including over 40 that had

A grille with chiseled satin chrome bars and scalloped dual reflector headlamps were key styling elements of the California Cruiser's front design. (Courtesy DaimlerChrysler Media Services)

The California Cruiser's seats folded flat to provide what Chrysler said was "the interior functionality of a 'surf wagon' ... and even the ability to convert to a hotel room for two." (Courtesy DaimlerChrysler Media Services)

been distributed by VXT to SEMA-member companies for customization and display.

This action was consistent with VXT's objective of developing cars and trucks highlighting Chrysler's personalization and customization initiatives, and coordinating relationships between Chrysler's resources and SEMA members and suppliers to produce special edition vehicles for shows. These initial activities also reflected Chrysler's increased emphasis on performance parts, accessories and customization. Earlier in 2002, as part of this philosophy, Chrysler had announced it would make vehicle technical

The California Cruiser was powered by the 4-cylinder, high-output turbocharged 2.4-liter engine. (Courtesy DaimlerChrysler Media Services)

Joining the 'California Cruiser' door-mounted identification was an art deco hood vent. (Courtesy DaimlerChrysler Media Services)

In September 2002, the PT Cruiser Convertible Styling Study was displayed at the Paris Auto Show in the new Inferno Red paint, along with a black cabriolet top and boot cover. The interior had a Light Pearl Beige color scheme with Inferno Red accents. (Courtesy DaimlerChrysler Media Services)

The PT Super Cruiser was finished in a Chrysler Group/ Rohm and Haas custom paint scheme of Octane Orange accented with Deep Royal Blue trim, which included glass and rubber additives. (Courtesy DaimlerChrysler Media Services)

specifications more widely available to SEMA members to encourage more aftermarket customization.

The formal announcement of VXT's creation (it had previously operated as Chrysler's 'Image Team'), was made by Dieter Zetsche at the SEMA show's opening 'Innovations Day' event. Seeming to have the PT Cruiser's origin, on-going evolution and future in mind, he declared that "designing and building cars and trucks that defy convention and challenge the status quo is something we love doing, something we're good at and something we're determined to do more and more of in the months and years ahead."

Zetsche identified several basic areas in which a company could focus its talents and energies in order to

Helping to put a new face on the Chrysler Group's Mopar parts and service brand at the 2002 SEMA show was this custom Mopar Chrysler Cruiser. (Courtesy DaimlerChrysler Media Services)

differentiate itself from other companies. These involved delighting customers, achieving lean processes in its operations, and producing "truly inspirational" products that people would line up to buy.

"In order to succeed," Zetsche asserted "you have to be competitive in all three areas and lead in one. We will definitely be competitive in operational excellence and the customer experience, but in the third area – product excellence – is where we're going to settle for nothing less than the leadership position."

Not surprisingly, two of the three VXT-developed vehicles, manifesting Zetsche's latter assertion, the PT Super Cruiser and the PT Big Sky, were based on the PT Cruiser. The third originated as a Dodge Stratus. The Super Cruiser was, like the California Cruiser, and the earlier GT Cruiser show car of 2000, a 2-door vehicle. It was powered by a turbocharged 2.4-liter engine equipped with a free-flow exhaust system, and was credited with over 300hp. The Super Cruiser had been built by Chrysler Group employees in Auburn Hills,

Michigan, including 10 engineers and 35 UAW (United Automobile Workers) members and was a fully functional automobile equipped with numerous features making it suitable for road racing. These included a six-point safety cage, six-point camlock harness, window nets, Lifeline fire system and Momo race seats and steering wheel.

The Super Cruiser was also equipped with a removable Infinity Entertainment Pak with a 22in LCD video screen, X-Box game console, 875 watt full-surround sound system, auxiliary batteries, folding chairs and cooler.

Bumpers were integral parts of the Super Cruiser's monochromatic front and rear fascias. The custom fiber hood had exterior gauges, a shift light set in a functional hood scoop and captive hood pins. A custom lightweight blue-tinted windshield was supplied by the Llumar Corporation, with the Chrysler Group fabricating the remaining windows in lightweight blue-tinted Plexiglass.

Additional exterior features of the Super Cruiser included sill extensions, wider fenders, 18 x 9.5in forged aluminum racing wheels, Michelin Pilot Sport Cup DOT (Department of Transportation) legal road-race tires, four-wheel 12.9in Brembo disc brakes with cross-drilled cadmium-plated rotors, a rear wing, and custom center-exit 4in exhaust pipes.

Contrasting with the Super Cruiser's performance-based theme, the second VXT PT Cruiser for SEMA '02, the PT Big Sky, had a luxury orientation. Its interior was finished in Light Pearl Beige with leather seating and door trim provided by the Seton Company of Troy, Michigan. Custom front seats with a WET Inc 'Comfort Cools' heating/cooling system were designed by Johnson Controls, Inc. The interior was also equipped with a Panasonic custom entertainment system with DVD video and a multi-channel surround system. This package also contained four LCD video screens, consisting of a 7in flip-out unit on the instrument panel, two additional monitors on the back of the front seats and a 15in removable package positioned in the cargo area. Along with these features, the Big Sky also had such performance-enhancing features as 18in BBS wheels, Goodyear Eagle F1 tires, and stainless steel brake rotors and calipers at all four wheels, as well as numerous distinctive styling effects.

The most apparent of the latter was its glass 'lamelia' roof system which opened wide enough for occupants front

With the exception of its carbon fiber trim package, the Mopar Chrysler PT Cruiser was equipped with Mopar accessories available at any Chrysler dealership. (Courtesy DaimlerChrysler Media Services)

The Kenne-Bell Chrysler PT Cruiser Turbo displayed at SEMA 2002 was inspired by the classic hot rods of the '60s. Along with a Golden Pearl paint, and Black LeMans stripes, it was equipped with 18in Oasis alloy wheels, low profile tires, and Force 10 stainless steel race brakes. (Courtesy DaimlerChrysler Media Services)

and rear to have a full view of the sky. The design of this roof was assigned to Webasto Roof Systems of Rochester Hills, Michigan, which devised a system of one stationary and four retractable units. The non-movable unit served as a vent, while the others could be stacked vertically at the rear of the window opening. Both the roof panels and the side windows were tinted with a new process developed by Solutia Automotive that laminated a color interlayer named

The stance of the Kenne-Bell Chrysler PT Cruiser Turbo was lower than a stock PT Cruiser due to its KW coil-over suspension. Other distinguishing features included a modified front grille, custom front fascia, hood and rear roll pan. The interior was fitted with Katzkin leather-wrapped racing seats, revised gauges, tinted windows, and a complete audio/video entertainment center. (Courtesy DaimlerChrysler Media Services)

Vanceva between two pieces of tempered glass, creating a tint matching the car's special Merlot paint color created by PPG. Compared to tempered glass, this new process weighed less, provided more UV protection, superior intrusion resistance, and improved sound deadening.

At the conclusion of the 2002 SEMA Show Webasto was the recipient of the Chrysler Group's Application Excellence for this system. The entries in this competition were judged by the Vehicle Excitement Team.

Also contributing to the Big Sky's unique exterior was a ground effects package provided by ASC of Southfield, Michigan. It included a rear fascia modified to accommodate an integrated rear bumper and a Boria dual exhaust system. The front fascia was also customized to accommodate a large opening fitted with a silver mesh insert. Wheel flares and fog lamps were also part of this package. Polished stainless steel surround trim accentuated the Solutia tinted windows. Both the side mirrors and bodyside molding were chrome-trimmed. Eager to enhance its relationship with SEMA members, Chrysler acknowledged the role of ASC Creative Services in the creation of the PT Big Sky. "While this one-of-a-kind PT Cruiser came from the Chrysler

Group," it explained that "ASC Creative Services performed the custom work and integration based on a design created in conjunction with the Chrysler Group."

As with the California Cruiser's two-door format, the provision of the Big Sky with an AWD system fueled speculation that a similar system might appear on subsequent/future production model PT Cruisers. Indeed, Chrysler indicated that reaction to the use of AWD on the Big Sky would be a factor in moving the concept toward production status.

Two years later, in April 2004, Chrysler Vice-President, Jeff Bell, in a interview with *Wards Auto* put an end to any hopes among PT Cruiser fans that an AWD model would be forthcoming. "I've got to be honest with you ... I didn't know there was a big demand for that. I don't have any data that tells me people are screaming for AWD, but I could be wrong. I haven't heard (customers) want AWD in that vehicle."

While Mopar had only one vehicle on display at SEMA – the Mopar Chrysler PT Cruiser – its presence coincided with Chrysler's announcement that Mopar would be playing an important role in the creation of future 'aspirational' vehicles.

A gathering of three Cool Cruisers. From left to right: a Woodie in Deep Cranberry Clearcoat, a Chrome Cruiser in Black, and a Dream Cruiser 2 in its exclusive Tangerine finish. (Author's collection)

Mopar traced its roots back to 1937 when the brand was created by combining key letters (MO and PAR) of the words motor and parts. Since that time, as the exclusive original equipment supplier of parts, components and accessories for Chrysler, Plymouth, DeSoto, Jeep and Dodge vehicles, Mopar had developed and marketed millions of OEP (Original Equipment Parts) through a global network of 10,000 authorized dealers, fully justifying the Chrysler Group's assertion that Mopar was its "Fourth Brand."

Mopar had been a SEMA show exhibitor since 1976, longer than any other Original Equipment Manufacturer (OEM), and Chrysler used the 2002 show to announce that Mopar was receiving a make-over. "The new look," it said, "reflects a revitalized mission – focused on renewing passion among existing owners – while at the same time demonstrating commitment to new markets and innovative ideas with parts for emerging vehicle categories ..."

Elaborating on this broad strategy, Christine Cortez, the Chrysler Group's Senior Vice President – Global Service and Parts, explained: "One of the ways is through the Mopar Speedshop. Creating a Mopar Speedshop in every retail store gives dealers an enthusiastic connection with customers. It's the idea of a store within a store; a boutique. We see the Speedshop as an interactive hangout for car nuts."

Additional comments by Cortez seemed tailormade to attract PT Cruiser fans to their local dealer's Mopar Speedshop. "We want to further enhance the lines of both performance parts and accessories under Mopar. We want to make it easy for customizers and enthusiasts to buy parts – both performance and accessories – from Mopar and personalize their vehicles their way. This will also be a great program for our dealers, pulling people into their stores to hang around and see what's new."

"SEMA is at the center of the automotive universe

This illustration of a 2003 PT Cruiser was included in Chrysler's all black-and white Drive & Love brochure, designed to express in words and photos the basic philosophy guiding the design of its automobiles. Setting aside the PT Cruiser's close association with the retro theme, Chrysler offered this view of the PT Cruiser as a gateway to the future: "Our designers and engineers are always working to move ideas forward in new and interesting ways. Like the PT Turbo. Under the cool exterior they've turned up the heat with a 215-peak horsepower 2.4-liter High Output 16-valve four-cylinder engine with intercooled turbocharger. In the process, we're inspiring the next generation." (Author's collection)

this week," she added. "This is the perfect opportunity to introduce our Chrysler, Jeep and Dodge dealers to the new Mopar. The new look of packaging, displays and in-dealership showcases are all here.

"We'd love to have customized vehicles on dealer showroom floors to draw customer traffic. Seeing all the tricked-up vehicles at the show, I think our more progressive dealers will say, 'Wow, I should do some of this stuff in my showroom.' They'll leave the show charged up to help us build our business in ways they haven't thought before."

To encourage this perspective, Mopar Accessories displayed several new appearance products for the PT Cruiser including Chrome Appearance Packages and 'baby moon' wheels.

The Mopar PT Cruiser effectively demonstrated the potential of Mopar Accessories to build showroom traffic. Except for a carbon fiber trim package, which was included as a design exercise, its distinctive appearance and features were due entirely to the application of readily available Mopar accessories. These included a rear spoiler, chrome fuel filler door, dual exhausts, 12-disc CD changer, illuminated door entry guards, and performance struts.

Never reluctant to offer PT Cruiser fans what they wanted, Chrysler had a slightly less powerful turbo along with a new Series 3 Dream Cruiser ready for introduction in 2004.

Both would be well received by PT enthusiasts, but there was unrest stirring in the ranks of the faithful, many of whom wondered, "When was Chrysler going to produce the PT Cruiser Convertible?"

Chapter 5 – "Wherever two or more PT Cruisers are gathered, you're guaranteed to have a good time"

A new turbocharged engine with 180hp @ 5200rpm and 210lb-ft of torque @ 2800-4000rpm was introduced as a standalone option for the 2004 Touring Edition and Limited Edition models. This engine, available only with the automatic transaxle, was intended to attract PT Cruiser buyers interested in performance mid-way between the 150hp 2.4-liter and the High-Output Turbo which was upgraded to 220hp for 2004.

The hefty $22,000-plus MSRP of the 2003 PT Turbo was one of the few miscues Chrysler made in the marketing of the PT Cruiser. In a June 2003 interview with Mary Donnelly of *Automotive News*, Gary Dilts, Chrysler Group Senior Vice President of Sales, acknowledged that the PT Turbo had been too expensive for many younger performance-oriented PT customers. "The big criticism of the PT Cruiser, especially from the youth market," he said, "was that it is not powerful enough. The turbo delivers significant power to the vehicle, but it also comes with an equipment package which raised the price $2500." The retail price of the 180hp engine option was $1280 for the Touring, and $1265 for the Limited.

PT Cruisers with this engine had a number of exterior identifying features including a body-color front fascia with a large lower opening, a '2.4L Turbo' liftgate badge, a large diameter chrome exhaust tip and new 16in chrome-clad aluminum wheels. Unlike the 220hp PT Turbo, which had a speedometer reading to 140mph/220kph, these Cruisers had the same speedometer with a maximum reading of 120mph/200kph as those with the standard 150hp engine.

Offering his perspective on the 180hp engine, Larry Lyons, DaimlerChrysler Vice-President, Small Vehicle Product Team Engineering, said: "Just as our High Output turbo engine pumped up the performance on the PT Turbo model last year, this new 180hp version will provide more punch to an already fun-to-drive vehicle."

Following up on these remarks, Tom Marinelli added that "the new 180hp engine option continues the PT Cruiser's reputation as the coolest, most unique car available at a great price.

"It's a vehicle that has helped the Chrysler brand's upscale momentum over the last years, and new options like the 180hp engine will make it appeal to an even broader customer base."

The new options alluded to by Marinelli also included a new body-color liftgate-mounted spoiler. Aside from its option-status for the Base, Touring and Limited models, it was also standard on the PT Turbo. All models were available with a factory-installed Sirius satellite radio receiver. This option, which had been introduced on the 2003 Dream Cruiser Series 2, included a one year subscription. Offered for all models except the Base PT Cruiser as a late availability option was a UConnect hands-free communication option. This system used Bluetooth technology and controls on the electrochromic (automatic day/night) rearview mirror to provide hands-free, in-vehicle communication. The audio, integrated into the car's electrical architecture, was heard through its speakers, with the customer's cellular phone located anywhere in the interior.

Content of the Chrome Accents option was expanded for 2004 to include bright pedals and a leather-wrapped steering wheel with Satin Silver painted spokes.

GT IN BRIGHT SILVER METALLIC

The entry level PT Cruiser had new body-color monotone front and rear fascias as standard equipment for 2004. Added to its standard safety equipment was the Sentry Key engine immobilizer. In 2003 it was available as part of the optional Base Power Convenience Group. A new sixteen-inch Aluminum Wheel/Touring Group option consisting of 16in painted cast-aluminum wheels, 205/55R16 all-season touring tires, and touring suspension was also available for the Base model. Also offered at extra cost for the Base model as well as the Touring and Limited Edition PT Cruisers with the standard 150hp engine was a new Disc/Drum ABS brake system. Previously, ABS had been offered only in combination with 4-wheel disc brakes.

When powered by the 180hp turbo engine the Touring and Limited models could be ordered with a performance four-wheel disc ABS brake system that included low-

Calling it "a dream come true," Chrysler added the 2004 Dream Cruiser Series 3 to its sequence of "dream team" limited production models on August 12, 2003. It had a unique Midnight Blue over Bright Silver paint scheme, tinted blue glass and 17in chrome-plated Empire cast-aluminum wheels. With the magic of digital imagery, a 2004 Series 3 Dream Cruiser replaced its predecessor as a companion car to PT Cruisers with the Woodgrain and Chrome Accent Group options. (Author's collection)

speed traction control. In addition, a new 16in chrome-clad aluminum wheel was optional for Touring Editions with the 180hp and standard for the 180hp Limited Edition Cruisers.

Numerous features previously optional for the PT Turbo (PT Cruiser sales literature identified this model as the GT), became standard for the 2004 model. They included the leather-trimmed interior with specially bolstered performance seats, a one-touch-open power moonroof and 17in chrome-plated aluminum wheels. Joining these items were several new standard features, including a leather-wrapped steering wheel with bright silver painted spokes, the bright pedal package and chrome door lock knobs. A new '2.4L Turbo High Output' badge was positioned on the liftgate to distinguish the PT Turbo/GT as the high-performance PT Cruiser model.

The color selection for PT Cruisers intended for sale both in North America and abroad was revamped for 2004 with Deep Plum Pearl Coat replacing Deep Cranberry Pearl Coat. Other changes included Bright Seamist Green Metallic Clear Coat in place of Steel Blue Pearl Coat and Stone White being dropped in favor of Cool Vanilla Clear Coat. Two additional new colors, Midnight Blue and Graphite Metallic were designated as late availability colors. Carryover colors included Electric Blue Pearl, Inferno Red Tinted Pearl, Midnight Blue Pearl, Bright Silver Metallic, Light Almond Metallic, and Black Clear Coat.

Chrysler's latest offering in its series of limited-production

PT Cruisers, the Dream Cruiser Series 3, was introduced on August 12, 2003, just in time for the annual Woodward Dream Cruise in Detroit. With Dream Cruiser Series 3 production beginning in August, Chrysler promised prospective customers that they would be arriving at Chrysler dealers "just in time for summer cruising." Production was limited to just 1300 units for the North American market, with Vehicle Identification Numbers (VIN) being reserved in a continuous sequence block to enhance the model's collectibility.

As expected, Chrysler officials had plenty to say about this new model's appeal. For example, Tom Marinelli said that "with this new version, we're giving PT Cruisers owners another limited-production Dream Cruiser vehicle already customized with the most exclusive options available on any 2004 Chrysler PT Cruiser.

"We received inspiration for this, the third member of our limited-production PT 'dream team', from the hundreds of Chrysler PT Cruiser owner events held across the globe. It's all about upping the ante and making your PT Cruiser just a bit more unique than the one parked next to you. Our new Chrysler PT Cruiser Series 3 does just that ..."

The Dream Cruiser's engine was the 220hp High Output Turbo engine. The standard transmission was the 5-speed Getrag manual. Also included in the Dream Cruiser's $28,810 MSRP (plus $590 destination charge) was four-wheel disc brakes, ABS with traction control, a power moonroof with an 'express-open' feature, a liftgate-mounted rear spoiler, AM/FM/six-disc changer radio and a factory-installed Sirius

The 2004 Dream Cruiser Series 3 interior featured Dark Slate leather seats with Light Slate accents and matching door trim panels. The instrument panel was accented with Midnight Blue cluster bezels matching the interior, and a passenger side airbag cover with a prismatic foil 'PT Cruiser' graphic. The leather-wrapped steering wheel had Satin Silver spokes. Additional bright interior appointments included a chrome AutoStick bezel for automatic transmission models and a Satin Silver shift knob. (Courtesy DaimlerChrysler Media Services)

The seats of the 2004 Limited Edition combined Capini leather and Preferred Suede Accents in Dark Taupe. (Author's collection)

satellite band digital radio system. The automatic 4-speed with AutoStick was available as an option.

Larry Lyons, after asserting that "with the increased horsepower from turbo-charging the engine and the 245lb-ft of torque at the most usable portion of the power band, this addition to the Dream Cruiser Series is certainly no 'sleeper'," adding that its appearance also made it a perfect "show and go" vehicle.

Its interior was equipped with Dark Slate leather seats (heated in the front), with Light Slate accents. The head

restraint's front surfaces were covered with a Light Slate material embossed with the Chrysler brand winged logo. Light Slate was also used for the door trim bolsters The door trim panels were finished in Dark Slate. Floor mats with embroidered silver Dream Cruiser logos maintained this two-tone theme.

The Dream Cruiser's leather-wrapped steering wheel with Satin Silver spokes joined other similar interior appointments, including a Satin Silver shift knob, bright pedals and bright inserts for the black front sill plates that were embossed with the winged Chrysler logo. Rounding out the Dream Cruiser's interior features were Midnight Blue instrument cluster bezels and a prismatic foil PT Cruiser graphic on the passenger side airbag.

The Dream Cruiser's exterior, an exclusive two-tone

The wheels and wheel covers available for the 2004 PT Cruiser. From left-to-right: the standard bolt-on 15in covers for the Base model; the Touring model's standard 16in cast aluminum painted wheels, the 16in chrome-clad aluminum wheel standard for the Limited and optional for the Touring; the 16in chrome-clad aluminum wheel optional for Touring with 180hp engine and standard on Limited when equipped with 180 engine, and the 17in chrome-plated aluminum wheel standard on the GT. (Author's collection)

Midnight Blue and Bright Silver color scheme with blue-tinted glass, was no less sensational and attention-grabbing than its interior. It was not mere happenstance if first-time observers of the Dream Cruiser 3 came away from the encounter sensing they had witnessed a bit of history being recycled since, as a Chrysler representative explained: "This new color combination hearkens back to the bold, multi-tone paint schemes the company made popular in the 1950s."

Elaborating on this comment, Dave McKinnon, Vice President, Small, Premium and Family Vehicle Design and Color Fabric Mastering, explained, "Chrysler hit its heyday with custom paint options in 1955, including bold, contrasting bodyside inserts called 'color sweeps' on its upscale Plymouth and Chrysler vehicles. That year Chrysler offered 56 solid hues, 173 two-tone color combinations and several three-tone choices, which usually included White, Black and one additional color like Fuchsia, Bright Yellow or Lavender.

"These combinations might seem a little flamboyant by today's standards, but they were extremely popular and helped the company sell 1.6 million vehicles in 1955, more than in any year prior to that time."

Other prominent exterior features of the Dream Cruiser included chrome horizontal front grille accents and bright bodyside moldings. Balancing the 'Dream Cruiser Series 3' identification on the liftgate's lower left side was a '2.4L Turbo/High Output' badge on its lower right side. Available for the first time on a production model PT Cruiser were the Dream Cruiser's standard 17in chrome-plated 'Empire' cast-aluminum wheels.

Following the introduction of the Dream Cruiser 3, a two-tone option was offered for the Touring, Limited and PT Turbo models in these combinations: Black over Bright Silver, Black over Inferno Red, Black over Electric Blue, Black over Bright Seamist Green and Black over Light Almond.

Just two days after the Dream Cruiser 3's debut, another low-volume PT Cruiser was announced as part of the Six-vehicle Limited Edition Platinum Series for 2004 that celebrated 20 years of Chrysler minivan history. Joining the PT Cruiser in this group was the Chrysler 300M, Sebring Convertible, Sedan and Coupé, and the Town & Country minivan. All were available in a three-color selection: Graphite Metallic, Bright Silver Metallic or Brilliant Black Crystal.

The Platinum Series PT Cruiser was powered by the 180hp turbo engine, and was equipped with an automatic transmission. Interior features included an AM/FM six-disc CD changer, radio with Sirius satellite radio capacity, unique two-tone leather seats with power-seat height adjuster, bright pedals, a leather-wrapped steering wheel with Satin Silver painted spokes, chrome door lock knobs, front door sill scuff

plates with bright winged logo inserts, a chrome shifter bezel and a Satin Silver shift ball.

The exterior featured special Platinum Series badging, chrome-clad wheels, chrome bodyside moldings and a chrome exhaust tip. The Platinum Series MSRP, including a $590 destination charge, was $24,965.

DaimlerChrysler selected the Frankfurt Auto Show to announce, on September 28, 2003, that PT Cruiser GT models powered by the High Output Turbo engine would begin arriving in European Chrysler dealerships beginning in October 2003. For the European market it was rated at 164kW (223hp) @ 5100rpm and 332Nm of torque @ 2400-4500rpm. The turbo

The Mopar PT Body Kit for the 2004 PT Cruiser consisted of the front and rear fascias, seen here along with side body sills. They could be purchased primed or in Silver Metallic, Inferno Red or Black. (Author's collection)

Mopar offered two types of entry guards for the PT Cruiser's front doors, to help protect the interior door sills from scratches. The brushed stainless steel unit at the left featured the PT Cruiser name. The second unit had the added quality of illuminating each time the door was opened and shutting off with the dome light. (Author's collection)

engine was paired to the heavy-duty Getrag five-speed manual transmission. Providing the GT with what Chrysler depicted as a "more European feel," were its specially tuned front struts and rear shocks for more body control, more responsive handling tires and adapted steering.

"With 'GT' being the traditional sign of a sportier model," explained a media representative, "the Chrysler PT Cruiser GT will capitalize on the vehicle's 'hot rod' character and add another dimension to the PT Cruiser phenomenon." The GT joined three other models, the Classic, Touring and Limited for the European market.

In the UK, these PT Cruisers were joined in May 2004 by a special edition Sport model. Based on the Classic version of the PT Cruiser, it featured an exclusive Graphite Metallic

speaker radio/CD player, four-wheel disc brakes and ABS, and electrically-heated retractable door mirrors.

Positioning the Sport model in the context of the PT Cruiser's impact upon Chrysler's image in the UK, Simon Elliot said: "The PT Cruiser has done much more than just generate excitement and emotion – it has changed the way that people view the Chrysler brand in the UK. The PT Cruiser maintains and builds upon Chrysler's strong reputation for delivering high specs for low cheques – providing high levels of standard specifications at competitive prices. The latest addition to the PT Cruiser line-up for 2004 – the PT Cruiser

On January 4, 2004, Chrysler Jeep in the UK announced the availability of this limited production PT Cruiser Sport special edition. Based on the PT Cruiser Classic model, it featured a roof-mounted body spoiler, 16in alloy wheels, an exclusive Graphite Metallic paint scheme, and a 'PT Cruiser Sport' badge. It was powered by the 2.0L petrol engine and listed for £13,995. (Courtesy Chrysler Media UK)

The prices of the 2004 PT Cruiser models and optional equipment for the US market.

Model	MSRP[*]
Base	$17,490
Touring Edition	$19,265
Limited Edition	$21,505
PT Turbo (GT)	$25,460
Dream Cruiser Series 3	$28,810

[*] The Destination Charge for 2004 was an additional $590.

Option	Retail price
Power Convenience Group (optional for Base only) included speed control, remote entry system, two transmitters, panic alarm and power door locks with central locking)	$705
16in Aluminum Wheel Touring Group (optional for Base only) included Touring Suspension, 16in painted cast aluminum wheels, 205/55R16 BSW all-season touring tires)	$570

This rear spoiler from Mopar was supplied pre-painted in a Clear Coat matching the PT Cruiser's body color. (Author's collection)

paint, 16in alloy wheels and a roof-mounted, body-color rear spoiler. The Sport was offered only with the 2.0-liter engine and 5-speed manual transmission. Major features of the Classic model that were shared with the Sport included a remote control Thatcham category alarm and immobilizer, front side airbags, airconditioning, six

Two views of a 2004 PT Cruiser GT equipped with the Mopar Dream Package accessory that consisted of the PT Body Kit, lighted door entry guards and rear spoiler. (Author's collection)

Light Group (optional for Base only) included overhead console with compass and temperature display, sliding sun visors with illuminated vanity mirrors, auxiliary 12-volt electrical power outlets, interior assist handles, and console flood lamp) $300

Chrome Accents Group (included Satin Silver shift knob, bright fuel filler door, front door sill scuff plates with bright winged logo inserts, chrome lock knobs, chrome PRNDL bezel for automatic transmission, body color/chrome front fascia, chrome bodyside moldings, eather-wrapped steering wheel with Satin Silver painted spokes, bright pedal package and chrome exhaust tip) $1295 [1]

2.4L 180hp turbocharged engine (Touring and Limited) $1280 [2]

Four-speed automatic transmission $850

Four-speed AutoStick transmission $440 [3]

Front side airbags (Base and Touring) $390

Disc/Drum ABS system (Base, Touring, Limited) 595 [4]

Four-wheel disc brake ABS system (Touring, Limited) $825 [5]

Power moonroof (Touring): $695

Navigation System $1200 [6]

AM/FM stereo radio with cassette and CD players (Base and Touring Edition) $100

AM/FM stereo radio with six-disc in-dash CD player $300 [7]

Sirius Satellite Radio with one-year subscription $325 [8]

UConnect hands-free communication system $360 [9]

Driver-seat power height adjuster (Touring Edition) $100

Heated front seats (Limited Edition and PT Turbo) $250

Woodgrain Exterior Accents Group $895 [10]

Deep tinted sunscreen glass (Base model) $295 [11]

Engine block heater $35

Two-tone paint (Touring, Limited and PT Turbo) $225

Rear spoiler (Base, Touring, Limited) $150

16in six-spoke chrome alloy wheel (Touring) $700 [12]

[1] Price listed is for Touring Edition. Price for Limited was $520; for PT Turbo, $400.
[2] Required 4-speed automatic transmission. Price listed is for Touring Edition. Price for Limited was $1265.
[3] Available for PT Turbo, only.
[4] Not available with turbocharged engine.
[5] Included traction control; required 180hp engine.
[6] Not available for Base model. Price listed is for Touring Edition. Price for Limited and PT Turbo was $1100.
[7] Price listed was for Base and Touring Edition. Price for Limited Edition and PT Turbo was $200.
[8] Required side airbags, not available in Arkansas or Hawaii.
[9] Not available for Base model. Required Bluetooth-enabled mobile phone. Included automatic day/night rearview mirror.
[10] Not available for PT Turbo or Chrome Accents Group.
[11] This glass was installed in the rear door, quarter and liftgate windows.
[12] These wheels were standard for the Limited Edition.

Sport – is helping us to build on the sales success of the PT in the UK."

With the 2004 model year in full swing, the Chrysler Group included a special PT Cruiser, the PT Coupé Concept, in a group of seven custom vehicles prepared for SEMA's annual early November Las Vegas extravaganza by its SkunkWerks operation. This volunteer group inside the Chrysler Group started around 2001 with members from Engineering, Marketing, Design, Product Planning, Mopar Performance, SRT (Street and Racing Technology) engineering and the Union Shops. It typically created niche derivatives based on existing products. Contrasting with the mild-mannered label of the PT Cruiser entry, several of the others had names stirring both the soul and imagination of the automotive enthusiast: Dodge Viper SRT-10 Carbon, Dodge SRT-4 Extreme, and Dodge Ram High Output 1500 Sportside. Not in the same league as these titles were the Jeep Liberator CRD Diesel, Chrysler Sebring Special, and Chrysler Pacifica Santa Monica.

Chrysler's consistently strong support of the SEMA show, and its involvement in the 2003 show demonstrated a dramatically expanding commitment to the development of high-performance products and components. "Not since the days of the muscle car," asserted a company representative, "have performance-oriented products been given such an

The PT Coupé Concept was one of seven SkunkWerks-designed show cars displayed at the 2003 SEMA show. (Courtesy DaimlerChrysler Media Services)

influential role at the Chrysler Group. Consumers experience it through performance parts from Mopar, the winning Dodge Motorsports cars and trucks on America's race tracks, and the Street and Racing Technology (SRT) niche vehicles developed by the company's Performance Vehicles Operations (PVO).

"We work closely with the Chrysler Group SkunkWerks team in looking at future directions for performance vehicles and parts," said Dan Knott, the PVO's Director. "Like PVO, the SkunkWerks team is composed of a group of dedicated enthusiasts that enjoy working on a wide range of special vehicle projects. They clearly have a grasp of what's hot in the aftermarket industry. The are really able to stretch their imagination, and that helps us significantly as we develop the next renditions of SRT vehicles and Mopar Performance Parts.

"It's important to note that several of the SkunkWerks

After the SkunkWerks team had finished crafting the Coupé Concept, little remained to indicate its origin as a PT Cruiser Convertible. (Courtesy DaimlerChrysler Media Services)

team members are PVO engineers," Knott added. "They walk the talk as PVO engineers during the day, and after hours they are enthusiasts working on SkunkWerks projects on their own vehicles. It all makes for lively idea generation between PVO and the SkunkWerks ream."

Ralph Gilles, who as the Director of Interior/Exterior Product Design and Specialty Vehicles, not to mention also serving as the leader of the SkunkWerks team, knew a few things about the nature and character of high performance vehicles, was eager to offer his thoughts about the value of small, highly motivated groups to the vitality of a large global corporation. "First and foremost, the one-off custom vehicles the Skunkwerks team creates are testbeds – dream applications, really – for future vehicle designs and Mopar Performance Parts that we use to gauge consumer interest. We are really able to push the envelope with these vehicles, by exploring a wide variety of new ideas that come from our engineering and design teams and from our supplier partners."

In spite of its unassuming and prosaic name, the PT Coupé Concept design manifested the philosophy expressed by Knott and Gilles. Moreover, having been developed in partnership with Decoma International, Inc, it benefited from the work between Chrysler's Vehicle Excitement Team and SEMA members that had earlier resulted in the creation of over one hundred custom Jeep, Chrysler and Dodge vehicles.

SkunkWerks developed its customized vehicles "straight from the factory," and for the PT Coupé, it selected the forthcoming PT Cruiser convertible as a starting point. The addition of a permanent hardtop transformed the convertible into a taut, close-coupled coupé whose sporting appearance was accentuated by a lowered suspension achieved by use of a Mopar coilover suspension kit. Incorporated into its truncated rear deck was a functional drop tailgate. The Coupé's wheel wells were filled with low-profile P235/35R19

Bridgestone tires mounted on 19 x 8in custom aluminum wheels supplied by Colorado Custom. The PT's 2.4 high-output turbocharged engine, equipped with a Mopar Stage 1 Turbo upgrade and a Borla dual tip exhaust system was credited with a 235hp rating. Upgraded braking capacity resulted from the use of two-piston caliper performance brakes from StopTech High Performance Brake Systems.

The Coupé's interior combined a 2+2 seating arrangement reminiscent of the classic GT Coupés of the 1950s and '60s, with a high-powered premium 900 watt audio system incorporating 18 'Infinity' speakers. Providing what Chrysler described as "backup assist" for the driver was a pop-out screen integrated with the rear view mirror that was connected to a camera positioned in the Coupé's rear spoiler.

Most of the interior, including the entire backseat area, was trimmed in Navy Blue leather, with the cockpit finished in a combination of Light Pearl Beige and Navy Blue leather.

Shortly after the SEMA show on November 22, 2003, the Second PT Block party was held at the Los Angeles Fairplex in Pomona, California. Three years later, a Street Cruiser Route 66 Edition would be offered, dedicated, said Chrysler, to "The Mother Road." In 2003, Chrysler had to be content by reporting that "thousands of Chrysler PT Cruiser owners and their families from across the country will cruise Route 66, 'The Main Street of America', to the second annual PT Block Party."

Like the initial Block Party, the theme of this event was decidedly nostalgic. The Fairplex was transformed into a '50s style neighborhood complete with a Mopar Speed Shop and adjoining drag racing track. But there were also

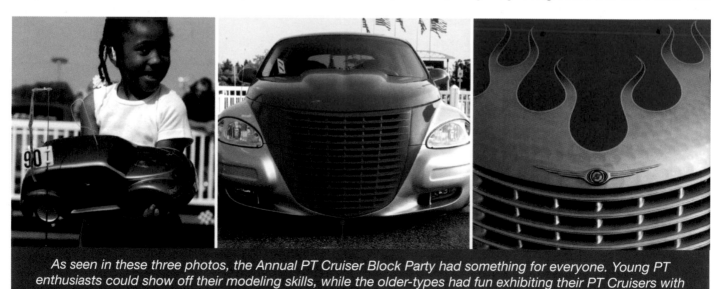

As seen in these three photos, the Annual PT Cruiser Block Party had something for everyone. Young PT enthusiasts could show off their modeling skills, while the older-types had fun exhibiting their PT Cruisers with paint schemes ranging from wild to wilder. (Author's collection)

Marv Brown of Camarillo, California (center) had the grand prize-winning ticket for a new PT Cruiser Convertible in the raffle held at the Second Annual PT Block Party on November 22, 2003. In early 2004, Brown picked up his new PT Cruiser at his local Chrysler dealership. Also seen here are Lou Bitoni (left), Senior Manager-Brand Events for Chrysler Group and, to Brown's right, Dietmar Exter, Vice President-Chrysler Brands Manager. (Courtesy DaimlerChrysler Media Services)

just enough modern happenings to remind everyone on hand that the PT Cruiser was first and foremost a thoroughly contemporary automobile. For example, PT Cruiser Concept cars were displayed alongside historic Chrysler vehicles, and activities out on the 'Strip' were dominated by the sights and sounds of the latest PT Cruisers, including the 180 and 220 horsepower turbo-charged models.

Once again demonstrating his awareness of the importance of the ardor of PT Cruiser owners to Chrysler's success, Tom Marinelli said: "PT Cruiser owners are some of our most loyal and enthusiastic customers. What better way to thank them for their devotion than to host an event that celebrates all the things that encompass the PT Cruiser lifestyle?

"The passion and excitement that PT Cruiser owners share for this vehicle truly demonstrates that there is nothing else like it on the road, and there is nothing like a PT Cruiser owner."

Eager to make this Block Party even more rousing for participants than the inaugural event, Chrysler stocked the Mopar Speed Shop with the latest products and made them available for either purchase or order. Also well stocked was the Chrysler Gift Gallery where the latest Chrysler and PT Cruiser themed apparel and accessories were available for purchase.

Contrasting with these stationary displays was the PT Turbo Drag Strip where attendees were given the opportunity to race the PT Cruiser GT on a special drag strip designed to highlight the GT's power.

The turbo engine's design was among the topics PT Cruiser owners could explore with Chrysler engineers and product planners who participated in the well-attended Engineering Round tables.

A major attraction of virtually all PT gatherings was the opportunity they offered owners to show their custom/ modified Cruisers and share ideas for future projects with other owners. Taking full advantage of this important element of PT ownership and brand loyalty, the Block Party offered a 'PT Cruiser Custom Court' featuring the 25 finalists of a PT Cruiser customization contest who were competing for the opportunity to have their car featured on the cover of *Cruiser Quarterly* magazine.

Throughout the day the 'Cruiser Kids Land,' an area with games and activities reserved for, in Chrysler's words, "the youngest PT Cruiser enthusiasts" was frequently visited by families with young children.

Winding up the day's activities was an outdoor music concert featuring performances by Little Anthony and the Imperials (*Tears on My Pillow*), Rare Earth (*Love Grows Where My Rosemary Goes*), Three Dog Night (*Celebrate*), The Association (*Cherish*) and Mitch Ryder and the Detroit Wheels (*Devil With a Blue Dress On*).

For one PT fan, Marv Brown, that was an extra-special time since he was the winner of a 2005 PT Cruiser, the grand prize in a raffle sponsored by Chrysler Financial to benefit the Surfrider Foundation. This organization, founded in 1984, was dedicated to the protection and preservation of oceans, waves and beaches.

After presenting Surfrider Foundation Executive Director Christopher Evans a check for $20,000, Dietmar Exler, Vice President, Chrysler Brands Marketing for DaimlerChrysler Services, said "Chrysler Financial is proud to support such a great environmental cause that is devoted to the protection on one of our greatest natural resources – our coastal environments."

Regardless of how close they lived to a shoreline, it's almost a certainty that virtually all of the over 7500 attendees returning home in the 2550 PT Cruisers that were present at the Block Party eagerly shared the news with friends and neighbors that they had been among the first to see the long-awaited, long-anticipated and long-overdue PT Cruiser Convertible.

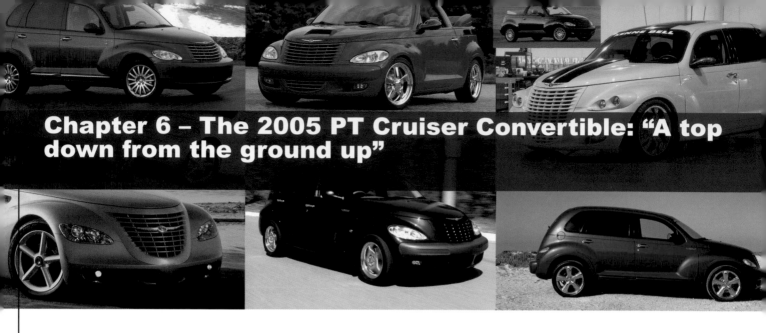

Chapter 6 – The 2005 PT Cruiser Convertible: "A top down from the ground up"

For anyone wanting to own one, the wait for a PT Cruiser convertible had been excruciating; considering that Chrysler had first shown a convertible version of the PT Cruiser at the New York Auto Show in April 2001, and, later at the March 2002 Geneva Show had announced its intention to build a production version. But finally, on Tuesday, January 6, 2004, the convertible debuted as a 2005 model at the North American Auto Show held in Detroit's Cobo Hall. According to a Chrysler representative: "The phenomenon began with the introduction of the 2001 Chrysler PT Cruiser sedan, but at a level cooler than a breeze through your hair and at a price to warm the heart."

Trevor Creed, perhaps aware that the Convertible's long gestation period had frustrated some PT Cruiser fans, provided this perspective of the production model's debut: "Our reputation for turning truly unique vehicles into significant production cars continues with the new Chrysler PT Cruiser Convertible. We wanted to maintain the memorable features

Visitors to Chrysler showrooms with an interest in the PT Cruiser Convertible were provided with a pre-introduction folder with this cover shot of an Electric Blue GT. Prospective buyers were advised that its MSRP was $29,695. (Author's collection)

CHRYSLER
PT CRUISER

COMING SPRING 2004

TO LEARN MORE VISIT CHRYSLER.COM/PTCRUISER OR CALL 800.CHRYSLER

But it was still early in calendar year 2004, and when that brochure was flipped over, there they were – those oft repeated and so familiar words "Coming spring 2004." At least they were accompanied by an attractive view of a top-up Touring model keeping company with the Electric Blue GT Convertible. (Author's collection)

everyone admired on the Styling Study, yet give customers a new interpretation of cool that they've come to expect from a Chrysler PT Cruiser."

When Convertible production had started at the Toluca plant in Mexico, in early 2004, the use of a rolling equipment changeover process resulted in no reduction in output. Heading this project was Tom LaSorda, who was familiar with the earlier crisis involving the installation of PT Cruisers at the plant. Obviously delighted by the ease by which the Convertible models were integrated into the PT Cruiser production process, he noted: "We are pleased with the smooth production launch of the PT Cruiser Convertible. The employees' dedication to customer satisfaction and the application of proven manufacturing processes and technologies have created a vehicle with the highest levels of quality and head-turning style that is part of the PT Cruiser heritage."

Central to the ease with which Convertibles began to roll off the assembly line was a cross-functional launch team that successfully maintained sedan production while managing the alterations required for the Convertible's launch. The

rolling changeover involving the addition of new assembly equipment and tooling along with their quality verification, as well as training for the new manufacturing processes, was implemented between the first and second work shifts and weekends.

Chrysler also took advantage of the addition of the Convertible to the PT Cruiser line to implement a number of changes at Toluca. Improved precision and efficiency resulted from the installation of new robotic equipment in the bodyshop's welding operations. The plant's areas dedicated to trim, chassis and final assembly were all expanded to accommodate both PT Cruiser models.

A new dedicated line, installed for the convertible's underbody assembly process, combined robotic and employee-manned workstations for welding the underbody, engine compartment and bodyside systems. A variety of 'error-prevention' devices incorporated into this process included clamps to guide panels into space, and sensors that ensured that all parts were in place before welding began.

This assembly line's unique design, by reducing floor space requirements, increased the plant's flexibility and

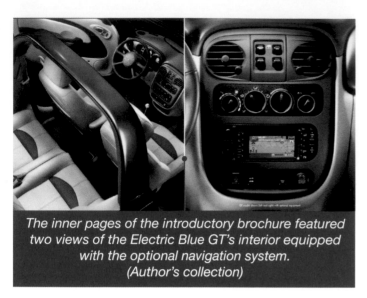

The inner pages of the introductory brochure featured two views of the Electric Blue GT's interior equipped with the optional navigation system.
(Author's collection)

efficiency as well as making it possible to build additional body lines within the plant at a minimal investment.

Productivity improvements in subsequent steps of convertible assembly process included the use by assemblers of a new ergonomic assist arm to position the top module for installation to the vehicle. A fixture then aligned the top to the rear quarter panels, while fasteners locked the top into the correct position. Using this device assured an accurate and repeatable fit to each Convertible.

Most of the Convertible's interior trim, including the new seats, was installed on the final assembly line. Workers put the seats in the body using a combination of new and modified articulated arms that protected the vehicle during their insertion. As part of a modified material delivery system the seats were now brought to the assemblers in a ready-to-install position.

Training for the employees at Toluca who would be assembling the convertible began early in the vehicle's development and eventually involved the plant's entire workforce. The first step involved the arrival of a select group of workers from Toluca at the Chrysler Group Pilot Facility at Auburn Hills, Michigan, where they co-developed and refined the Convertible build process. This Auburn Hills/Toluca group assisted in identifying the best aspects of the PT Cruiser sedan's assembly and incorporating them into building pilot models of the convertible.

Using knowledge and experience gained from this activity, the Toluca workers returned to the plant where they trained the rest of the workforce. All assemblers were also tested for knowledge of both the Convertible and manufacturing processes relating to their workstation.

Referring to Toluca's successful launch of the Convertible

with no interruption of production and its steadily improving performance, Roberto Gutierrez, Vice President, Mexico Manufacturing Operation, Chrysler Group, said: "The entire team at the plant contributed to the successful operations we've seen at Toluca Operations. From the ongoing production of the PT Cruiser to the rolling changeover, we achieved positive gains in productivity and quality without missing a day of production." Supporting his remarks was a corporate report that stated the warranty costs of the cars produced at Toluca were among the lowest of all Chrysler Group manufacturing plants in 2003. This followed a 20 per cent reduction in warranty costs between the 2000 and 2002 model years. The PT Cruiser was also still pleasing its owners. As Strategic Vision reported, the PT Cruiser tied for first place with the Volkswagen Golf and Pontiac Grand Am in the Compact Car category of its 2003 Total Quality Index.

Although its styling cues and contours were obviously derived from the sedan, the new Convertible's design, as well as its body components differed in many ways from those of the original version. For example, except for the taillights, nothing on the Convertible from the A pillar back was interchangeable with the sedan. Making certain that the public was aware of the dramatic distinctions between the two vehicles, Larry Lyons, Vice President, Small Vehicle Product Team, explained that "with more than half of its

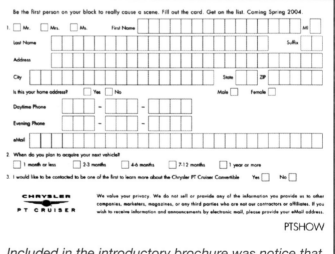

Included in the introductory brochure was notice that a $19,995, "Introductory Base Model" with limited availability, would be at select dealers beginning February 2004. Then came the clincher – an attached, postage-paid postcard that included a spot to check "Yes" to "be contacted as one of the first to learn more about the PT Cruiser Convertible."
(Author's collection)

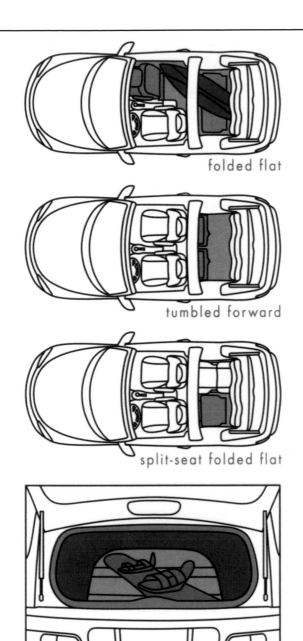

folded flat

tumbled forward

split-seat folded flat

pass-through

When he introduced the 2005 PT Cruiser Convertible at the Detroit Auto Show in January 2004, Larry Lyons, Vice President, Small Vehicle Product Team, explained that: "our engineers wanted to make the PT Cruiser Convertible a convertible that you can actually do things with. Nine different seat configurations and a pass-through trunk opening with enough room to store two golf bags make the car more versatile than its competitors." (Author's collection)

parts unique from the sedan, the new Chrysler PT Cruiser Convertible represents a vehicle specifically engineered with convertible drivers in mind. We engineered more stability into the body structure itself and fine-tuned the handling to deliver the type of ride a convertible deserves."

The extensive use of Computer Aided Engineering (CAE) refined the Convertible's body performance, assuring a high level of structural integrity. The outcome, a stiffer body with limited twist and bend, contributed to the Convertible's quiet ride, minimal body shake and ease of handling. Recalling this effort, Vice President Larry Lyons explained: "The traditional convertible challenge of how to tie the whole vehicle back together once the roof is gone was solved on a computer screen long before the first prototype models were produced. Creating a rigid structure using computer aided engineering helped us eliminate body twist and bend in the early phases of vehicle development."

Engineers took advantage of these attributes to tune the suspension for optimum handling and ride quality without incurring any negative impact upon the car's NVH. At the rear, again utilizing CAE, they stiffened the Watt's linkage and trailing arm mounting structures. By inserting bulkheads inside the longitudinal rail, the stiffness of the shock absorber's attachments was increased, helping to minimize noise transmission. Mounting the rear spring seats on the crossmember suspended on this rail also helped isolate the passenger compartment from noise transmitted through the rear suspension. A tauter front strut was also used. The natural frequency of these components was tuned to separate them from the noise and vibration inputs of tires and suspension components. This, in turn, allowed the suspension bushings to be tuned for the desired handling level without affecting NVH. The spring rates were adjusted to compensate for the convertible body's added mass. Concurrently, the sway bar rates were increased at the front and lowered in the rear to maintain ride balance.

Along with these components, the Convertible's powertrain, including its engine, transmission, driveline and engine accessories were engineered to minimize the levels of noise and vibration that they created. Typical of this effort was the design of the Convertible's air induction system that reduced airflow resistance and diminished induction noise. A large air cleaner housing mounted on the engine compartment's left front corner dampened incoming airflow pulsations. A tuning chamber in the cover enhanced its noise reduction ability. The housing's body mounting prevented it from becoming a potential engine noise amplifier, while rubber mounting kept it from transmitting induction noise to the body structure.

Combining the Convertible's distinctive sport bar with

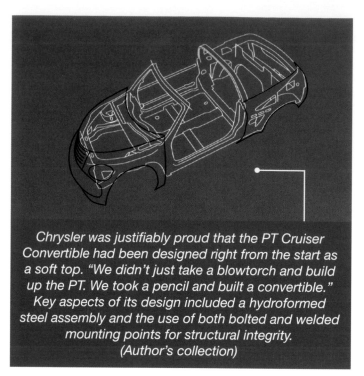

Chrysler was justifiably proud that the PT Cruiser Convertible had been designed right from the start as a soft top. "We didn't just take a blowtorch and build up the PT. We took a pencil and built a convertible." Key aspects of its design included a hydroformed steel assembly and the use of both bolted and welded mounting points for structural integrity.
(Author's collection)

uniquely designed joint that ran from the front hinge pillar through a hydroformed sill tube and into the B pillar. Even the Convertible's powertrain was utilized in this effort to make the characteristics of the Convertible's body as 'unconvertible' as possible. Towards this end, the engine mounts were tuned to use the powertrain as a mass damper to reduce body shake.

Speaking at the Convertible's Auburn Hills introduction in January 2004, Larry Lyons recalled that "our engineers wanted to make the PT Cruiser Convertible a convertible that you can actually do things with." Closely related to doing anything in a moving convertible, particularly when the top was lowered, was the ability to carry on a civilized conversation with other occupants. "One thing we know from our experiences with convertible customers," said Steve Bartoli, Vice President, Strategy, "is that convertibles are 'social vehicles,' which means passengers want to be able to talk to each other when riding in them, much like they would around a kitchen table. So we made sure Chrysler PT Cruiser Convertible passengers could carry on an open-air 'picnic table' conversation while driving, something other convertibles would be hard pressed to offer."

As part of this effort, the Convertible was one of the first Chrysler Group vehicles to be evaluated in the company's full-scale Aero-Acoustic Wind Tunnel Test Facility in Auburn

a stamped cross-vehicle kickup-reinforcement and the rear seat support added to the rigidity of the body's rear section. A new rear seat anchor structure also enhanced overall body rigidity. Contributing to door openings that resisted twisting and bending was a

"At the touch of a button, the top comes off and the sky pours in. You no longer live under a glass ceiling – or any ceiling. The sun warms your face as you take a breath of freedom. Now there's room, both around and above you. Room to roam. Room to live. The new PT Cruiser Convertible. You can finally breath again." Who could resist such tempting words when looking at this 2005 Electric Blue Convertible parked miles from the company of dull 4-door sedans?
(Author's collection)

Hills. The impact of the results upon the Convertible's design was sufficient to allow Chrysler to claim that the Convertible had "world-class wind noise reduction with top up and down." Contributing to this performance was a significant reduction in rear compartment turbulence resulting from the determination of the ideal tuning and placement of the sport bar. Specifically, the bar's design, location and height prevented air from tracking back into the rear seat vacuum, moving it instead over the passenger compartment.

Also identified as a result of the wind tunnel testings was the optimal boot fastening and attachment integrity. An improved mirror design and various body surface refininements minimized turbulence-induced noise.

In addition, several critical sections of the Convertible's design, from the glass to engine compartment, were also reviewed for opportunities to reduce noise levels with the top up or down. In developing the Convertible body, engineers, aware of the contribution weatherstripping had made to reducing interior noise levels of previous convertibles, made certain the PT Cruiser was tightly sealed against wind, road and engine induction sounds. A special 'C-channel' weather stripping completely wrapped the top edge of the side windows at the sealing edge of the convertible top. Compared to that of conventional weather stripping, its design was measurably superior in preventing water leaks as well as minimizing wind noise level. The section of stripping that came into contact with the door windows was treated with a special anti-stick coating making it easy to open and close the doors. Extensive door weather stripping also helped seal the interior from wind and water. This trim came into contact with the upper edges of the body sills to prevent road splash and road noise.

Body-mounted tubular weather strips sealed the sides and lower edges of the doors, while inboard lips overlapped the interior trim for a tidy appearance. Weather striping was also applied to the full perimeter of the engine hood and deck lid. Inside the cabin, extensive applications of acoustic material helped absorb, dampen or block noise from entering the passenger compartment.

Summing up these efforts, a company spokesman asserted that "extensive use of weather stripping, combined with rigorous sealing of body panel seams and gaps on the Chrysler PT Cruiser Convertible resulted in one of the most tightly sealed bodies of any DaimlerChrysler convertible."

Many additional aspects of the Convertible's design contributed both to its structural integrity and to reduced levels of NVH. The stiffness of the rear shock absorber attachments points was increased by inserting heat-expandable foam bulkheads inside the longitudinal rail. This, in turn, minimized the transmission of noise into the

A 2005 PT Cruiser Touring Edition Convertible powered by the 180hp Turbo engine. It is equipped with the Mopar PT Body Kit consisting of Front and Rear Fascia Treatments, and Side Sills that integrate into the front and rear wheel wells. It's also fitted with a Custom Graphics Package, a rear spoiler, and 16in 5-spoke chrome wheels. (Author's collection)

137

PT CRUISER GT CONVERTIBLE IN DARK PLUM

vibration transmission path into the passenger compartment.

Inside the cabin, extensive use of acoustic material helped absorb, dampen or block noise from external sources. Also contributing to NVH control was an array of small but noteworthy body features including seatbelt turning loops situated in a shallow pocket to lessen wind noise around the turning loop and attachment bolt, a stiff front bumper beam and attachments to the longitudinal rails, enhanced stiffening bead patterns on all inner body panels, and pass-through sealing on cowl-side inner wiring.

interior. Mounting the rear spring seats on a crossmember suspended between the longitudinal rails also helped isolate the passenger compartment from noise transmitted through the rear suspension.

In addition, both the desired level of steering column stability and less awareness of vehicle-operation sounds were achieved by combining a robust mounting of the instrument panel structural beam with a lightweight tubular steering shaft.

Along with paying close attention to these traditional methods of utilizing tight sealing of the body against intrusions of wind, road, and engine aspiration sounds, engineers also tuned the entire body structure to minimize transmission of outside noise into the passenger compartment. This latter effort involved using full body Finite Element Analysis (FEA) models to determine dynamic bending and torsional characteristics needed to achieve the team's NVH performance criteria. The natural frequencies of these characteristics were then separated from steering column, powertrain and suspension input frequencies and transmitted to the body structure at forty-seven attachment locations. Tuning each of these locations to separate its natural frequency from that of the input virtually eliminated that area as a potential noise and

This Dark Plum GT Convertible's interior combined Royale Grain leather seats in Light Pearl Beige with Dark Taupe accents. Also seen here is its satin silver spherical shifter knob. The seats were also offered in Dark Slate with Medium Slate accents.
(Author's collection)

Chrysler has no difficultly in associating the Convertible's dash panel with the best aspects of pre-World War Two automotive design. "A modern take on the 1930s heritage," it said, "is played out well in the interior design. The browless gauges are reminiscent of a time when interiors were as cool as exteriors." (Author's collection)

Incorporated into these efforts was DaimlerChrysler's goal of providing the newest PT Cruiser with a top quality convertible top system. "We searched the world and its supply base to assure we included the best available convertible technology in the new Chrysler PT Cruiser Convertible," recalled Larry Rybacki, Director of Small Vehicle Product Team Procurement and Supply. "From the world-class top to the new 'Smart' glass system, this vehicle represents convertible bests across the board."

Among the results of this effort was a six-point top attachment and a high-strength steel floating bow top retention system, both of which Chrysler claimed were US industry "firsts." The former feature allowed the entire mechanism (including hydraulics, headliner, weather striping and latching), to be installed in a single manufacturing operation.

The system's four extruded, high-strength steel roof bows and rails maintained the top's structural integrity when it was raised or lowered, while the rear bow 'floated,' creating a compact and clean top-down appearance.

The top's additional mechanical components included forged main control link and rails, a stamped top header and main pivot bracket, glass-stabilizing wide tension belts, and a one-piece stamped header.

A high-pressure, thermally protected electric pump mounted in the center of the vehicle quickly activated the top. Anti-chaffing hydraulic lines connected the pump to cylinders that raised or lowered the top. Both the pump and the hydraulic lines were secured in the bottom of the convertible top well. A noise-deadening cover was positioned above the pump to minimize noises produced during the top's operation.

The soft top's parts consisted of a three-layer premium cloth top with an insulated pad and full cloth headliner that helped isolate the cabin from road noise and extreme outside temperatures. Chrysler maintained that the top's layered cloth was far superior to vinyl, offering greater strength and durability, along with a soft-touch feel.

The heated and scratch-resistant glass backlight was urethane bonded in place, removing the need to disassemble the entire top if it required servicing. Also incorporated into the top were adjustable tension straps, a single center-mounted top release handle and side-glass weather stripping.

Operating the top was easy. A single O-ring release handle at the center of the windshield/header provided one-handed release of the two latches located at the top's front corners. The power top switch was located in the accessory switch bank in the instrument panel center stack. Latches at each corner of the A pillar secured the top when it was up.

The boot cover was specifically designed for easy installation and stowing. It's soft center section allowed the arms to rest together in a 'tuck in' fashion that reduced installation time and effort. One person could easily install the boot with just a couple of snaps when the top was retracted. To assure low wind noise, engineers performed extensive validation of the boot attachment setup in Chrysler's Aero-Acoustic Wind Tunnel Test Facility in Auburn Hills, Michigan. The boot, which was standard on Touring and GT and not available for the Base model, was color-coordinated to match the Convertible's interior/exterior packaging.

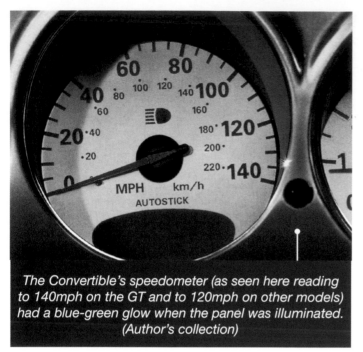

The Convertible's speedometer (as seen here reading to 140mph on the GT and to 120mph on other models) had a blue-green glow when the panel was illuminated. (Author's collection)

The use of 'smart glass' on the Convertible was due to the decision to use frameless glass in its doors. "Developing a glass system that didn't need a window frame was critical in helping retain the 'PT-ness' of the new Convertible," said Larry Lyons. "Smart glass technology and some engineering

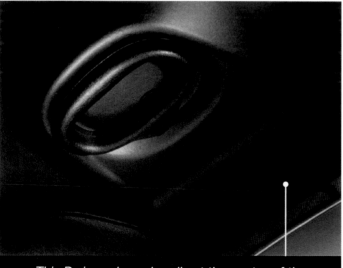

This D-ring release handle at the center of the windshield header provided a one-hand release of the convertible top's dual latches, positioned at its front posts. After the latches were released, a touch of the power switch, located in the center accessory switch bank, lowered the power top. (Author's collection)

ingenuity led to the same distinct Chrysler PT Cruiser profile on the Convertible as the segment-busting sedan."

The smart glass system functioned by lowering the windows slightly whenever the convertible top was lowered. Selection of the first detent on the convertible top switch lowered the front door and rear quarter windows by 1.6in (40mm) and 2.17in (55mm), respectively. All four windows lowered completely when the second detent was selected. When either door was opened, the door's glass lowered 0.39in (10mm), which prevented the glass from 'hanging up' on the top or upper window seals. The door glass remained in this position until the door was closed, when the glass rose to fully close the gap. As an added benefit, the system's thicker window glass increased vehicle rigidity and contributed to noise reduction in the cabin. Chrysler asserted that "this technology is a key contributor to superior wind reduction in the cabin and gives the Chrysler PT Cruiser Convertible one of the easiest door opening and closing efforts in the industry." Also making door closing more convenient was the geometry of the hinges that caused the doors to rise slightly when opened, thus taking advantage of gravitational force. Smooth operating linear door check arms held the doors open when the car was parked in an incline. A new arm on the door check strap increased the door's open angle (as compared to the sedan) for easier entry and exit.

Several features included in the Convertible's door structure were intended to assure its long term durability. Longitudinal beams, positioned inside the doors, contributed to maintaining the door opening's integrity at a level that Chrysler said gave the Convertible a lag resistance among the best of the soft tops in its class. In addition, the door inner panels were thicker at the hinge face and thinner elsewhere, which increased their strength and stiffness while reducing weight. The door hinge's design helped minimize the potential for sag. Its larger offsets also assured that the deep-draw front doors had sufficient space to clear the front fenders.

Dominating all aspects of the Convertible's design was the need to optimize occupant safety. This was achieved by combining numerous enhancements into its body structure for maximum occupant protection in the case of a collision, along with standard safety and security features designed to make the Convertible safe for occupants while on the road and secure when parked. "Every driver demands safety and security for themselves, their passengers and their cargo, and convertible owners are certainly no exception," said Larry Lyons. "The new Chrysler PT Cruiser Convertible includes the numerous safety features of the sedan version, as well as special high-strength steel applications for added protection without added weight."

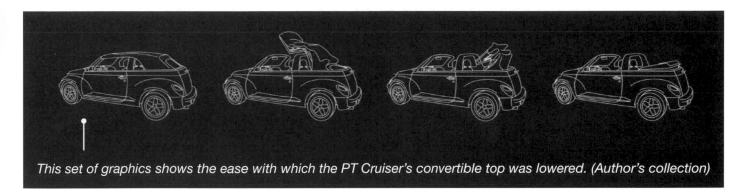

This set of graphics shows the ease with which the PT Cruiser's convertible top was lowered. (Author's collection)

The Convertible weighed 150 pounds more than the sedan, comparing favorably with the weight of the VW Beetle convertible which was 350 pounds more than the hardtop version. Credited with keeping the Convertible's weight under control while resulting in a safer and stiffer vehicle was the selective use both of the high strength steel mentioned by Lyons and body panels of differing thickness.

Rear impact protection was provided by a continuous beltline structure around the rear of the vehicle that tied into the B pillar and a hydroformed sill reinforcement. Along with the revised hinge pillar, the sill reinforcement helped deflect offset impact forces away from occupants. Strengthening the rear faces of the front wheel wells also provided a load path through the front tires into the sills.

Chrysler used this illustration to demonstrate the contribution the sport bar played in directing air flow over the open compartment of the PT Cruiser. "Instead of wind and noise going over the windshield and down into the cab," it explained, "they now have to reckon with the sport bar, thus forcing them over the sport bar – well above and away from the cabin." (Author's collection)

Emphasizing this design approach, Steve Speth, Director, Vehicle Compliance and Safety Affairs, explained: "To protect occupants, the Chrysler PT Convertible was designed and tested with strict safety and impact goals in mind from the onset of its development. From the front, to the rear, to the side, structural enforcements were included for added protection in the unfortunate case of an impact."

A new wraparound stamped structure at the beltline tied directly into the kickup structure between the front and rear floorpan also improved the management of offset impact forces. While the rear seat structure was designed to allow cargo pass-through into the trunk, it also incorporated integrated seatbelt anchors and contributed to body torsional rigidity. The longitudinal beams in each front

Anyone familiar with automotive navigation systems was likely to agree with Chrysler's assertion that "the convenience and security offered by the available navigation/CD player system is immeasurable ..." (Author's collection)

The Sport Bar's overhead directional spotlights were an industry first in a convertible. The Sport Bar also helped reduce turbulence. Larry Lyons, Vice President, Small Vehicle Product Team, explained that: "the combination of the sport bar design and position, together with enhancements to the body structure, resulted in an exceptionally quiet ride. While on-the-road experience is what ultimately matters, we performed extensive wind tunnel testing to assure our customers a quiet ride, top up or down." (Author's collection)

door distributed collision energy to the rear of the vehicle. A tunnel reinforcement crossmember and floor reinforcements minimized floorpan wrinkling in the footwell areas.

The form of the Convertible's quarter trim panels played a major role in optimizing its interior volume. But more importantly, they also protected passengers in the event of a side impact through the inclusion of energy-absorbing foam inserts on the backside of the panels. A similar foam insert was also included on the backside of the door trim panels for the same purpose. The use of additional foam in these areas also prevented contact with the convertible top mechanism in side impact collisions.

Safety engineers also incorporated two unique transverse beams into the Convertible's body structure. Both tied into the floorpan (one at the center tunnel, the other at the kickup crossmember). Positioned directly in line with side-impact forces, they helped the front door side-impact beams and the basic body structure to maintain overall vehicle integrity during a side-impact collision.

In addition to these components designed into its body structure, the Convertible also had a number of standard and optional safety features. 'Unibelt' three-point belts with low-tension retractors provided primary passenger restraint in all seating positions. The optimum position of the front seatbelt turning loops was maintained by attaching them to the sport bar. Next generation driver and passenger airbags were standard on the Convertible. Outboard, front seat mounted supplemental side airbags were standard on GT models and optional for the Touring Edition. In the event of an accident resulting in an airbag deployment, the Convertible's dome light illuminated and the door locks unlocked, making it easier for emergency personnel to assist the occupants.

Although it didn't play the starring role, that was given to the new Chrysler 300C, the PT Cruiser Convertible was a visible participant in the Chrysler Group's first of three 'Premiere/Nights/Days Celebrations' that began on April 22, 2004. The purpose of this project was to financially support educational outreach programs, including school field trips. Playing off the 300C name, Chrysler contributed a '300C-Note,' or $30,000, to the Orlando Museum of Science and Technology. While this check was being received by the Museum at Central Florida Chrysler/Jeep/Dodge in Orlando, over 2100 other Chrysler dealerships were hosting over four million invited guests to what was described as "the biggest product offensive in Chrysler Group History, [a] sneak preview" of new Chrysler vehicles, some on display before they were widely available.

"In the cities and towns that are home to Chrysler Group

offices and dealerships, we strive to be good neighbors," said Eric Ridenour, Chrysler Group's Executive Vice President for Product Development as he presented the check to Dr Brian Tonner, the President of the Science Center. "Through these donations," he explained, "we hope we can inspire young people to embrace science and math, and possibly pursue careers in the automotive industry."

Dr Tonner was equally enthusiastic about the possible outcomes of this effort. "The Chrysler Group," he said, "is helping us to reach tens of thousands of young people with the message that there is great opportunity in high technology fields like the automotive industry. Their support will have a great impact on the future of our area youth."

When the PT Cruiser soft top debuted, the convertible segment of the new-vehicle market was relatively small at about 300,000 units annually. Sales in the luxury speciality segment had increased nearly 40 per cent in the past four years. Chrysler sold almost 44,000 Sebring Convertibles in 2002 and had a 14.5 per cent share of the convertible market, the highest for any nameplate.

Chrysler was confident that the new PT Cruiser would attract buyers from not only all segments of the convertible market, but because of its heritage, would also appeal to those who had not previously considered owning a convertible. Chrysler depicted PT Convertible buyers as: "Unique as the vehicle itself. They defy demographics, fitting instead into a psychographic of fun-loving, confident, style-conscious consumers that goes beyond age, sex or income."

Expanding on this perspective, Jeff Bell said that "because of its unique blend of customized styling and versatile packaging, we expect the Chrysler PT Cruiser Convertible can and will crisscross the customary divisions within the convertible segment. The PT Cruiser Convertible features like best-in-class rear leg room, a quiet ride and more pass-through space will appeal to convertible customers no matter where they fall in the segment.

"There's only one way to top the original Chrysler PT Cruiser sedan, and that's by losing the top," Bell continued. "We consider the new PT Cruiser Convertible the ultimate factory-backed customization of the ultimate segment-buster and see it as an opportunity to expand on the original PT Cruiser frenzy."

In the midst of the summer convertible driving season, Chrysler conducted an on-line survey that included an invitation for visitors to vote for the most popular song for top-down cruising. Having earlier introduced both the 2005 PT Cruiser and Crossfire convertibles, Chrysler was ideally suited to promote 'Top Down Days,' which were depicted as the nation's official celebration of the 2004 convertible driving season. Selected as the best song for cruising was

Surfin' USA by the Beach Boys. The Beatles' hit Here Comes the Sun and Take It Easy by the Eagles were chosen as the second and third top songs respectively.

The best place to drive a convertible, with 46 per cent of the votes, was on a winding road. Close behind at 38 per cent was the beach. Red was selected as the most popular convertible color by 44 per cent of the voters. Star gazing topped the list of best things to do in a convertible with the top down, followed closely by singing along with the radio. Overwhelmingly, 67 per cent of respondents preferred to let their hair blow free while driving in a convertible.

Almost two million visitors to www.topdowndays.com played to win the Top Down Sweepstakes by clicking on floating balloons that revealed either a fun convertible fact or an automatic entry into the sweepstakes. The winner of the sweepstake's top prize, a 2005 PT Cruiser Convertible, was Frances Blalock of Pink Hill, North Carolina. "I've always wanted a convertible," she said, "and look forward to enjoying the top down weather while cruising around with my friends."

The Convertible was available in three models: Standard, Touring and GT. The Standard version, was powered by the familiar 150hp engine linked to a 5-speed manual transaxle. Its $19,995 MSRP (the destination charge was an additional $590), included a power top, sport bar with integrated dome lights, solar-tinted 'smart glass,' rear glass window with defroster, cloth seats with driver manual lumbar adjuster, rear 50/50 split fold and tumble seats, pass-through cargo area, power exterior mirrors, touring-tuned suspension, and body-color fascias and bodyside moldings.

The next step up the Convertible hierarchy, the Touring model, also had the 150hp/manual transaxle combination as its standard powertrain, but was offered with the 180hp turbo engine and automatic transaxle as an option. Its MSRP

This badge, installed on the GT's tailgate, indicated it was powered by the 220hp turbocharged High Output engine, which Chrysler described as "downright nuclear." (Author's collection)

PT CRUISER GT CONVERTIBLE IN INFERNO RED

These travelers seem to be thoroughly enjoying their journey in an Inferno Red 2005 PT Cruiser Convertible. If this trip is of any duration, it's likely that those in the back will appreciate Chrysler's success in providing the convertible with rear seats that carried two adults quite comfortably. Also seen is the Convertible's boot. Its semi-rigid self-supporting arms gave the Convertible a distinctive appearance when in place. When removed, the boot could be stored in the trunk. (Author's collection)

of $22,900 (plus the $590 destination charge), added to or upgraded all the Standard model's features with these items: convertible top boot, 16in painted cast aluminum wheels, speed control, security alarm, fog lights, floor mats, and an AM/FM stereo radio with CD player.

The GT model's standard equipment included, in addition to that of the Touring version, both the 220hp turbocharged engine and 5-speed Getrag G288 manual transmission. The shifter had an audible acknowledgement feature that sounded after the lever was moved to the reverse gate. Other key standard features added to or replacing certain items found on the Tourer included a performance-tuned suspension

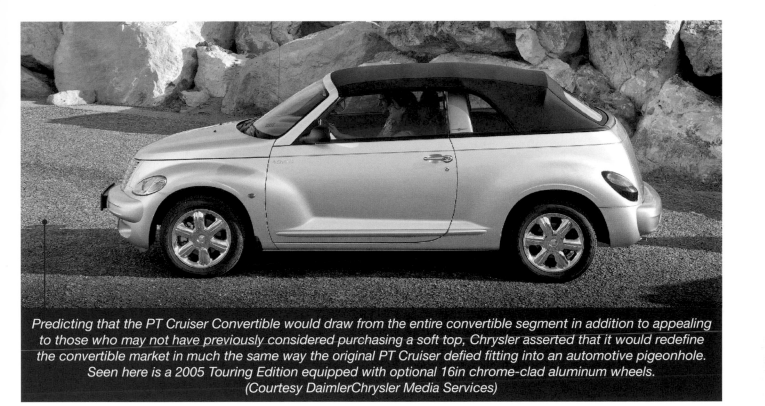

Predicting that the PT Cruiser Convertible would draw from the entire convertible segment in addition to appealing to those who may not have previously considered purchasing a soft top, Chrysler asserted that it would redefine the convertible market in much the same way the original PT Cruiser defied fitting into an automotive pigeonhole. Seen here is a 2005 Touring Edition equipped with optional 16in chrome-clad aluminum wheels. (Courtesy DaimlerChrysler Media Services)

with ABS 4-wheel disc brakes, low-speed traction control, chrome-accented grille and fascia, 17in 'Empire' painted cast aluminum wheels, all-season performance tires, a 2.75in chrome-plated stainless steel exhaust tip, leather-wrapped steering wheel, leather seats, driver seat power height adjuster, unique silver painted shift knob, 'GT' embroidered floor mats, supplemental side airbags, AM/FM stereo radio with CD and cassette player, and driver and front passenger side airbags. The GT's MSRP was $27,565, plus the $590 destination charge. All models had a remote power deck lift release. The switch was mounted in the lockable glove box.

Standard on the Touring Edition and GT models was a Vehicle Theft Security System (VTSS), which was also identified as the Security Alarm System. VTSS secured the deck lid by disconnecting its power source. This was accomplished by activating VTSS using the key fob, the exterior door key cylinder or the interior door lock switch. Power was restored to the deck lid release by disabling the VTSS. This feature also emitted both audible and visible signals if unauthorized entry into the vehicle was attempted.

Taking aim at the Volkswagen New Beetle and Mustang convertibles, Chrysler pointed out that the PT Convertible's 84.3cu-ft interior volume was greater than that of the VW (79.6cu-ft) and the Mustang (79.0cu-ft). It also noted that among these three convertibles, the PT Cruiser was the only one to have a true pass-through luggage volume of 13.3cu-ft, and nine different seat configurations. "Like the sedan," explained Larry Lyons, "the new Chrysler PT Cruiser Convertible has more versatility built into it than a Swiss Army Knife. Maintaining multiple seat configurations and unparalleled cargo storage in a convertible was a challenge our engineering team met with all the success of the four-door version."

To accommodate passengers and cargo as needed, folding and tumbling either or both of the Convertible's rear 50/50 split seats resulted in numerous interior configurations. Each section could be folded flat independently to form a load-carrying surface. If tumbled forward they provided cargo pass-through from the trunk. When in their upright position, each seat back latched to the center of the body structure. Knobs located in the trunk released each seat back for folding. To keep items in the rear cargo secure when the top is down, the trunk release button is located in the lockable glove box.

Aware that customers of the Convertible would be anticipating rear seating accommodations in line with those of the original PT Cruiser, engineers designed seats with the same height as the sedan's. The seat's 40.9 inches of leg room was significantly greater than that of the convertible models of the VW Beetle (30.9in), and the Ford Mustang

All 2005 PT Cruiser Convertibles had fog lamps as standard equipment. (Courtesy DaimlerChrysler Media)

(29.9in). Elaborating on this aspect of the Convertible's design, Larry Lyons said: "Our customers are accustomed to the exceptional roominess of the PT Cruiser, so it was imperative that we give them all the space and comfort they deserve in the new PT Cruiser Convertible, too."

"Our engineers used the transverse structural beam as the rear mounting surface for the front seats, which left the floor clear from sill to tunnel and created roomy footwells for best-in-class rear leg room."

Chrysler anticipated that a key element of the Convertible's appeal would be the results of its creators' effort to make the appearance of its exterior and interior as seamless as possible. "The new Chrysler PT Cruiser Convertible opens up the sedan's styling to reveal an exterior and interior design that's coordinated when the top is down," said Dave McKinnon. "This creates a connection between two usually separate environments, which is essential in developing a distinctive convertible design ..." Another example of this approach was the high-gloss finish on the instrument gauge bezel and the airbag door. In most color schemes their color was keyed to the Convertible's exterior, which, said Chrysler, "helps bring the outside color to the inside of the vehicle when the top is down."

When the top was lowered, it was difficult for viewers to not focus on the Convertible's hydroformed steel color-keyed sport bar that was positioned between the front and rear seats. Its outer surface, color-keyed to the exterior, had a high gloss finish. Its inner surface was lined with a textured three-piece polypropylene trim matching the interior trim color. The bar was equipped with two flush-mounted

The Touring Edition 2005 PT Cruiser had this standard 16in painted cast-aluminum wheel. (Author's collection)

This 17in painted cast-aluminum wheel was standard for the GT Convertible. (Author's collection)

This 17in chrome-clad aluminum wheel was optional for the GT Convertible. (Author's collection)

Fresno cloth seats were standard for the 2005 Touring Edition Convertible. They are seen here in Dark Slate Gray. (Author's collection)

overhead courtesy lamps. Both the design and location of the bar were cited as contributing to dramatically limiting wind buffeting which, in turn, enhanced vehicle quietness and passenger comfort. The sports bar also added to the car's transverse body stability and served as a position for the seatbelt turning loops.

The Convertible also had plenty of nooks and crannies ideal for stowing a wide variety of items, including a cubby bin at the base of the center stack, a locking bin-type glove compartment with storage clips specifically designed for a tire gauge or pen/pencil, under-seat storage drawer with slots for cassette tapes and CDs, door storage pockets, four cup holders, coin holder, pen tray, miscellaneous storage bin, cubby bin at rear of center console, and a driver seat back storage pocket.

The Convertible's initial selection of exterior colors consisted of Black, Bright Silver Metallic, Cool Vanilla, Dark Plum, Electric Blue, Light Almond, Pearl Metallic, Midnight Blue, Graphite Metallic and, except for standard models,

Inferno Red. Later, when the entire line of 2005 PT Cruisers was announced on September 1, 2004, Inferno Red was listed as available for all three Convertible models.

Development of the Convertible's interior was directed by Senior Design Manager Jeffrey Godshall who explained: "Inspired by two-tone color combinations of earlier automotive eras, we've achieved a luxurious interior design ... Together with the circular patterns and features first introduced on the sedan, the complementary color combinations continue the modern approach to heritage design on the all-new convertible version."

The low-back seats of the Standard and Touring model were covered in a Dark Slate Gray cloth with a Fresno print. Two color schemes were offered for the GT model's Royale Grain leather seats: Dark Slate with Medium Slate accents on the seats and doors, or Light Pearl Beige/Dark Taupe with seat and door accents in Dark Taupe. 'Halo-design' door trim panels continued this two-tone color scheme. The doors had long, vinyl-covered armrests with open-grip areas that had a concave depression behind them for comfortable hand clearance. A red reflector at the rear of the door trim panel provided a warning to approaching night time traffic when the door was open.

The MSRP of the Convertible models was as follows:

Model	MSRP *
Standard	$20,045
Touring	$23,815
GT	$28,570

* Included destination charge of $640

Feature	Standard	Touring	GT
Exterior:			
Unique doors with 'smart glass'	S	S	S
Unique rear quarter panels with passenger-side fuel filler door	S	S	S
Locking rear 'Top Cut' deck lid	S	S	S
Power folding soft-top with textile cover, insulated headliner and serviceable glass backlite	S	S	S
Sport bar with Chrysler wing badge located above beltline	S	S	S
Body-color monotone painted front fascia with integral lower grille with horizontal chrome accents	NA	NA	S
Body-color monotone painted front fascia	S	S	NA
Body-color monotone painted rear fascia	S	S	S
Front fog lamps	NA	S	S
Quad halogen headlamps	S	S	S
LED CHMSL	S	S	S
Body-color upper grille with horizontal chrome accents	NA	NA	S
Body-color upper grille	S	S	NA
Chrome door handles	S	S	S
Body-color bodyside moldings	S	S	S
Black dual power remote control fixed mirrors	S	S	S
Variable intermittent wipers	S	S	S
Solar tinted glass	S	S	S
Power front door windows with driver and passenger auto down	S	S	S
Power roll down rear quarter glass (automatic with top operation)	S	S	S
Fixed mast fluted antenna	S	S	S
Chrysler wing badge on hood	S	S	S
'PT Chrysler' bright badge on front doors	S	S	S
'Touring Edition' bright badge on deck lid (left side)	NA	S	NA
'GT' bright badge on deck lid (left side)	NA	NA	S
'2.4L Turbo' bright badge on deck lid (right side)	NA	O	NA
'2.4L Turbo High-output' badge on deck lid (right side)	NA	NA	S
Bright Chrysler wing badge integral with deck lid fixed pull cup	S	S	S
Convertible boot cover [1]	NA	S	S
Interior:			
Enhanced New Generation front airbags [2]	S	S	S
Cloth performance seats	S	S	NA
Leather/vinyl performance seats	NA	NA	S
Rear seat fixed bolster with integrated headforms	S	S	S
Under passenger seat storage drawer	S	S	S
Driver seat manual lumbar adjuster	S	S	S
Heated driver and passenger seats	NA	NA	O
Front and rear floor mats with 'GT' embroidery	NA	NA	S
Carpeted passenger compartment	S	S	S
Rear window defroster	S	S	S
Power door locks	S	S	S
Sentry key theft deterrent system	S	S	S
Security alarm system	NA	S	S
Remote keyless entry system	S	S	S
AM/FM radio with cassette player	S	NA	NA
AM/FM radio with CD player	NA	S	NA
AM/FM radio with cassette and CD player	NA	O	S
AM/FM radio with integral six-disc CD changer	NA	O	O
AM/FM radio with CD player, navigational system	NA	O	O
Six speaker premium sound system	S	S	S
Driver seat power height adjuster	NA	O	S
Driver and front passenger supplemental airbags	NA	O	S
Child seat anchor system	S	S	S

Feature	Standard	Touring	GT
Speed control	NA	S	S
Light Group	S	S	S
Prismatic rearview mirror with compass/temperature/map/reading lights	S	S	S
Remote power deck lid release switch	S	S	S
Front door trim panels with storage pockets, bolsters, reflectors and door lock knobs	S	S	S
Full length low center console with cup and coin holders, storage trays and power outlet	S	S	S
Tachometer	S	S	S
Locking glove box	S	S	S
Instrument cluster with 120mph speedometer, 'white faced' gauges and low fuel light	S	S	NA
Instrument cluster with 140mph speedometer, 'silver faced' gauges low fuel light and '2.4L Turbo' in script	NA	NA	S
Rear quarter trim panels with integral arm rests	S	S	S
Power top switch	S	S	S
Rear seat ventilation ducts	S	S	S
White round 'ball' shifter knob	S	S	NA
Silver painted shifter knob	NA	NA	S
Vinyl steering wheel	S	S	NA
Leather wrapped steering wheel	NA	NA	S
Tilt steering column	S	S	S
Air conditioning	S	S	S
Console flood light	S	S	S
Cargo light	S	S	S
Theater dimming lights in sport bar	S	S	S
Sun visors with driver and passenger covered illuminated vanity mirrors	S	S	S
Front and rear floor mats	NA	S	NA
Tires:			
Goodyear Eagle LS P195/65R15 All-Season	S	NA	NA
Goodyear Eagle LS P205/55R16 All-Season	NA	S	NA
Goodyear Eagle RS-A P205/50HR17 Extra Load All-Season			

Feature	Standard	Touring	GT
Performance	NA	NA	S
Powertrain:			
2.4-liter engine/5-speed manual transmision	S	S	NA
2.4-liter engine/4-speed automatic transmission	NA	O	NA
2.4-liter turbo engine/4-speed automatic transmission	NA	O	NA
2.4-liter High-Output turbo engine/5-speed Getrag manual transmission	NA	NA	S
2.4-liter High-Output turbo engine/4-speed manual transmission with AutoStick	NA	NA	O
'2.4L Turbo' embossed on engine intake manifold	NA	O	S
2.75in diameter chrome-plated stainless steel exhaust tip	NA	O	S
2.25in diameter stainless steel exhaust tip	S	S	NA
Power assisted disc/drum brakes	S	S	NA
Power assisted ABS disc/drum brakes	NA	O	NA
Turbo ABS 4-wheel disc brakes and low-speed traction control	NA	O	S
Power assisted steering	S	S	S
Touring Suspension	S	S	NA
Sport Suspension	NA	NA	S
Front and rear stabilizer bars	S	S	S
15 x 6in steel wheels with bolt-on covers (six-spoke)	S	NA	NA
16 x 6in painted cast aluminum wheels (seven-spoke)	NA	S	NA
16 x 6in chrome-clad aluminum wheels (six-spoke)	NA	O	NA
17 x 7in 'Empire' painted cast aluminum wheels (five-spoke)	NA	NA	S
17 x 7in 'Empire' chrome-plated cast-aluminum wheels (five-spoke)	NA	NA	O
Steel compact spare wheel	S	S	S

[1] Both early specifications released on January 28, 2004, as well as the dealer reference material for

the 2005 Convertible indicated that the boot wasn't available for the base model. However, a Convertible sales brochure, (Form No 74-383-2502), dated 01/04, cited it as included in the standard equipment of all three models.
[2] If the airbags deployed in an accident, the Convertible's dome light illuminated and the doors unlocked.

Outside North America, the Convertible was sold as the Cabrio. When the Cabrio (available in left-hand drive only), made its European debut in early March 2004 at the 74th Salon International de l'Automobile in Geneva, the Chrysler Group announced that it would be available in more than 30 markets worldwide. In that context, Thomas Hausch, Executive Director of International Sales and Marketing for the Chrysler Group, noted: "This exciting newcomer embodies the reborn 'spirit of Chrysler' and takes our brand into another segment so far unexplored by Chrysler around the world. It is going to be an immensely satisfying car to own, throughout all seasons – a car with huge appeal to the individuals who traditionally buy Chrysler products and also to the host of customers considering the purchase of a C-segment convertible for the very first time."

Shown in Dark Slate Gray is the GT's leather performance seat. (Author's collection)

The PT Cruiser Convertible was identified as the Cabrio model for markets outside North America. This example has an Inferno Red exterior. (Courtesy DaimlerChrysler Media Services)

Limited (2.4-liter*):
Maximum power:	143hp DIN (105kW) @ 5200rpm	
Maximum torque:	158lb-ft (214Nm) @ 4000rpm	
0-100km/h (62mph):	10.3 seconds (manual),	
	12.2 seconds (automatic)	

Fuel consumption (liters/100km)	Manual	Auto
Combined cycle	9.9	10.8
Ex-urban cycle	7.7	8.7
Urban cycle	13.6	14.5
Combine CO_2	234g/km	258g/km

* This engine replaced the 134hp/139lb-ft 2.0-liter 4-cylinder engine as the European-market PT Cruiser's standard engine for the 2005 model year.

GT (2.4-liter turbo-charged)
Maximum power:	223hp DIN (164kW) @ 5100rpm
Maximum torque:	332Nm @ 3950rpm
Top speed;	200km/h (125mph)
0-100km/h (62mph):	7.6 seconds

Fuel consumption (liters/100km)	
Combined cycle	9.9
Ex-urban cycle	8.2
Urban cycle	13.2
Combine CO_2	235g/km

For prospective owners in markets beyond North America, Chrysler offered this summary of the technical specifications and performance.

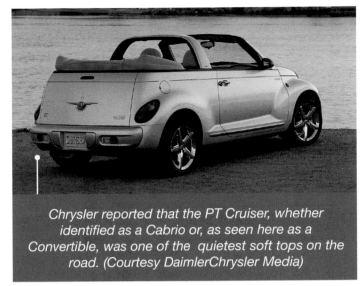

Chrysler reported that the PT Cruiser, whether identified as a Cabrio or, as seen here as a Convertible, was one of the quietest soft tops on the road. (Courtesy DaimlerChrysler Media)

Two versions of the Cabrio were initially available, the Limited and the GT. The Limited was powered by the normally-aspirated 2.4-liter engine with either a manual or automatic gearbox. The GT had the High-output turbocharged engine driving through the Getrag 5-speed manual transmission.

On October 30, 2004 Chrysler UK reported that it planned to import up to 100 left-hand drive 2.4-liter Cabrios into the UK during the coming year. When these models began arriving in the UK in March 2005, they were priced at £17,495 with the 5-speed manual transmission and £18,295 for the automatic gearbox version. Confident that the market for the Cabrio would far exceed its limited availability, and aware that a right-hand drive version was forthcoming, Simon Elliott said: "The new Chrysler Cabrio retains many of the unique styling elements of the original PT Cruiser, while

the designers have put an immense amount of thought into making this one of the quietest soft-tops around. The Cabrio develops the outspoken retro design of the original PT Cruiser even further, to create a very practical yet distinctive vehicle."

As in previous years, Chrysler selected Detroit's annual Woodward Dream Cruise as the site, on August 17, 2004, to unveil the latest PT Dream Cruiser model. Few automotive enthusiasts were surprised that the Series 4 model was a Convertible. Its Lava Red exterior and matching Maroon cloth top were joined by chrome grille accents and 17in Satin Silver painted 15-spoke wheels with smooth silver center caps. The decklid-mounted Dream Cruiser Series 4 badge had Deep Lava accents. Light Pearl Beige leather performance seats had perforated inserts with 'half-moon' maroon accents. When the top was lowered, a Light Beige convertible boot coordinated with these seats. Included in the front seat head restraint was an embossed Dream Cruiser logo in a contrasted Light Pearl Beige thread. The same color was used for the Dream Cruiser logo embroidered into the standard Dark Taupe floor mats. The instrument panel had Deep Lava Red accents with a prismatic foil PT Cruiser graphic on the passenger side of the dashboard.

It's unlikely that few PT Cruiser enthusiasts, after giving this model the once over, disputed Jeff Bell's assertion that it "sizzles." Referring to its interior/exterior color combination, he added that "this PT Cruiser is hotter than a volcano both inside and out."

For the North American market, each example had a reserved, sequenced Vehicle Identification Number (VIN), as well as a special owner's manual holder in Light Pearl Beige embossed with the Dream Cruiser Series 4 shield logo.

The US MSRP for the Dream Cruiser was $30,260 when fitted with the 5-speed Getrag manual transaxle and $30,700 for models with the 4-speed automatic transaxle with AutoStick. Both prices included $590 for destination. Production of the Dream Cruiser was capped at 1700 units.

Supporting Chrysler's description of the Dream Cruiser 4 as the 'Ultimate PT Convertible' was an array of standard equipment that began with all the standard features of the 2005 GT convertible. Since that included the 220hp high-output turbo engine, it had, said Larry Lyons, "plenty of power burbling under the hood." Standard for the Dream Cruiser were heated front seats and an AM/FM radio with in-dash six-disc CD changer. Models with the automatic transaxle had a chrome shifter bezel.

Specifically designed for the Dream Cruiser was a premium Infinity audio system unit with 368 watts peak system power and dual voice-coil rear 6 x 9in speakers. Its installation in the Dream Cruiser was the first use in a PT Cruiser of an eight-channel digitally amplified system that was acoustically tuned to the vehicle interior, maximizing audio output and clarity while minimizing distortion. This audio system had speed dependent bass boost that automatically elevated the bass as the vehicle's speed increased. This system also was made available as an option for the Touring and GT Convertible models.

On November 4, 2004, as part of the Legends Gala charity auction held in New York City to support the Ovarian Cancer Research Fund, a Dream Cruiser Series 4 received a top bid of $37,000. Overall, the Gala, which was a glamorous event supported by celebrities from fashion, modeling and music, raised a record amount of nearly $4.4 million. Acknowledging the Cruiser's contribution by the Chrysler Group, the Fund's Executive Director, Jamie Boris, said: "The Legends Gala is so important in the fight against ovarian cancer. This year it was extra special, we not only raised a record amount of funding for our cause, but also had strong support from companies like the Chrysler Group." In response, Chrysler/Jeep Vice President Jeff Bell noted: "We are very happy to have had the opportunity to donate the inspiring Limited Edition 2005 Chrysler PT Cruiser Dream Cruiser Series 4 to benefit such an inspirational cause."

As it had done with previous Dream Cruisers models, DaimlerChrysler offered the latest version as the Street Cruiser Series 4 for markets outside North America. The PT Cruiser's competitiveness in those regions was further strengthened with the introduction of a lower-priced Cabrio, the Touring model, on March 1, 2005. Its trim and appointments were similar to those of the Touring Sedan. Highlights included cloth seats, a body-color painted grille, 16in painted aluminum wheels and a stainless steel exhaust tip. The only engine offered for the Cabrio Touring, which was marketed only for a limited time in the spring, was the 143hp 2.4L in combination with the 5-speed manual or 4-speed automatic transmission.

Debuting in November 2004 at the SEMA show in Las Vegas, was the Chrysler PT Speedster, an example of what happens when the Chrysler Group's SkunkWerks used a PT Cruiser Convertible to transform its vision of performance and style into sheet metal reality.

Ralph Gilles, Director, Interior/Exterior Product Design

Regardless of the position of its top, the PT Dream Cruiser Series 4, with its 220hp engine and Deep Lava Red paint, heated up Woodward Avenue in Royal Oak during the 10th Annual Woodward Dream Cruise. (Courtesy DaimlerChrysler Media)

and Specialty Vehicles explained that "the Skunkwerks team combines the best of engineering discipline with the excitement and pizzazz of the creative process." In that context, Chrysler described the Speedster as "developed by and for true hot rod enthusiasts." With the exception of items such as its custom scooped hood by Quality Metalcrafters, most of the Speedster's performance components were available to PT Cruiser owners from Mopar. The use of a Mopar Performance Parts Stage I Turbo Upgrade Kit and a Borla dual exhaust system raised the output of the Speedster's 2.4-liter turbocharged engine to 235hp and 260lb-ft of torque. Four-wheel slotted disc brakes with twin-piston calipers were supplied by Stainless Steel Brakes.

A Mopar Performance Stage 2 coilover suspension kit gave the Speedster a low profile, which was accentuated by a Mopar deck lid spoiler. Additional components supplied by Mopar included a sway bar kit, turbo boost gauge, blow-out valve, and a Hurst short-throw shifter. Budnik Wheels provided custom 18in wheels which carried Bridgestone Fusion XRiP235/40R18 tires. Custom badging was by Craft Originators. The Speedster's interior appointments included Falcon Enterprises custom floor mats and Katzkin leather seats. Equally eye-catching was its custom two-tone Brilliant Black over Viper Red exterior paint scheme.

Not withstanding the sensational look and performance of the PT Speedster, and the success of the PT Cruiser Convertible, the original 5-door PT Cruiser had been

on the market essentially unchanged in appearance, since early 2000, a long time for any automobile, even for one as popular as the Cruiser.

With its first major redesign scheduled for the 2006 model year, DaimlerChrysler decided that it was time to play to the PT's strength – its outstanding value for the money – and offer a revised line-up of PT Cruiser models beginning at just $13,995.

The Chrysler PT Speedster, finished in a Black and Viper Red two-tone paint scheme, was one of six vehicles from Chrysler's SkunkWerks on display at the 2004 SEMA show. Parts supplied by Mopar included a Stage 1 turbocharger which raised horsepower to 235, a Stage 2 coilover suspension kit, and an anti-sway bar. A set of 18in Budnik wheels was also installed. (Courtesy (DaimlerChrysler Media)

Admittedly, the changes in the 2005 PT Cruiser sedans were of the variety easily eluding casual onlookers, but delighting dedicated dyed-in-the wool devotees of the annual model introduction. But that didn't deter Jeff Bell from declaring that "the PT Cruiser is the best small car alternative in the United States. With more size, more flexibility and more power than other small cars, the vehicle represents one of the best values in America."

Warranting Bell's ebullience was a realignment of the PT lineup that offered an entry model for under fourteen thousand dollars. Although this PT Cruiser's standard equipment included an AM/FM radio with cassette, a 65/35 folding rear seat, 15in wheels and wheel covers, there were, as compared to the comparable 2004 model, several items deleted from its content. These consisted of bodyside moldings, airconditioning (available as an option), rear shelf panel, fold-flat front passenger seat and under-seat storage bin.

Coinciding with this move aligning the PT Cruiser in the heart of the market's compact car segment, was a strengthening of its position in the upper end of this hotly

Chrysler referred to the 2005 PT Cruiser GT as the "maximum-strength power" model. This example is finished in Bright Silver Metallic. Both the rear spoiler and moonroof were standard on the GT. (Author's collection)

contested field. This was accomplished by making many changes in the Touring Edition's standard and optional equipment as well as adding a second Limited Edition 'G' CPOS Package and enhancing the equipment content of the existing 'F' CPOS Touting Edition Package.

Highlights of changes made in the content of the Touring Edition are indicated by this comparison of the 2004 and 2005 models:

Feature	2004	2005
Tires	P205/55R16 89T BSW AST	
	P195/65R15 89T BSW AST	
Suspension	Touring	Normal duty
Speed control	Standard	Optional
Sunscreen glass	Standard	Optional
Fog lamps	Standard	Not available
Security alarm	Standard	Not available
Light Group	Standard	Optional
Moonroof	Optional	Not available
Moonroof Group	Not available	Optional

A new exterior color, Linen Gold Pearl Coat, joined the following for all 2005 models: Electric Blue Pearl Coat, Inferno Red Crystal Pearl Coat, Midnight Blue Pearl Coat, Dark Plum Pearl Coat, Bright Silver Metallic Clear Coat, Black Clear Coat and Cool Vanilla Clear Coat. Bright Seamist Green, Light Almond and Graphite were no longer offered. With the exception of Inferno Red, which was not offered for the Base Convertible, all models were available in any of these colors. In addition, two-tone paint combinations of Black over Bright Silver, Electric Blue, Inferno Red or Linen Gold were offered for the GT, Limited Edition and Touring Edition sedans.

The full range of standard and optional equipment of the 2005 PT Cruiser line.					
Feature	Base	Touring	Limited G Pack	Limited K Pack	GT
2.4L/5-speed manual	S	S	S	NA	NA
2.4L/4-speed automatic	O	O	O	NA	NA
2.4L HO/5-speed manual Getrag)	NA	NA	NA	NA	S
2.4L HO Turbo/4-speed automatic (AutoStick)	NA	NA	NA	NA	O
2.4L Turbo Supplemental side impact	NA	NA	O	S	NA

The 2005 PT Cruiser GT's Royale leather seats in Dark Slate Gray. Also seen are the GT's bright silver dash panel inserts. (Author's collection)

Feature	Base	Touring	Limited G Pack	Limited K Pack	GT
airbags	O	O	S	S	S
Airconditioning	O	S	S	S	S
Brakes:					
Power front disc/rear drum	S	S	S	S	NA
Power front disc/rear drum with anti lock	O	O	O	O	NA
Performance power 4-wheel disc, anti lock, low-speed traction control [1]	NA	NA	O	O	S
15-gallon fuel tank	S	S	S	S	S
Normal duty suspension	S	S	NA	NA	NA
Touring duty suspension	NA	NA	S	S	NA
Sport suspension	NA	NA	NA	NA	S
Interior features:					
Assist handles	NA	O	S	S	S
Bodyside moldings (body-color)	NA	S	S	S	S
Chrome Accents Group [2]	NA	NA	O	O	O
Chrome horizontal grille accents	NA	NA	P	S	P
Overhead console [3]	NA	P	S	S	S
Power door locks [4]	NA	S	S	S	S
Engine block heater	O	O	O	O	O
Chrome-plated stainless steel exhaust tip	NA	NA	S	NA	NA
Chrome-plated stainless steel 2.75in diameter	NA	NA	O	S	S
Fog lamps	NA	NA	S	S	S
Deep-tint sunscreen glass [5]	NA	O	S	S	S
HomeLink universal garage door opener	NA	NA	O	O	O
2.4L Turbo liftgate badge	NA	NA	P	S	NA
2.4L Turbo High Output liftgate badge	NA	NA	NA	NA	S
GT liftgate badge	NA	NA	NA	NA	S
Limited Edition liftgate badge	NA	NA	S	S	NA
Touring Edition liftgate badge	NA	S	NA	NA	NA
Light Group [6]	NA	O	S	S	S
Chrome lock knobs	NA	NA	O	S	S
Dual power exterior mirrors	NA	S	S	S	S
Power moonroof (with one-touch-open and sliding sunshade)	NA	O	O	S	S
Moonroof Group [7]	NA	O	NA	NA	NA
Bright pedals	NA	NA	P	P	S
Power outlets [8]	NA	P	S	S	S
Remote Keyless Entry System [9]	NA	S	S	S	S
Seat trim material:					
Metro II/Solar cloth	S	S	NA	NA	NA
Fresno cloth	NA	NA	S	NA	NA
Royale leather trim with Preferred Suede accents	NA	NA	NA	S	NA
Royale leather trim with 'Axis' perforated inserts	NA	NA	NA	NA	S
Fold-flat front passenger seat	NA	S	S	S	S
Heated driver's and front passenger seats	NA	NA	NA	O	O
Driver-side manual lumbar support	NA	NA	S	S	S
Driver-side power					

Feature	Base	Touring	Limited G Pack	Limited K Pack	GT
seat height adjuster	NA	O	S	S	S
2-way outboard rear adjustable low-profile rear head restraints	S	S	S	S	S
Security alarm system	NA	NA	S	S	S
Rear shelf panel	NA	S	S	S	S
Shifter knob [10]	S	S	S	NA	NA
Shifter knob [11]	NA	NA	P	P	S
Sound systems:					
AM/FM stereo radio with cassette and CD players	S	NA	NA	NA	NA
AM/FM stereo radio with CD player, CD changer controls	NA	O	S	S	S
AM/FM stereo radio with CD player and full-map GPS navigation	NA	NA	O	O	O
IRIUS satellite radio system	NA	O	O	O	O
AM/FM stereo radio with 6-disc CD player	NA	O	O	O	O
Electronic speed control with steering wheel mounted controls	NA	O	S	S	S
Leather-wrapped steering wheel	NA	NA	S	NA	NA
Leather-wrapped steering wheel with Satin Silver spokes (included in Chrome Accent Group)	NA	NA	P	P	S
Under front passenger seat storage drawer	NA	S	S	S	S
Sun visors with illuminated mirrors (included in Light Group)	NA	P	S	S	S
Tires:					
P195/65R15 89T BSW all-season touring	S	S	NA	NA	NA
P205/55R16 89T BSW all-season touring	NA	NA	S	S	NA
P205/50R17 all-season performance	NA	NA	NA	NA	S
Low-speed traction control [12]	NA	NA	O	O	S
Wheels:					
15in steel with bolt-on wheel covers	S	S	NA	NA	NA
16in silver-painted aluminum	NA	NA	S	NA	NA
16in 6-spoke chrome-clad aluminum with 2.4L naturally-aspirated engines	NA	NA	O	NA	NA
17in aluminum-clad	NA	NA	NA	NA	S
16in chrome-clad aluminum 6-spoke with 2.4L Turbo	NA	NA	O	S	NA
Woodgrain Exterior Accents [13]	NA	NA	O	O	NA

[1] Required Turbo engine on Limited Edition models.
[2] Included door sill scuff pads with bright insert with wing logo, silver shifter knob, chrome lock knobs, chrome PRNDL bezel (with automatic transaxle), bright pedals, body-color grille with chrome horizontal accents, chrome bodyside molding, body-color front fascia with chrome horizontal accents on lower grille opening, leather-wrapped steering wheel with Satin Silver spokes, chrome 16in wheels, and bright fuel filler.
[3] Included dual map courtesy lamps, digital display for

compass and outside temperature (also included in Light Group).

4 Speed sensitive with central locking.

5 Installed in rear passenger doors, rear quarter windows and liftgate.

6 Included an overhead console with dual map courtesy lamps, digital display for compass and outside temperature, dual illuminated visor-mounted vanity mirrors, instrument panel and cargo-mounted 12V power outlets and assist handles.

7 Included power moonroof with one-touch-open feature, sliding sunshade and Light Group.

8 Consisted of instrument panel and cargo area-mounted12V power outlets.

9 Provided controls for illuminated entry system, door and liftgate locks, panic alarm, and Security Alarm System. Included 2 transmitters and rolling code technology.

10 Color-keyed to interior (either Dark Taupe or Dark Slate), ball-type with chrome shifter lever.

11 Satin silver, ball-type with chrome shift lever; includedin Chrome Accent Group.

12 Packaged with Performance ABS brakes for 2.4L Turbo equipped vehicles.

13 Not available with Chrome Accent Group.

This Walter P Chrysler signature badge was affixed to the exterior of all members of Chrysler's 2005 Signature Series, consisting of special editions of the 300, Town & Country, Pacifica, Sebring Sedan, Sebring Convertible, and PT Cruiser. It "conveys," said Chrysler, "pride, craftsmanship,heritage and value". "Each of the Signature Series models," it also noted, "reflects the original vision of the Chrysler brand's founder, Walter P Chrysler: precise engineering and great design."
(Author's collection)

The PT Cruiser's 2005 model year wound down with the announcement on October 15, 2004 of the Limited Edition PT Cruiser Signature Series model. Additional Signature Series models included versions based on the 300 Touring, Sebring Touring Convertible and Sedan, Pacifica Touring and the Town and Country and Town and Country Touring minivans.

The Cruiser's Signature Series Package, which listed for $3085, included a no-charge navigation system, power moonroof, Walter P Chrysler signature badges, Sirius satellite

All 2005 Signature Series vehicles had two-tone leather-trimmed interiors. Additional features of the PT Cruiser version included a GPS navigation system, Sirius Satellite radio, the Chrome Package, 16in chrome-clad wheels, AM/FM/CD radio with six speakers, leather-wrapped steering wheel, and a power moonroof. All of the PT Cruiser's exterior colors were available and, in place of the standard 150hp engine, the 180hp turbo version could be ordered. (Author's collection)

radio, Chrome Package, two-tone Dark Taupe/Light Pearl Beige leather-trimmed seats, driver and front passenger side airbags, driver power height adjuster, 16in chrome-clad wheels, HomeLink universal transceiver, AM/FM/CD radio with six speakers, and a leather-wrapped steering wheel. The Signature Series PT Cruiser was available in all of 2005's exterior colors.

A few weeks earlier, Chrysler invited PT Cruiser owners and their families to the third annual Chrysler Block Party held at Six Flags Great American in Gurpee, Illinois on September 25. This had been the location of the first Block Party and, from that perspective, Jeff Bell observed that "the Chrysler Block Party is not only a unique event for car enthusiasts to show off their vehicles and learn more about new products, but it's also a great chance for families to spend quality time together in an extremely lively environment. It's a great party for all ages."

The day's format and activities followed the pattern of the previous gathering, but a few enhancements were evident. *Car and Driver* and *Road & Track* magazines joined together to sponsor several driving courses where guests over the age of 18 could test not only the latest PT Cruiser, but also several other vehicles, including the Chrysler 300, and Crossfire Roadster and Convertible.

Prices of the 5-door 2005 PT Cruisers and their options for the American market.	
Model	MSRP*
Base	$14,170
Touring Edition	$16,205
Limited Edition	$18,205
GT	$ 23,705
* Included $640 Destination Charge	
Option	Price
4-speed automatic transmission (Base, Touring, Limited)	$825.00
4-speed automatic transmission with AutoStick (GT only)	$550
Quick Order Group 2CK [1]	$1855
Airconditioning (Base)	$1000
Engine block heater	$35.00
AM/FM stereo radio with CD	$125.00
AM/FM stereo radio with CD and cassette	$150.00
AM/FM stereo radio with 6-disc and cassette	$300.00 [2]
Sirius satellite radio	$195.00
UConnect	$360.00
Option	Price

Front side airbags	$390.00
Linen Pearl Gold Metallic paint (Base and Touring)	$150.00
Inferno Red Crystal Pearl paint (Base)	$225.00
Black/Electric Blue Pearl Two-Tone	$695.00
Black/Linen Gold Metallic Two-Tone	$845.00
Black/Inferno Red Crystal Pearl Two-Tone	$920.00
Black/Bright Silver Metallic Two-Tone	$695.00
Light Group	$350.00
Moonroof Group	$1100.00
Power moonroof	$750.00
Rear spoiler (Limited)	$150.00
Chrome-clad aluminum 6-spoke 16in wheels (Limited)	$700.00
Chrome Accents Group	$1220.00 [3]
Power driver's seat height adjuster	$100.00
Heated front seats	$250.00
Royal leather-trimmed Light Pearl Beige seats	$1175.00 [4]
Anti-lock braking system	$595.00
Anti-lock 4-wheel disc brakes	$825.00
Deep tinted rear glass	$350.00
Speed control	$250.00
180hp Turbo engine	$1280.00 [5]
Navigation system	$1200.00 [6]
Universal garage door opener	$90.00
Woodgrain Exterior Accents	$895.00

[1] Available for Limited. Included Royale leather rim with Preferred suede accents seating, power moonroof, and chrome exterior trim.

[2] Price listed is for Touring model. If ordered for Limited or GT the price was $250.00.

[3] Price listed is for Limited. Price for GT was $400. For Limited models with the 2CK Group, the cost was $210.

[4] Included driver seat power adjuster and leather wrapped steering wheel.

[5] Price listed is or the Touring Convertible. If ordered for the Limited sedan the price was $1175.

[6] Price listed is for Touring convertible. Price for the Limited and GT sedans was $1100. Included AM/FM stereo radio and CD player.

Preceding the availability of the LHD Cabrio had been the debut of the other PT Cruiser models for the UK in December 2004. Replacing the previously used 2.0-liter gasoline engine was the 2.4-liter engine familiar to PT owners in the United States.

A 2005 PT Cruiser Limited Edition in Cool Vanilla. This example is equipped with the optional Moonroof, 180hp turbo engine, and 16in chrome-clad aluminum wheels. (Author's collection)

The 2005 Limited Edition's standard Metro Cloth seats in Dark Taupe. Royale leather-trimmed seats with Preferred Suede accents were also available. (Author's collection)

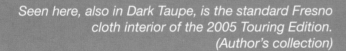

Seen here, also in Dark Taupe, is the standard Fresno cloth interior of the 2005 Touring Edition. (Author's collection)

For the UK market, this engine was rated at 141hp @ 5200rpm and 158lb-ft of torque @ 4150rpm, which compared favorably with the 134hp and 139lb-ft of torque of the departing 2.0-liter engine.

The accompanying table gives a comparison of the performance of these engines along with that of the 2.2-liter CRD and supports both Chrysler's assertion that the "driveability of the PT will be enhanced" by the 2.4 liter engine, and that the CRD provided "brisk acceleration, smooth high speed cruising and abundant pulling power."

Powertrain	2.4/5-speed manual	2.4/4-speed automatic*	2.2/5-speed manual
0-62mph	10.6sec	11.5sec.	12.1sec.
Max. speed	121mph	106mph	114mph

* Equipped with AutoStick.

Engine performance comparison table

UK-market PT Cruiser prices

Model	On the road price [1]
2.4 Classic Edition (manual transmission)	£12,995
2.4 Touring Edition (manual transmission)	£14,525
2.4 Touring Edition (automatic transmission)	£15,325
2.4 Limited Edition (manual transmission)	£16,025
2.4 Limited Edition (automatic transmission)	£16,825
2.2 CRD Classic Edition (manual transmission)	£14,225
2.2 CRD Touring Edition (manual transmission)	£15,725
2.2 CRD Limited Edition (manual transmission)	£17,225
2.4 GT Special Edition [2] (manual transmission)	£14,995
Options:	
Special paint	£230
Electric sunroof (Limited models only)	£500

[1] This price included a 12-month Road Fund License (£160 annually for models with the gasoline engine and £155 for those with diesels), and, if applicable, a First Registration fee of £38. Eager to emphasize the competitiveness of these prices, Simon Elliott, Managing Director for the Chrysler Group in the UK said: "There are no price changes for 2005, with the new 2.4-liter engine costing exactly the same as the outgoing 2.0-liter unit".

[2] GT models for the UK market were not turbocharged. Coinciding with Chrysler's announcement of the Cabrio's' limited availability in LHD form in the UK on October 30, 2004, had been the introduction of this special edition GT model. It was based on the Touring Edition and featured a body-colored rear roof mounted spoiler, sports suspension and 17in alloy GT wheels. It was offered only with the 5-speed manual transmission and the 2.4-liter engine.
The GT's color selection was limited to Black and Dark Plum with a Dark Slate Gray cloth interior. Along with the other PT Cruiser wagons, the GT went on sale in December, 2004.

Helping to explain the reasons for the pricing variation of the latest PT Cruisers for the UK market is this summary of their equipment specifications:

Model Feature	Classic	Touring	GT	Limited
ABS-4-wheel disc brakes	S	S	S	S
Fog lamps	NA	S	S	S
Headlamp leveling system	S	S	S	S
Side airbags	S	S	S	S
15 x 6in steel wheels, 185/55RHR15 tires	S	NA	NA	NA
16 x 6in alloy wheels, 205/55R16 tires	NA	S	NA	NA
17 x 7in GT alloy wheels, 205/55R17 tires	NA	NA	S	NA
16 x 6in chrome finish alloy wheels, 205/55R16 tires	NA	NA	NA	S
Body-color bumper and bodyside moldings	S	S	S	NA
Body-color bumpers and chrome bodyside moldings	NA	NA	NA	S
Chrome-plated exhaust pipe	NA	NA	NA	S
Chrome fuel filler door and horizontal grille bars	NA	NA	NA	S
Roof mounted rear spoiler	NA	NA	S	NA
Electric sunroof	NA	NA	NA	Opt
Airconditioning	S	S	S	S
Removable rear parcel shelf	S	S	S	S
Cruise control	NA	S [1]	S	S
Leather wrapped steering wheel	NA	S	S	S
Steering wheel with silver spokes	NA	NA	S	S
Overhead console with compass	NA	S	S	S
Front door brushed steel scuff plates with PT Cruiser graphic	NA	NA	NA	S
Chrome door lock knobs	NA	NA	NA	S
Chrome gear knob	NA	NA	S	S

This PT Cruiser GT's color, Linen Gold Pearl Coat, was new for 2005. (Author's collection)

PT Cruiser GT in Linen Gold Metallic

Model Feature	Classic	Touring	GT	Limited
Driver's seat lumbar support	NA	NA	NA	S
Leather and suede faced seats, heated front seats	NA	NA	NA	S

[1] Automatic transmission only.

On July 1, 2005, at the height of the summer sales season, Chrysler UK introduced a very limited edition (only 100 were available) PT Cruiser Nintendo DS model. These Cruisers, originating as Classic, Touring or Limited models, depending on the participating dealer's inventory, featured privacy glass, unique badging, and two Nintendo DS game consoles. Only two exterior colors, Black or Silver were available. Prices began at £12,995.

Along with collaborating with Nintendo in the development of the Nintendo DS, Chrysler UK also prepared a trio of special customized versions that were part of Nintendo's

Standard for the Base and Touring Edition 2005 PT Cruisers was this 15in bolt-on wheel cover. (Author's collection)

2005 PT Cruisers with the Limited Edition G Package had this 16in silver-painted cast-aluminum wheel. (Author's collection)

Included in the Limited Edition K Package was this 16in chrome-clad aluminum wheel. It was also offered as an option for 2005 PT Cruisers equipped with the Limited Edition G Package. (Author's collection)

All PT Cruisers with the Limited Edition G Package, regardless of engine, could be ordered with this optional 16in chrome-clad aluminum wheel. (Author's collection)

The 2005 PT Cruiser GT was fitted with this standard 17in chrome-plated aluminum wheel. (Author's collection)

A trio of appealing 2005 PT Cruisers. From left-to-right: a Limited Edition in Linden Gold Metallic with the Woodgrain Accent Group; another Limited Edition in Black with the Chrome Accent Group, and a GT in Black over Inferno Red Pearl two-tone. (Author's collection)

For 2005, Mopar continued to provide owners of PT Cruisers with a wide range of accessories. Seen here are three popular items. From left-to-right: the chrome grille accents, a chrome fuel filler door, and the rear spoiler. (Author's collection)

biggest ever sampling campaign, its "Touch Me Tour". Through August 18, these PT Cruisers would make "Pull Up and Play" appearances at many of the UK's most popular extreme sports and lifestyle events, such as the Goldcoast Oceanfest and BMX Racing European Championship. Each PT Cruiser was equipped with a dozen Nintendo DS units showcasing games including *Ridge Racer DS, PacPix, Star Wars Episode III, Revenge of the Sith* and *Splinter Cell: Chaos Theory*.

Jeff Bell's comment when he had introduced the Signature Series model in mid-October, 2004, that "it takes a special product to bear the name of our founder," was applicable to every PT Cruiser. Since its debut as a 2001 model, the PT Cruiser had become one of the most widely recognized automobiles of the modern era. Buoyed by an array of factory-customized versions and the new convertible, the public's enthusiasm for the Cruiser had been maintained at a high level.

For 2006, the PT Cruiser would receive its first major redesign; always a risky move with any high-volume vehicle, but even more so when it involved a car that had become a corporate icon. Would the new PT Cruiser still be "cooler than cool," or would PT mania finally cool off?

Chapter 8 – "A reimagined American favorite"

The PT Cruiser began its sixth model year in a form that visually set it apart from its predecessors. Along with a refreshed exterior, the latest PT Cruiser's interior was all-new, its high-output turbo engine more powerful, and its audio system selection updated.

Speaking at the 2006 model's Press introduction at Auburn Hills, Michigan, on June 16, 2005, Jeff Bell explained that "we completely upgraded the Chrysler PT Cruiser for 2006. We increased the horsepower, refined the exterior and updated every interior detail to assure that the new 2006 Chrysler PT Cruiser continues to lead the segment in style, versatility, quality and performance."

A 2006 PT Cruiser GT in Linen Gold Pearl. (Author's collection)

A 2006 PT Cruiser Base model in Marine Blue Pearl. (Author's collection)

The standard 17in chrome-clad cast-aluminum 15-spoke wheel of the 2006 GT. (Author's collection)

The GT's High-Output Turbo engine was rated at 230hp @ 5100rpm for 2006. (Author's collection)

The GT shared these new round fog lamps with the Limited models for 2006. They were not available for the Base and Touring Edition models. Also see here are the Cruiser's new headlamps. The "scallops" along the lower edge were described as providing the latest models with a "face of Chrysler" look. (Author's collection)

This Bright Silver Metallic GT's ready-to-leap posture made it hard to resist Chrysler's invitation to "get in, close the door and experience the newly restyled 2006 PT Cruiser GT. Prepare for the biggest dose of excitement ever built into one high-spirited, economically smart, bantamweight vehicle." (Author's collection)

With the model lineup carried over from 2005, all PT Cruisers had new front and rear fascias, as well as a new front grille with a larger Chrysler wing across its top and chrome accents on its horizontal bars. New headlamps with 'scallops' along the bottom edge were used for what was described as a "face of Chrysler" look. The Limited and GT models had new round fog lamps. Neither the Base nor Touring Edition models were available with fog lamps. Along with the Limited model they were fitted with a new strip spoiler mounted on the rear of the roof panel that improved their aerodynamics.

Among the features identifying the latest GT Cruiser were its standard 17in, 15-spoke, chrome-clad aluminum wheels. The tail lights on all models were modified to accommodate white turn signal lenses with an amber bulb.

The power ratings of the GT's High-Output Turbo engine were increased to 230hp @ 5100rpm, up from 220hp @ 5100rpm. Peak torque remained unchanged at 245lb-ft @ 2400-4400rpm.

Debuting as exterior colors for 2006 were Marine Blue Pearl and Magnesium Pearl. They replaced Midnight Blue and Dark Plum.

Leading the list of changes made in the Cruiser's interior was the replacement of Dark Slate Gray and Taupe/Light Pearl Beige with two new colors Pastel Slate Gray and Pastel Pebble Beige. A 'Bauhaus' color fabric was standard for the Base and Touring models. Limiteds had seats in an 'Alias' cloth fabric as standard with Royale leather trim with Preferred Suede accents optional. Exclusive to the GT were seats in two-tone 'Royale' leather with 'Axis' perforated inserts.

Interior/exterior color selection for 2006.

Model	Base/Touring	Limited Edition	GT
Interior color*	Pastel Slate Gray	Pastel Slate Gray	Pastel Pebble Beige
Exterior color			
Black	X	X	X
Bright Silver Metallic	X	X	NA
Cool Vanilla	X	X	X
Electric Blue Pearl	X	X	NA
Inferno Red Crystal Pearl	X	X	X
Linen Gold Pearl	NA	NA	X
Magnesium Pearl	X	X	NA
Marine Blue Pearl	X	X	NA

* The instrument panels had color-keyed inserts for PT Cruisers with Marine Blue, Electric Blue, Inferno Red, and Magnesium exteriors. Those finished in Linen Gold, Bright Silver, Black and Cool Vanilla received neutral inserts.

X Available
NA Not available

The instrument panel on all models had larger gauges with silver faces, white night lighting, new flush shut off rotating air vents, and an analog clock with the Chrysler signature winged logo. Replacing the old center console with its seat-mounted armrests and front passenger seat storage bin was a unit with a padded fore/aft sliding armrest and a covered two-tier storage tray combining a shallow 'clamshell' top bin suitable for concealing small items, with a deeper lower receptacle capable of holding six CDs. If the optional battery-fed power outlet for cell phones was ordered, it was installed on the console. The radio was mounted higher in the center stack above the HVAC controls. Common to the center stack on all models was a Satin Silver bezel, the GT model's was distinguished by its Mini-Carbon technical pattern.

The capacity of the glove box was increased. Its door now had a dampened movement. A passenger grab handle was added to the right side of the instrument panel, making it easier for passengers to get in or out of the car. A new coin holder and two fold-out cupholders were provided for rear seat occupants. The rear window switches were positioned higher on the back of the center console for easier access. The front cup holders on the Limited and GT had bright accent rings. These two models also had a new 6-way power driver's seat with manual lumbar support. All models except the Base had new front courtesy/map lamps. Power speed sensitive door locks and a power accessory delay were standard on all models. A key with integral fob for the remote keyless entry and Sentry Key Engine Immobilizer were standard for all models but the Base.

New radio options for 2006 included a Boston Acoustics premium sound system with six speakers, a

A 2006 PT Cruiser GT in Inferno Red Crystal Pearl. (Author's collection)

subwoofer (positioned in the left rear quarter trim, it was the first production-offered subwoofer on a PT Cruiser), and a 368 watt amplifier that Chrysler assured buyers would "modernize the driving experience." The rear door speakers were repositioned in the rear doors for improved bass response, most notably in the back of the cabin.

An audio input jack was added to the base AM/FM single CD radio enabling it to be used with virtually all audio input sources, such as portable MP3, cassette or CD players. This marked 2006 as the first time all PT Cruiser radios had

The instrument panel of a 2006 PT Cruiser GT in Pastel Pebble Beige. Its speedometer reads to 140mph and the Satin Silver gearshift knob controls either a Getrag 5-speed manual transmission or, as seen here, the AutoStick transaxle. (Author's collection)

this feature. All radios also now had MP3 play capability. The AM/FM radio with a 6-disc CD changer that was optional for all but the base model PT Cruisers could also play CDs burned with MP3 files.

Standard for all PT Cruisers except the Base models was a new Electronic Vehicle Information Center (EVIC), enabling owners to easily customize and adjust its settings that included compass and temperature display, audio

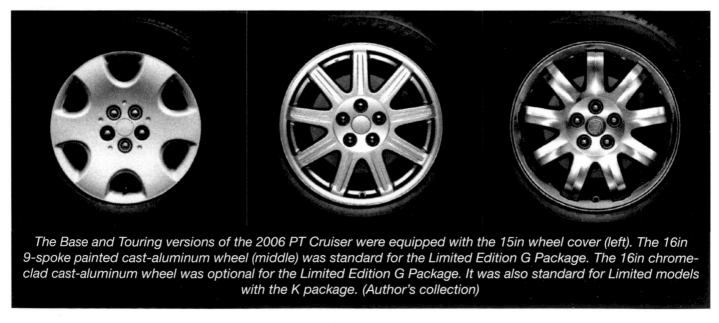

The Base and Touring versions of the 2006 PT Cruiser were equipped with the 15in wheel cover (left). The 16in 9-spoke painted cast-aluminum wheel (middle) was standard for the Limited Edition G Package. The 16in chrome-clad cast-aluminum wheel was optional for the Limited Edition G Package. It was also standard for Limited models with the K package. (Author's collection)

A 2006 PT Cruiser Touring Edition in Inferno Red Crystal. (Author's collection)

Feature	Base	Touring	Limited		GT
			G	K	
Side airbags	O	O	S	S	S
Airconditioning	O	S	S	S	S
Antilock brakes [1]	O	O	O	NA	NA
Antilock brakes [2]	NA	NA	O	O	S
Body-color bodyside moldings	NA	S	S	S	S
Chrome Accents Group [3]	NA	NA	O	O	O
Electronic Vehicle Information Center (EVIC)[4]	NA	S	S	S	S
Engine block heater	O	O	O	O	O
Chrome-plated stainless steel exhaust tip	NA	NA	S	NA	NA
Chrome-plated stainless steel exhaust tip, 2.75in diameter	NA	NA	O	S	S
Fog lamps	NA	NA	S	S	S
Deep-tint sunscreen glass [5]	NA	O	S	S	S
HomeLink universal garage door opener (visor-mounted)	NA	NA	S	S	S
Illuminated entry	NA	S	S	S	S
2.4L Turbo liftgate badge	NA	NA	P	S	NA
2.4L Turbo High-Output liftgate badge	NA	NA	NA	NA	S
GT liftgate badge	NA	NA	NA	NA	S
Limited Edition liftgate badge	NA	NA	S	S	NA
Touring Edition liftgate badge	NA	S	NA	NA	NA
Front courtesy and map lights	NA	S	S	S	S
Chrome lock knobs	NA	NA	P	NA	NA
Dual power exterior rearview mirrors	NA	S	S	S	S
Auto day/night interior rearview mirror	NA	NA	P	P	P
Power moonroof with one-touch-open					

The full list of feature availability for the 2006 PT Cruiser sedans (excluding the convertible models)

information, fuel economy, distance to empty and elapsed time.

The multistage driver and front passenger airbags installed in the 2006 PT Cruisers were the latest models utilizing what was identified as the Occupant Classification System (OCS) and a lower driver's inflatable knee blocker. OCS determined the conditions for activation or deactivation of the passenger-side front airbag based on the weight of the occupant. It might not activate the airbag if the occupant had incorrect seating posture or was moving in the seat. Owners were advised to observe the airbag light to determine if the OCS was making the proper decision.

For 2006, the Limited's standard equipment included a six-way power driver's seat, a new six-spoke design for its 16in aluminum wheels, and sport cloth seats finished in a new 'Alias' feature fabric. The Limited's CPOS 'K' option was upgraded for 2006. It included the 180hp turbo engine, 2.75in diameter chrome-plated stainless steel exhaust tip, fog lamps, automatic transmission, a Royale leather-trimmed interior with Preferred Suede inserts on the seats, four-wheel disc brakes with low-speed traction control, and many of the Chrome Accents Group elements, including chrome lock knobs, and 16in chrome-clad 9-spoke aluminum wheels.

Feature	Base	Touring	Limited		GT
			G	K	
feature and sliding sunshade	NA	O	S	S	S
Bright pedals	NA	NA	P	P	S
Power outlets [6]	NA	S	S	S	S
Remote Keyless Entry	NA	S	S	S	S
Seat trim material					
Bauhaus cloth	S	S	NA	NA	NA
Alias cloth	NA	NA	S	NA	NA
Royale leather trim with Preferred Suede accents	NA	NA	NA	S	NA

This Inferno Red 2006 GT is equipped with wheels supplied by Mopar. (Author's collection)

Feature	Base	Touring	Limited		GT
Royale two-tone leather with Axis perforated inserts	NA	NA	NA	NA	S
Fold-flat front passenger seat	NA	S	S	S	S
Heater driver and front passenger seats	NA	NA	NA	O	O
Driver's manual lumbar adjuster	NA	NA	S	S	S
Driver's 6-way power seat	NA	NA	S	S	S
Security alarm system	NA	S	S	S	S
Rear shelf panel	NA	S	S	S	S

Feature	Base	Touring	Limited		GT
			G	K	
Color-keyed shifter knob (Pebble Beige or Pebble Slate Gray)	S	S	S	S	NA
Satin Silver ball-type shifter knob	NA	NA	P	P	S
Sound systems					
AM/FM radio, single CD player	S	S	S	S	S
AM/FM stereo radio with 6-disc CD player with MP3 play capability	NA	O	O	O	O
Sirius satellite radio system	O	O	O	O	O
Boston Acoustics Group [7]	NA	O	O	O	O
Speed control	NA	O	S	S	S
Rear spoiler	NA	NA	O	O	S
Leather-wrapped steering wheel	NA	NA	S	S	NA
Leather-wrapped steering wheel with Satin Silver spokes	NA	NA	P	P	S
Sliding sun visors with illuminated mirrors	NA	S	S	S	S

The Satin Silver center stack of the 2006 PT Cruiser Touring Edition. Supporting its promotion of the Touring Edition as offering "great content at a great price," Chrysler called attention to its signature Chrysler wing badge clock and chrome-trimmed air conduits that contributed to the stack's "command central" look. (Author's collection)

Feature	Base	Touring	Limited		GT
			G	K	
Normal duty suspension	S	S	NA	NA	NA
Touring suspension	NA	NA	S	S	NA
Sport suspension	NA	NA	NA	NA	S
Tires					
P195/65R15 89T BSW all-season touring	S	S	NA	NA	NA
P205/55R16 89T BSW all-season touring	NA	NA	S	S	NA
P205/50R17 all-season performance	NA	NA	NA	NA	S

A 2006 PT Cruiser Limited in Cool Vanilla. Seen on this example are its standard 16in cast-aluminum wheels and moonroof. It is also equipped with the optional liftgate-mounted Sport Spoiler. (Author's collection)

This 2006 PT Cruiser Limited Edition has the leather-trimmed performance seats included in the K Package. (Author's collection)

The 2006 PT Cruiser GT interior was available in Pastel Gray Beige or, as seen here, in Pastel Pebble Beige. (Author's collection)

Feature	Base	Touring	Limited		GT
			G	K	
Traction control [8]	NA	NA	P	P	S
UConnect [9]	NA	NA	O	O	O
Wheels					
15in steel wheels with bolt-on wheel covers	S	S	NA	NA	NA
16in silver-painted 9-spoke aluminum wheels	NA	NA	S	NA	NA
16in chrome-clad 9-spoke aluminum wheels	NA	NA	O	S	NA
17in chrome-clad 15-spoke aluminum wheels	NA	NA	NA	NA	S

Legend
S standard
NA Not available
O Optional
P Included in Package Option

[1] Front disc/rear drum brakes.
[2] 4-wheel disc brakes with turbo engine applications.
[3] Included door sill scuff pads with bright insert with wing logo, silver shifter knob, chrome lock knobs, chrome PRNDL bezel for automatic transaxle, bright pedals, chrome bodyside moldings, leather-wrapped steering wheel with Satin Silver spokes, chrome 16in wheels (Limited 'G'), bright fuel filler door.
[4] This reconfigurable display included compass/

temperature, audio information, average fuel economy, distance to empty, elapsed time and personal settings.

[5] This glass was installed in the rear passenger doors, rear quarter windows and liftgate.

[6] Consisted of three 12-volt outlets, located in center stock, center console bin and cargo area.

[7] Included 6 premium speakers, subwoofer in left rear quarter trim and 368 watt amplifier.

[8] This low-speed system was packaged with Performance ABS brakes for 2.4L Turbo engined Limited Edition PT Cruisers.

[9] This hands-free communication system included an automatic day/night rearview mirror.

A 2006 PT Cruiser Convertible GT in Bright Silver Metallic. If anyone was hesitating before opting for a new PT Convertible, Chrysler offered this food for thought "Ask anyone who has ever owned one – there is nothing like a drop-top. Especially this one." (Author's collection)

The PT Cruiser Convertible shared the sedan model's updates for 2006. Alluding to these changes, Jeff Bell commented "The 2006 Chrysler PT Cruiser Convertible maintains its one-of-a-kind styling and flexibility. For 2006, we've increased the horsepower, refined the exterior and undated the interior to ensure that the PT Cruiser Convertible continues to grow in the hot small specialty car segment."

The Convertible was available in four variations for 2006; Base Convertible D Package, Base Convertible E Package, Touring Edition, and GT. Their standard and optional features are shown in the accompanying table.

The extent to which the latest PT Cruiser offered a far different driving experience from that of its predecessors was emphasized by Larry Lyons at its media introduction in mid-June 2005. "In addition to the exterior and interior changes

Convertible's standard and optional features

Feature	D Package	E Package	Touring Edition	GT
150hp engine/5-speed manual transmission	S	NA	NA	NA
150hp engine/4-speed automatic trans	NA	S	NA	NA
180hp turbo engine/ 4-speed automatic transmission	NA	NA	S	NA
230hp turbo engine/ 5-speed manual transmission	NA	NA	NA	S
230hp turbo engine/ 4-speed automatic trans with AutoStick	NA	NA	NA	O

The instrument panel of a 2006 GT Convertible equipped with the Getrag 5-speed manual transmission. The panel is finished in Pastel Pebble Beige. The panel inserts are in Light Pewter. Bright Silver was also available. The mini-carbon pattern of the center panel instrument bezel was exclusive to the GT models. (Author's collection)

Feature	D Package	E Package	Touring Edition	GT
Power front disc/rear drum brakes	S	S	S	NA
Power front disc/rear drum with antilock	NA	O	NA	NA

This 2006 PT Cruiser GT has a Linen Gold Pearl exterior and a Pastel Pebble Beige interior with two-tone leather-trimmed seats. (Author's collection)

Feature	D Package	E Package	Touring Edition	GT
Performance 4-wheel disc brakes with antilock and low-speed traction control [1]	NA	NA	O	S
Engine block heater	O	O	O	O
Speed control	NA	NA	S	S
Touring suspension	S	S	S	NA
Sport suspension	NA	NA	NA	S
Low speed traction control	NA	NA	P	S
'2.4L Turbo' badge	NA	NA	S	S
'GT' badge	NA	NA	NA	S
'High-Output' badge	NA	NA	NA	S
'Touring Edition' badge	NA	NA	S	NA
Convertible top boot cover	NA	NA	S	S
2.25in stainless steel exhaust tip	S	S	S	NA
2.75in chrome-plated stainless steel exhaust tip	NA	NA	S	S
Body-color bodyside moldings	S	S	S	S
Chrome grille accents	S	S	S	S
Solar-control glass in all windows	S	S	S	S
Fog lamps	NA	NA	S	S
Dual power exterior mirrors	S	S	S	S

A 2006 Touring Edition Convertible in Black. From this perspective, the Turbo-engined Cruiser, if projected back in time to a dimly-lit American street of the late '30s, might have motored almost unnoticed past groups of busy pedestrians. (Author's collection)

Feature	D Package	E Package	Touring Edition	GT
Tires				
P195/65R15 all-season touring	S	NA	NA	NA
P205/55R16 89T all-season touring	NA	S	S	NA
P205/50R93H extra-load all-season performance	NA	NA	NA	S
Wheels				
15in steel wheel with silver-painted bolt-on wheel cover	S	NA	NA	NA
16in silver-painted aluminum	NA	S	S	NA
16in chrome-clad aluminum	NA	NA	O	NA
17in silver chrome-clad aluminum	NA	NA	NA	S
Airconditioning	S	S	S	S
Bright pedals and				

Feature	D Package	E Package	Touring Edition	GT
12V power accessory outlets (center console, instrument panel and storage area)	S	S	S	S
Color-keyed ball-type shift knob	S	S	S	NA
Satin Silver ball-type shift knob	NA	NA	NA	S

This 2006 Touring Edition Convertible combines a Marine Blue Pearl exterior with an attractive Pastel Slate Gray cloth interior. (Author's collection)

Feature	D Package	E Package	Touring Edition	GT
120mph speedometer	S	S	S	NA
140mph speedometer	NA	NA	NA	S
Vinyl steering wheel	S	S	S	NA
Leather-wrapped steering wheel with Satin Silver spokes	NA	NA	NA	S
Leather-wrapped steering wheel [2]	NA	NA	P	NA
Tachometer	S	S	S	S
Heated driver and front passenger seats [3]	NA	NA	O	O
Driver-side 6-way power seat	NA	NA	O	S

Feature	D Package	E Package	Touring Edition	GT
lock knobs	NA	NA	NA	S
Analog clock with Chrysler wing badge	S	S	S	S
Floor console	S	S	S	S
Cup holders (front, 3, rear, 2)	S	S	S	S
Power door locks (speed sensitive)	S	S	S	S
Electronic Vehicle Information Center	S	S	S	S
Front and rear floor carpeted mats	NA	S	S	S
Front and rear floor mats with 'GT' embroidery on front mats	NA	NA	NA	S
HomeLink Universal Transceiver	NA	NA	O	S
Sport bar dome lighting	S	S	S	S
Covered illuminated visor vanity mirrors	S	S	S	S

This 2006 GT Convertible is equipped with several Mopar accessories including 16in 5-spoke chrome wheels, a windscreen, rear spoiler and a rear bumper step pad. The windscreen was designed to reduce wind and noise for both the driver and passenger. It was constructed of nylon and included two Velcro straps that attached to the sport bar, and a heavy nylon cover that snapped behind the back of the convertible top to channel wind away from the seating area. (Author's collection)

With the exception of the base sedan model, all 2006 PT Cruisers had the EVIC system as standard equipment. Seen here are its compass and temperature features. Additional functions included audio information, average fuel economy, distance to empty and elapsed time, as well as numerous individualized settings. (Author's collection)

Feature	D Package	E Package	Touring Edition	GT
Color-keyed instrument panel inserts [4]	P	P	P	P
Light Pewter instrument panel inserts [5]	NA	NA	P	P
Bright Silver instrument panel inserts [6]	P	P	P	P
Rear 50/50 Fold-and-Tumble rear seats	S	S	S	S
Bauhaus cloth seats [7]	S	S	S	NA
Royale leather-trimmed seats with two-tone perforated Axis inserts [7]	NA	NA	NA	S
Royale leather-trimmed seats [8]	NA	NA	O	NA
Sound systems				
Boston Acoustics Audio System	NA	NA	O	O
AM/FM stereo radio with CD player and MP3 input jack	S	S	S	S
Six speakers	S	S	S	S
Airbag side-impact protection for front outboard occupants [9]		O	O	S
Remote keyless/ illuminated entry	S	S	S	S
Security alarm	NA	NA	S	S

[1] Turbo engine applications.
[2] This wheel was included in the Touring Edition's leather trimmed seating option.
[3] These were available only with leather-trimmed seating.
[4] These were included with Electric Blue, Inferno Red, Magnesium and Marine Blue exteriors.
[5] These were included with the Linen Gold exterior.
[6] These were included with Bright Silver, Black and Cool Vanilla exteriors.
[7] These seats were available in either Pastel Pebble Beige or Pastel Slate Gray.
[8] These seats were available only in Pastel Pebble Beige.
[9] This features was included in the Touring Edition's leather-trim option.

This Inferno Red 2006 GT is equipped with the Chrome Accent Package that was available as a Mopar accessory. It included chrome door spears, chrome fuel filler door, chrome exhaust tip, illuminated door entry guards, and 16in 5-spoke chrome wheels. (Author's collection)

higher performing, with 20 per cent more air flow, and quieter that the system of 2005.

Wind noise was also reduced by the use of redesigned inner belt seals in the doors and additional foam in the A pillars. Summing up the benefits of these changes, Lyons said "The interior of the 2006 Chrysler PT Cruiser is up to five decibels quieter, depending on driving conditions."

The Touring version of the PT Cruiser was again available in both Signature Series and Street Cruiser form for 2006. The Signature Series listed for $18,900 with automatic transmission and $18,065 with the manual 5-speed gearbox. The package included 16 x 6in chrome-clad aluminum wheels, P205/55R16 BSW all season touring tires, bright exhaust tip, cloth low-back bucket seats, deep tint sunscreen glass, front bright accent ring cupholder, chrome PRNDL bezel (on models with automatic transmission), leather-wrapped steering wheel, 6-way power adjustable driver's seat with manual lumbar adjuster, Sirius satellite radio with one-year subscription, speed control, and supplemental side airbags.

The latest Street Cruiser model, the Street Cruiser Route 66 Edition, was introduced at Detroit's annual Woodward Dream Cruise on August 16, 2005. "Like the historic highway it's named after, the new 2006 Chrysler PT Street Cruiser Route 66 Edition celebrates the journey as well as the destination, " said Jeff Bell. "With its proud heritage styling, colorful exterior and fun-to-drive character, Chrysler PT Street Cruiser captures the adventurous essence of Route 66, it's Route 66 personified."

The Route 66 Edition's MSRP was $19,185 with the manual 5-speed

and the boost in power, " he said, "the 2006 Chrysler PT Cruiser offers an overall quieter driving experience because of the many reductions we've made in road, wind and powertrain noise. Customers won't necessarily see these improvements listed in a dealer brochure, but they will hear the difference when they get behind the wheel."

Making a major contribution to the latest model's noticeably lower level of road noise was an all-new acoustic package which included improved sealing around the doors, windows, rear floor pan and reverberant cavity area, as well as increased sound absorption in the trim panels. A measurable reduction in powertrain noise was achieved by installing additional dashboard insulation and using improved sealing around the heating, ventilation, and airconditioning (HVAC) system, which was both

Seen on this 2006 PT Cruiser GT Convertible are several Mopar accessories including the 16in chrome wheels, windscreen, fog lamps, front air deflector and rear spoiler. (Author's collection)

A 2006 Signature Series PT Cruiser Touring Edition in Inferno Red. Its 16in chrome-clad aluminum wheels, P205/55R16 BSW tires and chrome exhaust tip were included at "no extra charge, "representing, said Chrysler, a $1255 value. (Author's collection)

The Route 66 Street Cruiser for 2006 was the eleventh unique version of the PT Cruiser since its introduction in 2000. Its predecessors included the Flames, Woodie, Dream Cruiser Series 1, 2, 3, and 4, Two-tone PT Turbo and Chrome Accents models, and the Convertible. (Courtesy UK Chrysler Press Office)

Declaring the Route 66 Street Cruiser "the coolest of cruisers, " Chrysler asserted that it had "a heritage of hip street style." Clearly visible in this view are its Solar Yellow disc brake calipers. (Author's collection)

transmission, or $20,020 if ordered with the 4-speed automatic. The destination charge was an additional $640.

Both versions were equipped with a sports suspension and four-wheel anti-lock brakes with low-speed traction control. The Street Cruiser was powered by the 2.4-liter, 150hp engine.

Exclusive to the Route 66 was a Solar Yellow exterior

color which was also used for its grille and brake calipers. Additional exterior features included solar-tinted sunscreen glass, lift gate-mounted spoiler and 17in all-season tires. Brightwork accents consisted of chrome bodyside moldings, a chrome exhaust tip and 17in chrome-plated, five-spoke 'Empire' aluminum wheels. A unique 'Street Cruiser' badge with Solar Yellow accents was positioned on the lift gate. 'Route 66' edition badges were located on the front doors.

Both the instrument cluster bezel and passenger airbag door (with a PT Cruiser graphic), of the Route 66 were finished in Solar Yellow. 'Alias' premium cloth seats in Pastel Slate Gray were specified. The door trim was also Pastel Gray, while the vinyl bolsters were Medium Slate. The Street Cruiser was also equipped with a leather-wrapped steering wheel with Satin Silver spokes, six-way power driver seat with manual lumbar support, front seat-mounted side airbags, remote keyless entry, Sentry Key engine immobilizer and speed-sensitive power door locks, as well as the safety features common to all 2006 PT Cruisers. Its standard audio system was an AM/FM radio with six-disc CD play and MP3 capability. It also had an audio-input jack that could be used to connect a portable MP3 player or other auxiliary audio devices.

Prices and options of the 2006 PT Cruisers.	
Model	MSRP (excludes $640 destination charge)
Sedans	
Base	$14,210
Touring	$16,280
Touring Signature Series	$18,900
Limited	$18,695
GT	$23,445
Convertibles	
Base (D-package)	$19,890
Base (E-package)	$20,715
Touring Convertible	$23,405
GT Convertible	$28.860

Option	Price
Airconditioning	$1000
Automatic transmission	$825
Anti-lock brakes	$595
Anti-lock brakes (front and rear disc brakes with traction control)	$825
Side airbags	$390
Sirius satellite radio	$195
Hawaii destination charge	$50
Engine block heater	$35
Power moonroof	$750
Boston Acoustics Group	$695
Heated front seats	$250
Deep tint sunscreen glass	$350
AM/FM 6-disc MP3 radio	$300
Speed control	$250
Quick order package 2CG [1]	$2105
Quick order package 2CK [2]	$3260
Quick order package 2CR [3]	$550
Chrome Accents Group	$1070 [4]
16in x 6in aluminum chrome-clad wheels	$700
UConnect hands-free communication	$360
Rear sport spoiler	$150

[1] Available for Limited only. Included 4-speed automatic transmission and 2.4-liter, 180hp turbo engine.

[2] Available for Limited only. Included 4-speed automatic transmission, 2.4-liter, 180hp turbo engine 16in x 6in chrome-clad aluminum wheels, chrome lock hubs, bodyside chrome molding, bright front door sill scuff pads and leather trimmed seats with preferred suede.

[3] Available for GT, included standard equipment and automatic transmission.

[4] If ordered on Limited with 2CK, or on the GT, the price was $210. The content of the Chrome Accents Group consisted of door sill scuff pads with bright inserts and Chrysler wing logo, chrome door locks, chrome shift surround (automatic transaxle), bright pedals, chrome body moldings, leather-wrapped steering wheel with Satin Silver spokes, 16in chrome-clad aluminum wheels (Limited Edition 'G' package), and chrome fuel filler door.

The 2.2-liter CRD engine available for European markets was upgraded for 2006. It had 150hp, 25 per cent more than in 2005. (Courtesy UK Chrysler Press Office)

This tailgate badge on a 2006 PT Cruiser Limited, available for sale in the UK, identifies it as being powered by the 2.2-liter Common Rail Diesel engine. (Courtesy UK Chrysler Press Office)

Model	Top speed
2.4/manual	121mph (195km/h)
2.4/automatic	106mph (171km/h)
2.2/manual	113mph (181km/h)

At the same time it was, along with the 2.4 engine, Euro4 compliant for exhaust emissions, as well as having a reduced high frequency combustion noise when compared to the previous CRD engine.

PT Cruisers, including the Route 66, destined for sale in Europe continued to have suspension systems that were

The Route 66 PT Cruiser began arriving in several markets beyond North America at the end of the year. This international version was offered in Black as well as Solar Yellow and with a choice of the naturally-aspirated 2.4-liter engine or the 2.2-liter CRD turbo engine that was uprated from 121hp to 150hp for the 2006 models, an increase of 25 per cent. Peak torque remained unchanged at 300Nm (221lb-ft), but it was now produced from 1600-3000rpm. Previously, the range had been 1600-2600rpm. These upgrades provided the CRD-engined PT Cruiser with impressive fuel economy (47.2mpg in the combined cycle test), and improved performance. Matched with the five-speed manual transmission, this engine reduced the zero to 60mph acceleration time from 12.1 seconds in the previous model to an estimated 10.8 seconds. This placed it in very close performance proximity to a 5-speed manual/2.4-liter gasoline-engined PT Cruiser which was credited with a zero to 62mph time of 10.6 seconds.

The CRD's top speed compared favorably with those of the manual and automatic transmission versions of the 2.4-liter Cruiser:

Comments by Steve Gray, who succeeded Simon Elliott as the Managing Director of Chrysler Group UK, amply describe the appeal of the 2006 PT Cruiser. "The exterior of the latest PT Cruiser has been freshened up for 2006, but our designers have made sure that we haven't lost the car's unique looks. Nearly all PT Cruiser customers tell us that one of the key reasons they buy a PT is the stunning design." (Courtesy UK Chrysler Press Office)

Although the PT Cruiser will be forever associated with the age of retro styling, it never appeared old-fashioned or out of date. On the contrary, its lines and forms were as refreshingly modern as those evident in contemporary architectural designs. (Courtesy UK Chrysler Press Office)

specially tuned to meet European expectations. Compared to US models, the European PT Cruisers had revised damping, greater front and rear roll control and, as the accompanying chart comparing PT Cruisers for the UK and US markets illustrates, tires with differing specifications.

After acknowledging the attributes of the latest 2006 PT Cruiser, Simon Elliott, who was still serving as Managing Director of Chrysler Group UK, turned his attention to the Route 66. "The exterior of the latest PT Cruiser has been freshened up for 2006, " he said, "but our designers have made sure that we haven't lost the car's unique looks. Nearly all PT Cruiser customers tell us that one of the key reasons they buy a PT is the stunning design. A special edition – the 'Route 66' makes an ever stronger visual statement with bright yellow paint, a large spoiler and big alloy wheels."

Availability of Route 66 models in the UK began in November, 2005, in 2.2 CRD or 2.4 gasoline engine form. The 2.4 manual transmission version was priced at £15, 440. With an automatic transmission its price was £16,240.

Model	Tire
UK/Classic	P195/65R/15 Goodyear Eagle LS
UK/Touring and Limited	P205/55R/16 Goodyear Eagle NCT-5
US/Base and Touring	P195/65R15 89T Goodyear Eagle LS, All-season Touring
US/Limited	P205/50R16 89T Goodyear Eagle LS, All-season Touring
US/GT	P20550HR17 Goodyear Eagle RS-A, All-season, extra load

The 2.2 CRD with the five-speed manual gearbox listed for £16,640.

Adding to the PT Cruiser's appeal in markets beyond North America was the availability of the Cabrio in right-hand drive form. These PT Cruisers began arriving in the UK in

The liftgate badge on this 2006 PT Cruiser, a right-hand drive Limited model for the UK market, reads 'Limited 2.4L' indicating it's powered by the 141hp gasoline engine. Limited and Touring models with this engine were available for the UK market with either a five-speed manual or the 4-speed automatic transmission. Respective 0-62mph times were approximately 10.6 and 11.5 seconds. (Courtesy UK Chrysler Press Office)

The 2.4-liter engine as installed in a 2006 PT Cruiser with right-hand drive. Its DIN rating was 143. (Courtesy UK Chrysler Press Office)

UK PT Cruiser sedan prices.

Model	OTR Price	
	Manual transmission	Automatic transmission
Classic 2.4	£12.995	NA
Touring 2.4	£14,525	£15, 325
Limited 2.4	£16,025	£16, 825
Classic CRD 2.2*	£14,225	NA
Touring CRD 2.2	£14,225	NA
Limited CRD 2.2	£17,225	NA

* Approximately 40 per cent of PT Cruisers sold in the UK through the start of the 2006 model year were diesel-powered.

Options
Special paint
Electric moonroof (Limited only)

The Chrysler Group launched the RHD 2006 PT Cruiser Cabrio in the UK at the end of April 2006. "With its power folding top and versatile cargo-carrying ability," said a press representative, "the PT Cruiser Cabrio provided a very effective way for customers to make a real statement." (Courtesy UK Chrysler Press Office)

March 2006. This development was particularly welcomed by Simon Elliott. "The PT Cruiser Cabrio is a spacious four-seat soft-top, and few, if any other Cabrios on sale today," he said, "can rival this car for its combination of stunning good looks, inspiring performance and immense practicality."

Destined to be a far less-common sight on the UK's

The 2006 PT Cruiser Cabrio's all-new interior and its availability in RHD expanded its appeal to customers in the UK. With nine different seating combinations, a tip-and-slide front passenger seat, and rear seats that could be split 50/50 as well as folded and tumbled to add to the Cruiser's luggage accommodations, it was both functional and fancy. (Courtesy UK Chrysler Press Office)

All 2006 PT Cruiser Limiteds for the UK market had this 18 x 6in chrome-finish alloy wheel as standard equipment. (Courtesy UK Chrysler Press Office)

roads than any of these Cabrios was the limited edition PT Cruiser Sunset Boulevard model which was introduced in early July 2006. Only 150 examples were available. All were equipped with a sports suspension, "enhanced exterior styling, and upgraded equipment levels." With the 2.4-liter engine and manual transmission, the Sunset Boulevard listed for £15,485. If the automatic transmission was preferred, the price moved up to £16,285. The 2.2 CRD/manual transmission combination was offered at £16,640. All were available in a standard Black Clear Coat or an optional Inferno Red exterior.

Production of the 2007 model year PT Cruisers began at the Toluca assembly plant in July 2006. Three new exterior colors debuted for 2007 Pastel Yellow Clear Coat, Tangerine Pearl Coat, and Opal Pearl Coat.

Carried over from 2006 were these five colors Marine Blue Pearl Coat, Inferno Red Crystal Pearl Coat, Bright Silver Metallic Clear Coat, Black and Cool Vanilla Clear Coat.

The Base models now had a soft-touch electric liftgate switch and the remote keyless entry system. All models now had a standard console flood lamp. A new 'YES Essentials' seat fabric was standard on the Limited model and optional for the Touring. Models equipped with the Boston Acoustics Audio Group had a

'Boston Premium Audio' badge added to their center stack bezel.

The first of the 2007 PT Cruiser models, the Street Cruiser Pacific Coast Highway Edition, made its debut on August 15, 2006 at the start of Detroit's annual Woodward Avenue Dream Cruise. Doing the honors was Larry Lyons, Vice-President – Front-wheel-drive Product Team. "The Chrysler PT Cruiser gives car buffs here at the Chrysler Group the opportunity to factory customize a classic," he said. "In fact, the Pacific Coast Highway Edition is our 12th edition of the segment-busting Chrysler PT Cruiser since it was first introduced in 2000."

The inspiration of this Cruiser, the Pacific Coast Highway, was regarded as one of the most unique highways in the United States. It was also one of the longest, extending from sunny southern California to the northern forests on the Canadian border. As they made their way along this road, drivers and passengers were treated to both spectacular ocean views and scenic landscapes.

Illustrating Chrysler's dedication of the latest PT Cruiser to this picturesque driving route was its Ocean Blue exterior, complemented by numerous bright accents, including a chrome grille, door handles, bodyside moldings and a bright exhaust tip. A lift-gate-mounted 'Street Cruiser' badge with Ocean Blue accents was complemented by 'Pacific Coast Highway Edition' badges. Also adding to this PT Cruiser's

Perhaps the Cabrio's versatility made it easy to justify its purchase to skeptical neighbors who considered practicality and common sense of paramount importance. But there were those magical moments, spontaneous, unexpected and unforgettable, when owners experienced the real reason for owning a Cabrio. (Courtesy UK Chrysler Press Office)

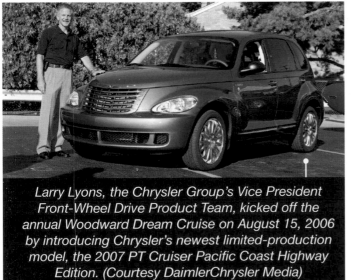

Larry Lyons, the Chrysler Group's Vice President Front-Wheel Drive Product Team, kicked off the annual Woodward Dream Cruise on August 15, 2006 by introducing Chrysler's newest limited-production model, the 2007 PT Cruiser Pacific Coast Highway Edition. (Courtesy DaimlerChrysler Media)

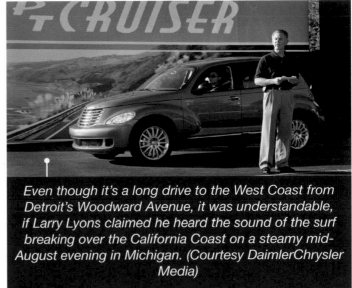

Even though it's a long drive to the West Coast from Detroit's Woodward Avenue, it was understandable, if Larry Lyons claimed he heard the sound of the surf breaking over the California Coast on a steamy mid-August evening in Michigan. (Courtesy DaimlerChrysler Media)

visual impact were its 17in, platinum-clad, 15-spoke wheels.

Chrysler described the Pacific Coast Edition's two-tone Slate Gray/Pastel Slate Gray interior as "a breath of fresh air." Medium Slate Gray 'Albi II' premium cloth seats with Ocean Blue Alias seat inserts complementing the exterior included a six-way power driver seat and driver manual lumbar adjuster. The Pastel Slate door trim had Medium Slate vinyl bolsters. The instrument panel featured a Satin Silver cluster bezel with an Ocean Blue overlay and a Satin Silver passenger airbag door.

Joining these features was a leather-wrapped steering wheel and Satin Silver brightwork for the steering wheel spokes, cupholder rings, door lock knobs, automatic shift bezel and shift ball. A bright Chrysler winged logo accented the front door scuff pads.

Both a Sirius Satellite radio and an AM/FM radio with a single disc CD player and MP3 player capability were standard. An audio input jack that could be used to connect with portable MP3 players or other auxiliary audio devices was also provided.

Since it was based on the 2007 Chrysler PT Cruiser Touring model, the Pacific Coast Highway Edition has these additional items as standard equipment

Power windows with automatic down function on both front windows.
65/35 fold/tumble/removable rear seats.
Center console with sliding armrest and storage.
Chrysler signature analog clock.
Airconditioning.

Electronic vehicle information center.
Illuminated visor mirrors.
Courtesy map lamps.
Rear door speakers.
Power outlets in console and rear cargo area.
Interior assist handles.
Fold-flat passenger seat.
Power mirrors.
Rear area shelf panel.

Powering the Pacific Coast Highway Edition was the familiar 4-cylinder, 2.4-liter, 150hp engine. It was available with either the 5-speed manual or 4-speed automatic transmissions. With the 5-speed manual, Chrysler reported the PT Cruiser achieved 29mpg on the highway – "just perfect," it said, "for long cruises down the Pacific Coast."

The Pacific Coast Highway Edition's MSRP was $20,735 for the manual transmission version and $21,570 for the automatic transmission model. Both prices included a $640 destination charge.

Summing up its virtues, David Rooney, Director – Chrysler Marketing and Global Communications, said "The Chrysler PT Street Cruiser Pacific Coast Highway Edition celebrates another great American road, a tradition we started with our PT Cruiser Dream Cruiser series and continued with last year's Route 66 Edition."

Borrowing from Jeff Bell's earlier comments about the Route 66 PT Cruiser, Rooney's final comments, while directed towards the latest limited edition PT Cruiser also articulated the PT Cruiser's timeless appeal and charm "It celebrates," he said, "the journey as well as the destination."

PT CRUISER

Earlier in the summer, Chrysler took an an early model Pacific Coast Highway Edition to California to be photographed at one of its namesake's spectacular ocean views. Inset: The spectacular badge of the latest limited edition PT Cruiser. (Courtesy (DaimlerChrysler Media)

The Pacific Coast Highway Edition's seats were finished in Medium Slate Gray Albi II premium cloth with Ocean Blue Alias inserts. (Courtesy DaimlerChrysler Media)

The interior of the Pacific Coast Highway Edition featured a Satin Silver cluster bezel with an Ocean Blue overlay, a leather-wrapped steering wheel with Satin Silver spokes, and a Satin Silver passenger side airbag door. (Courtesy (DaimlerChrysler Media)

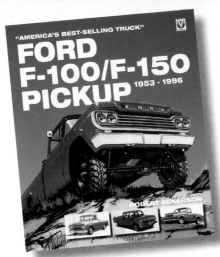
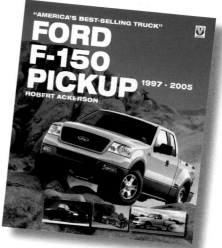
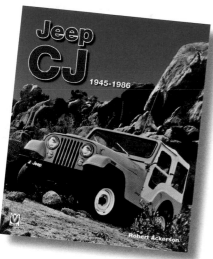
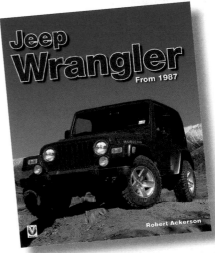

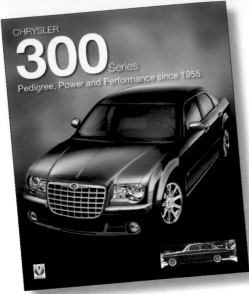

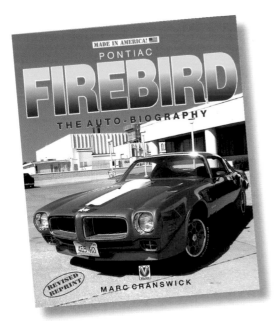

Index